JESUS THE SAVIOR

JESUS THE SAVIOR

The Meaning of Jesus Christ for Christian Faith

William C. Placher

Westminster John Knox Press
LOUISVILLE • LONDON

Book design by Sharon Adams
Cover design by PAZ Design Group
Cover illustration by Georges Rouault: Christ on the Cross, *from the Bridgeman Art Library International Ltd.*

First edition
Published by Westminster John Knox Press
Louisville, Kentucky

This book is printed on acid-free paper that meets the American National Standards Institute Z39.48 standard. ♾

PRINTED IN THE UNITED STATES OF AMERICA

04 05 06 07 08 09 10 — 10 9 8 7 6 5 4

Library of Congress Cataloging-in-Publication Data

Placher, William C. (William Carl), 1948–
Jesus the savior : the meaning of Jesus Christ for Christian faith / William C. Placher.
p. cm.
Includes bibliographical references.
ISBN 0-664-22391-5 (alk. paper)
1. Jesus Christ—Person and offices. I. Title.

BT203.P53 2001
232'.3—dc21 2001026111

for my mother

If God had a face, what would it look like?
and would you want to see
if seeing meant that you would have to believe
in things like heaven and in Jesus and the saints
and all the prophets? . . .
What if God was one of us,
just a slob like one of us,
just a stranger on the bus
trying to make his way home?

—"One of Us," lyrics by Eric Bazilian,
sung by Joan Osborne

Let the same mind be in you that was in Christ Jesus,
who, though he was in the form of God,
did not regard equality with God
as something to be exploited,
but emptied himself,
taking the form of a slave,
being born in human likeness.
And being found in human form,
he humbled himself
and became obedient to the point of death—
even death on a cross.

—Philippians 2:5–8

Contents

Preface

During the years I have been working on this book, I have also been thinking a lot about how to write theology: who should be its audience? what should be its form?

Many people outside of Christian churches want to know more about Christian faith; they are often particularly intrigued by the person Jesus. But the "public face" of Christianity they encounter too often comes only from television evangelists, and repels at least as many intellectually interested outsiders as it attracts.

Within Christian churches, I continue to find, when I visit local congregations, large numbers of laypeople interested in thinking seriously about their faith. It is therefore depressing how few of their pastors have read much theology since seminary and how little help most denominations provide laypeople (or pastors) for reflection on their faith. (I should acknowledge that there are currently some signs of change for the better in this regard, but still on too small a scale.)

Curious outsiders and reflective insiders alike, then, want to think more about Christian faith, and at the heart of that faith lies the figure of Jesus. "Theology" is a word that scares off many people, but "theology" really just means reflecting on faith, and I'm convinced many people want to do that. So I've tried to write a book for anyone who wants to learn more concerning what Christianity has to say about Jesus.

It's customary to distinguish among books written for laypeople, for pastors, for college students, or for seminarians. As a layperson myself, I'm skeptical of the distinctions. If the issues and the technical terms get explained along the way, any intelligent person can follow even complicated arguments, and I'm not persuaded that clergy or academic institutions have cornered the market on intelligence. Theology that engages laypeople may well be the right theology for a seminary classroom.

An earlier version of some of this material was presented as the 2001 M. E. Osterhaven lectures at Western Theological Seminary. A grant from the Lilly Endowment enabled me to spend some months visiting the Office of Faith and Worship of the Presbyterian Church (USA), Westminster John Knox Press, and *Christian Century* to learn about how theology can reach an audience beyond the academic world. I am grateful to friends old and new at all those places for their hospitality and patience and to Craig Dykstra and Chris Coble at the Lilly Endowment not only for giving me the money but also for asking me such good questions along the way. I hope this book reflects some of what I learned.

It is hard to write about Jesus. There are the intellectual challenges of thinking through difficult issues and deciding how to deal with the nearly infinite body of material already written about him. There are also the problems of writing about just one aspect of Christian faith; I was particularly conscious while writing this book of how connected what Christianity says about Jesus is to what it says about the Trinity and the last things. But those would be topics for other books, so, awkwardly, I had to try to say enough about them to get on with the topic at hand without getting completely sidetracked.

More than that, however, it is hard to write about Jesus because one keeps facing one's own inadequacies and failures in the face of the challenges he poses. Writing about Jesus, I kept learning not only that I was not smart enough, but also that I was not good enough. Writing books, like everything else in Christian life, depends on grace. But even with grace, sometimes you only get by with a little help from your friends. That too, of course, is grace.

My friends in the Yale-Washington Theology Group read an early version of the manuscript, and I am grateful to those who attended the session where we discussed it: Jim Buckley, David Dawson, Joe DiNoia, Dave Gouwens, George Hunsinger, Bruce Marshall, Mike Root, and Ron Thiemann. From conversations with George Hunsinger over the years, I have learned many things about Christology that I should have learned by reading Karl Barth more carefully.

As I was completing this manuscript, Keith Baird retired after twenty-five years as my physician, so this seems a good time to express thanks to him. Stephanie Egnotovich has been a marvellously supportive and helpful editor; nearly every paragraph of this book is better because of her thoughtful comments. Raymond Williams has now been my colleague for over twenty-five years and has given me more personal and professional support than I know how to measure. My friend and colleague Steve Webb, as always, was my first and best reader. My mother has complained that my more recent books have grown more technical and less easy to read. I have tried to improve this time out. For that reason, and a lifetime of other reasons, this book is for her.

W. C. P

Introduction: Even His Name Means Salvation

One of Frederick Buechner's sermons tells about watching Federico Fellini's film *La Dolce Vita* in a college town movie theater. In the opening scene a helicopter is carrying a statue of Christ, hanging from a kind of halter, through the sky of Rome to its appointed place atop a church. Some workmen look up and say, "Hey, it's Jesus," and laugh and wave. The helicopter passes above some young women sunbathing, and swoops down as the pilot and co-pilot try to get their phone numbers. The youthful audience was laughing at the ironies.

> But then the helicopter continues on its way, and the great dome of St. Peter's zooms up from below, and for the first time the camera starts to zoom in on the statue itself with its arms stretched out, until for a moment the screen is almost filled with just the bearded face of Christ—and at that moment there was no laughter at all in that theater full of students and their dates and paper cups full of buttery popcorn and La Dolce Vita college-style. Nobody laughed during that moment because there was something about that face, for a few seconds there on the screen, that made them be silent—the face hovering there in the sky and the outspread arms.[1]

"Jesus, Jesus, Jesus—there's just something about that name," go the words of an old revival song. And so it seems. At unexpected moments, even in the midst of a sexually daring Italian movie, people can find themselves somehow face to face with Jesus. Sometimes, more than that, they can't quite forget that face, and their encounter with Jesus changes their lives.

Even in our supposedly secular culture, *Time* and *Newsweek* find occasions to run cover stories about Jesus, because it always increases the newsstand sales. Movies about Jesus, bold historical books that claim to recover the "true Jesus" fascinate us endlessly. The desperate turn to him for hope. The "successful," looking for some meaning to their lives and disappointed with the gimmick or the guru of the month, wonder if this strange teacher from so long ago is more complex than their half-forgotten Sunday School memories imply.

For Christians, the impact of Jesus goes beyond fascination to faith. For two thousand years now, they have sought to follow him, even when that path leads to dark places. And still today:

> an addict sweating in a jail cell reads a small New Testament with desperate hope;
>
> Christians in a Chinese village emerge from two generations of frightened secrecy, and the world discovers their faithfulness;
>
> the presidents of several large corporations meet regularly over lunch for prayer and Bible study, and, perhaps to their own amazement, they start thinking about how to live and work differently;
>
> Christians in a hospice care for patients dying of AIDS.

Addicts, villagers, corporate presidents, caregivers—all of them turn to Jesus for inspiration.

But who is this Jesus? Popular culture, religious tradition, and historical research generate such a wide array of images of him. How can we find out who Jesus really was and is?

Coming to Know Jesus

One answer would be to turn to the historians. Jesus was, after all, a historical figure. He lived in a Roman province in the first century. A good many historians have recently written books about him. But unfortunately, each book seems to reach a different conclusion. Was Jesus basically a political revolutionary? a Cynic philosopher? a liberal Jewish Pharisee? a Middle Eastern magician? Scholars make apparently plausible arguments for these and many other theses, each seeming to refute the others.

It's part of the job of historians to be skeptical about their sources. But if we decide to be fundamentally skeptical about the New Testament, then there just isn't enough evidence to know very much about Jesus at all. Some Christian texts from outside the New Testament provide a few historically plausible sayings of Jesus, but not nearly enough to piece together his life or teaching. Some non-Christian sources (Roman or Jewish works) make passing references to him, but their reports are third and fourth hand and dependent on Christian sources. Archeological evidence provides information about the world in which Jesus lived, and that can sometimes illumine parts of his story, but the archeologists have given us no direct information about him.

A few basic facts about Jesus are historically as well established as nearly anything in ancient history. But try to go into more detail and things quickly become problematic. Different scholars may pick their own favorite clues and hints, and develop their hypotheses on that basis, but the wide divergence of their conclusions shows that, if we start anywhere but the New Testament, we will not reach any consensus about a detailed picture of Jesus.[2]

I therefore *will* begin with the New Testament and the creeds and theologians that have interpreted it in the light of Christian faith. I will assume that at the core of things, Christian teaching has correctly understood Jesus. As a Christian, I believe that. Those who do not share that faith may still find it interesting to know, amid all the other available portraits of Jesus, what the Christian tradition has had to say about him.

In proposing this starting point, I do *not* mean that the New Testament, or its interpretation in the Christian tradition, is historically accurate in all the stories it gives us about Jesus. "We know," even the great sixteenth-century Reformer John Calvin wrote, "that the Evangelists [the authors of the Gospels] were not very exact as to the order of dates or even in detailing minutely everything that Christ said or did."[3] The Gospel writers were not writing modern biographies or histories; when they did their work, many of the rules of modern history had not yet even been established.

Instead, they were writing from experience; their lives had been changed forever by what they had learned about Jesus. They felt convinced that they knew who he was—and they were willing to die for that conviction.

Determined to convey to others what they believed, they took anything they could find or invent—accurate reports of events, anecdotes, good stories that might or might not be true, legends, old prophecies, the products of their own imaginings—anything that would somehow communicate their understanding of Jesus. Their results take a very different form from the work of most modern historians, but that doesn't necessarily make them less truthful. Sometimes, after all, a vivid anecdote or an artist's quick sketch can capture a person better than a long list of facts or a formal photograph.

In terms of the person Jesus was, what he stood for, why he matters—never mind the details, never mind the genre of the various stories (history, poetry, legend, all of the above)—my working hypothesis in this book is that we come away from the New Testament with most of the right answers to the really important questions.

Why do I believe that? Let me admit at the outset that I do not know how to prove it. By and large, people come to believe what Christian faith teaches about Jesus when a moment of light enters a dark period of their lives, when the pattern of Christian faith suddenly seems to make sense of things for them, or when they see how faith in Christ has transformed the lives of others—not by reading books like this one.[4] Christian faith has long talked about such transformations as "the work of the Holy Spirit," as a way of indicating that they are God's work, not ours. I am not the Holy Spirit, and I don't pretend to be, so I can't promise that this book will change anyone's life.

I do have some stories to tell, stories about Jesus. Christians down the centuries have found those stories so compelling that they wanted to become his disciples. Hearing or reading what the Bible says about Jesus changed the way they understood the world and lived their lives in such fundamental ways that they could not believe that that portrait was false. Such transforming experiences still happen, however unpredictably. At least I can try to get the stories right enough to give them the chance to do their work.

Beyond that, I can at least show that these stories are not dull. In today's context this in itself seems worth doing. Part of our fascination with many of the new books headlining shocking discoveries about who Jesus really was is surely that we have fallen into the habit of thinking that what Christianity has to teach about Jesus is a bit boring. Many of us think we learned it in Sunday School, after all—and our memories of the experience are not inspiring. Or we hear Christian preachers talking about Jesus in a way that makes him seem safe, comfortable, reassuring—and therefore not very interesting. If we think that such a boring Jesus is the best Christianity has to offer, little wonder that we look elsewhere for something more exciting.

In the New Testament, however, Jesus inspires love, hatred, and fear, but never boredom. The political and religious authorities of his time conspired to kill him. He challenged some of his contemporaries' most basic assumptions about God and how to live one's life, and he continues today to challenge many of the most pervasive assumptions of our culture. For example, we tend to think of Christianity as the business of respectable, church-going folk. He particularly welcomed the outcasts and oppressed of his society into his company. Many Christians today comfortably go about our ordinary business and still think of ourselves as his followers. He calls on those who would follow him to take risks; he will not tolerate our complacency. Many contemporary Americans—whether Christians or non-Christians—imagine the Bible a conservative book that comforts those who want to preserve the status quo. But the Jesus it presents shook up his society and would shake up ours if we read about him more carefully.

To be sure, generalizations about the Bible or the Christian tradition are always dangerous. The New Testament itself includes four very different Gospels, in addition to letters, hymns, sermons, stories of the early church, and more. Christian writers since New Testament times have belonged to different denominations, been shaped by different intellectual contexts, and brought different personal perspectives to their reflections on Jesus. I will draw here on many different strands of the Christian tradition, but I will no doubt attend more to the parts of it I know best. I am writing in a North American context. I read mostly books in English. Since I am Presbyterian, the Reformed tradition founded by John Calvin will have particular prominence. If I were a German Lutheran or an African Roman Catholic, I would have written a very different book.

Still, some basic elements do run rather consistently through many different interpretations of Christian faith. To start with, Christians believe that Jesus is the Savior. Even his name—probably something like "Yehoshua" in the language of his time—means "the Lord saves." It was a common enough name in first-century Palestine, but right on the first page of the New Testament we get a signal of its importance. In the first chapter of the Gospel according to Matthew, an angel tells Joseph to give the boy this name and explains that the name refers to "saving" because he "will save his people from their sins" (Matt. 1:21). As one contemporary biblical scholar writes, "of all the traits Matthew ascribes to Jesus in the course of his story, the one most fundamental is that he is 'saving.'"[5] Who he is cannot be separated from what he does, and even his name means salvation.

Jesus' Story: Incarnation, Ministry, Cross, Resurrection

Christian faith, in other words, implies that knowing who Jesus, the human being who lived in first-century Palestine, *was* cannot be separated from knowing who he *is* and what he *does* for people even today. Philipp Melanchthon, a Lutheran theologian of the sixteenth century, put it this way: "To know Christ is to know his benefits."[6] That is, if you learn all about Jesus but then say, "That's interesting, but it has nothing to do with my life" (has no "benefits"), then Christians will believe you have not understood him rightly. Therefore subsequent chapters of this book will move back and forth between Jesus' story and its implications for our stories.

If Jesus is the savior, what does it mean to "save"? The Greek word can mean "save," "keep from harm," "rescue," "heal," or "liberate." One could be "saved" from drowning, from sickness, from slavery, from sin, or from the power of evil. As a Christian at the beginning of the twenty-first century, I would explain "salvation" like this:

People today sometimes feel rather satisfied with ourselves; other times we despair. Particularly if we live in circumstances where our lives are comfortable, we think the world looks good. With all our modern technology, we think human beings have helped make it that way, and we feel proud of ourselves.

Alternatively, we can think of ourselves as engaged in meaningless lives on a tiny planet travelling randomly through the cosmos, and find that all the things that were supposed to give life value turn to ashes in our hands.

The Bible gives a picture of our condition that evokes neither self-satisfaction nor despair. We human beings, it says, are in a mess. Our fundamental problem is that we were designed to be creatures of God, to have God at the center of our lives, but we have turned away from God. Like the "prodigal son" in the New Testament parable, we have left home and find ourselves lost, trapped, in a "far country." We try to find fulfillment in things other than God—in wealth, fame, or what the world calls "success"—but none of it finally satisfies, for these are not the ends for which we were made. Desperate, we turn away not only from God, but from our neighbors, becoming ever more self-centered.

We were meant to be in relation with God, but somehow we have wandered off on the wrong path. We cannot figure out what shape our lives should take. Even if we have led respectable lives, as the world judges such things, we know in dark moments how deep are our hidden flaws and how much more we could have done to help others. We fearfully wonder what, if anything, awaits us after death. Such symptoms manifest themselves more clearly in some of us than in others, but they are the human condition.

But Jesus is the savior. He offers hope that gets beyond our failures and our fears. Some have heard the good news of the salvation he brings and seek to follow him. Others may have their condition transformed without even knowing it. The Christian tradition has taught that Jesus is *the* Savior, and not one of many, but it has *not* consistently taught that Jesus only saves Christians. Issues about non-Christians will come up again later in this book; for now, I will just note that saying Jesus is the savior does not imply that non-Christians are not saved. Indeed, the more we learn about Jesus, and through Jesus about God, the less we are inclined to set *any* limits on divine love. We Christians, luckily for us, have heard and believed the good news that Jesus saves. That does not mean that he saves only us, or that no one else will ever get good news.

If Jesus saves (whomever he saves), then, how does he do it? "How has Christ abolished sin, banished the separation between us and God, and acquired righteousness to render God favorable and kindly toward us?" John Calvin asked in the sixteenth century. "To this we can in general reply that he has achieved this for us by *the whole course of his obedience*."[7] In all of Jesus' life, he was obedient to God, and it was the whole course of that life that accomplished our salvation.

Sometimes Christians lose sight of the importance of the whole course of Jesus' obedience and focus on just one event or aspect of his life. In many old evangelistic hymns, for instance, it was only the cross that mattered. For a certain kind of liberal Protestantism, it is a selection of Jesus' teachings that really defines who he is and why he is important. For some Greek Orthodox Christians the emphasis falls on the moment of Jesus' birth. But much of the tradition, like Calvin, says: Christ saved us by living out the whole of his life in obedience to God, following God's plan for him.

Therefore the account of what Jesus did for us inevitably takes the form of a story, for only stories can trace a long series of events. The New Testament gives us stories of Jesus, and stories about Jesus are also stories about how he saves us.

The differences among the four Gospels already indicate that that story can be told in many different ways, and for two thousand years Christians have continued to find new ways of telling it. Versions faithful to the New Testament, however, include at least four episodes. These elements are central to the four Gospels and consistently appear in short summaries of Christian faith in the New Testament and in Christian creeds. They are the titles of the four parts of this book: incarnation, ministry, the cross, and resurrection.

Incarnation: "Incarnation" means "becoming embodied," and Jesus' story begins when the Savior becomes a human being, body and all. "[T]he Word became flesh," John's Gospel says, "and lived among us" (John 1:14). **In the incarnation, Jesus revealed God's identity and transformed what it meant and ever after would mean to be human by uniting humanity with divinity.**

Ministry: By "ministry" I mean what Jesus said and did up to the time of his death—how he proclaimed the reign of God, healed the sick, joined all kinds of people for meals, taught love and judgment and forgiveness, angered many of the authories of his time, and so on. The Gospels tell us very little of his childhood but focus on his activities during the last year or few years of his life. In presenting sayings and deeds from that part of his life, they show us that Jesus was not just *any* human being, but *this* one in particular. We have to take account of the sorts of things he said and did if we want to understand who he was. **In his ministry, Jesus teaches us to hope for God's reign and anticipates it in his own activity.**

The Cross: Jesus died on a cross. No matter what else gets left out, that part of the story is always central. When one of his disciples, Thomas, saw him after his death, according to John's Gospel, the way he really knew it was Jesus was by the nail holes in his hands and feet and the wound in his side (John 20:27). Who is Jesus? Whatever else, Jesus is the one who was crucified. **On the cross, Jesus suffers in a way that can help other sufferers know they are not alone, reconciles us to God, and redeems us from the powers of evil.**

Resurrection: Also, and just as important, as the Apostles' Creed puts it, "And the third day, he rose again from the dead." If Jesus' life is not to be just one more tragic story in a world of tragic stories, then it cannot end with the cross. Jesus must be one who lives again after his death. **In the resurrection, Jesus triumphs over death and evil.**

So—incarnation, ministry, cross, resurrection—these provide a basic framework by which to organize stories about Jesus' life, "the whole course of his obedience," and in learning through these stories who he is, we learn how he is our Savior.

Three Contexts: Israel, the Church, Our Lives

I began with Frederick Buechner's story about an encounter with Jesus in a college town movie theater. Consider another story about meeting Jesus, this one from Luke's Gospel. It is a few days after Jesus' death, and his disciples, who had loved him and centered so many of their hopes around him, have fallen into a despair which strange rumors that his tomb has been found empty have not yet transformed. Two of them are walking away from Jerusalem to a little village called Emmaus when a stranger joins them on the road.

> And he said to them, "What are you discussing with each other while you walk along?" They stood still, looking sad. Then one of them, whose name was Cleopas, answered him, "Are you the only stranger in Jerusalem who does not know the things that have taken place there in these days?" He asked them, "What things?" They replied, "The things about Jesus of Nazareth, who was a prophet mighty in deed and word before God and all the people, and how our chief priests and leaders handed him over to be condemned to death and crucified him. But we had hoped that he was the one to redeem Israel." . . . Then he said to them, "Oh how foolish you are, and how slow of heart to believe all that the prophets have declared! Was it not necessary that the Messiah should suffer these things and then enter into his glory?" Then beginning with Moses and all the prophets, he interpreted to them the things about himself in all the scriptures.
>
> As they came near the village to which they were going, he walked ahead as if he were going on. But they urged him strongly, saying, "Stay with us, because it is almost evening and the day is now nearly over." So he went in to stay with them. When he was at the table with them, he took bread, blessed and broke it, and gave it to them. Then their eyes were opened, and they recognized him; and he vanished from their sight. They said to each other, "Were not our hearts burning within us while he was talking to us on the road, while he was opening the scriptures to us?"
>
> (Luke 24:17–21, 25–32)

Whatever the historical truth of this story, it surely was intended to convey something about how some early Christians came to their faith. Unlike the college students watching an image of Jesus in Fellini's film, Cleopas and his friend are not just momentarily intrigued. They will follow this Jesus the rest of their lives, wherever that leads them. For them, he is not just a figure in the past; he still lives. In other words, it is not just that *they* remember *him*, but *he* can continue to act on and for *them*. He is the savior.

Part of the reason the mysterious experience of Cleopas and his friend could be transformative was the rich context it had for understanding who Jesus is. He was not just a haunting image on a movie screen. In this story: (1) Jesus interpreted his life as a fulfillment of hopes of Israel; (2) he shared a meal with them that anticipated one of the sacraments of the church; (3) he changed the direction of their lives, and their hearts burned within them. No matter the risk involved in following this teacher who had been so recently executed by the authorities, they returned to Jerusalem as his disciples.

Christian faith holds that, if we know who Jesus really is, we will believe that he has saved us, and we will want to follow him. Knowing him begins with knowing his own story, but that story needs to be understood in the context of (1) Israel, (2) the church, and (3) our own lives. I have already outlined the four basic parts of this book: incarnation, ministry, cross, resurrection. Part 1, on the incarnation, is the most complicated, for to explain what it means that God became human, I must first define the terms and say something about both God and humanity. In parts 2, 3, and 4 (on ministry, cross, and resurrection), in addition to discussing Jesus himself, I will set Jesus in the three contexts I just mentioned as appearing in the story of the walk to Emmaus—Israel, the church, our lives.

Israel is Jesus' most obvious context. He was a Jew—a teacher or rabbi whose ways of thinking about God, history, and himself were shaped by the Jewish scriptures. After his death, his followers initially interpreted his significance by using Jewish categories. They called him "the Christ"—the Greek word "Christos" is a translation of the Hebrew word "Messiah," which means "anointed one." In ancient Israel prophets, priests, and monarchs were all anointed with oil as a symbol of their chosenness by God.[8] "Messiah" had come to have particular meanings in the Jewish tradition—more of that in later chapters—but at least it harkened back to those three anointed offices of prophet, priest, and king. Calvin therefore understood Jesus, in the context of Israel, in terms of these three "offices." We might think of them as three jobs Jesus had. In his ministry, particularly through his teaching, he functioned as a *prophet*; in his death on the cross, he was at once *priest* and sacrifice; he was raised from the dead to rule like a *monarch* from the right hand of the one he called his Father.

Second, Christians understand Jesus in the context of the church. Following Jesus does not mean just an individual spiritual or ethical journey—it involves joining the community of those who are his disciples. Knowing about him includes understanding what it means to follow him, and that means understanding him in the context of this community.

But anyone can claim to be following Jesus. How do we know which followers count as "church"? Here too I think that Calvin gave a good answer. He said that the church is defined by three basic characteristics he called its "marks": the pure preaching of the word and the proper administration of what he thought were the two sacraments—baptism and the Lord's Supper.[9] In parts 2, 3, and 4, along with explaining Jesus in terms of the three "offices" of prophet, priest, and king, I will also relate three parts of his story to these three marks of the church. In his ministry, Jesus was preaching; in the Lord's Supper Christians share in the body and blood he sacrificed on the cross; in baptism, his followers are united with Christ to share in the hope of his resurrection.

Third, understanding Jesus involves thinking about what he means for the day-to-day affairs of the lives of his disciples. How should people live differently if they are trying to follow Jesus? Here I don't think there is any short list of answers; I can only offer a few examples of questions about ethical behavior. Still, it would distort the picture badly to say that following Jesus just means joining the church. Christian discipleship also means thinking differently about all kinds of questions concerning how Christians ought to live. This book would be incomplete without at least a few examples.

Again, I will make some correlations with the stages of Jesus' life to illustrate how his life has implications for our lives today. If God became human in the incarnation, I explain in part 1, that says something about the value of the life of every human being, with consequences on issues from abortion to capital punishment. As we trace the course of Jesus' ministry, we will come to recognize how much controversy he evoked, and how often he sided with the outcasts of his culture. In part 2, I will thus consider homosexuality, one of the most controversial issues facing the church today, and one where Christians often condemn some who stand as outcasts in our society. Jesus went to the cross as a condemned criminal, so in part 3 I consider ethical questions about criminal justice and prisons. In the resurrection, Jesus triumphed over evil, but he triumphed without the use of violence. Part 4 will therefore consider Christian attitudes toward war and violence.

If you're the sort of person who can see things better in chart form, then the book will have a structure like this:

1. Jesus is God. Jesus is human.
   Jesus united God and humanity, with implications for the value of human life.

	In Jesus' life	*In Israel*	*In the church*	*Ethical issue*
2.	ministry	prophets	preaching	homosexuality
3.	cross	priests	Lord's Supper	prisons
4.	resurrection	monarchs	baptism	war

Readers may be relieved to know that I will not follow these topics in the same order in every chapter, and that some will get more attention than others. The logic of particular stories sometimes supersedes that of this structure.

Throughout, my focus is on Jesus. What does Christian faith have to say about him? How does he save us? What does it mean to follow him? The answers to these questions, I believe, offer a glorious hope, but they also challenge us by presenting a picture of a sometimes unexpected and discomforting Jesus. Following him, it turns out, leads people to the company of outcasts and outsiders. As we trace the whole course of his obedience, after all, we come to resurrection only on the other side of the cross.

PART 1

Incarnation

Incarnation

Christians believe that in Jesus of Nazareth, a Jewish rabbi who lived in the first century, God was among us as a human being, like us in all things but sin, really God, but also really human. Part of what it means to be human is to have a body, so theologians talk about God becoming human as "incarnation"—literally, "becoming embodied." Jesus' story began when God became incarnate.

For the very first Christians, Jesus' humanity would have been the easy part to believe. They had travelled with him on the dusty roads of Galilee, seen him grow tired, shared supper with him. Most important, they knew he had died on a cross. You cannot kill God, or even an angel. It is human beings who die. He must have been human.

Yet at the same time Jesus challenged some of the forms of knowledge *about* God and how to live in obedience *to* God that Jews believed they had received *from* God—matters related to law, temple, or Sabbath—as if Jesus now had a greater authority than any of those other divinely given authorities. But how could that be, unless he was divine? After his resurrection, his followers prayed to him and trusted in him for their salvation. Unless he was God, such prayers and trust were idolatry, a terrible sin.

As early as we know about Christians, however, they were calling Jesus "God." The first surviving Christian sermon from outside the New Testament proclaimed, "We must think of Jesus Christ as we do of God."[1] The first reference we have to Christians from a Roman source occurs in a letter, written about 112, from a Roman governor named Pliny to the Emperor Trajan. Pliny has encountered some Christians and wants to know whether to arrest them. He doesn't know much about them, but he has established that "it was their habit on a fixed day to assemble before daylight and recite by turns a form of words to Christ as a God."[2]

Those early Christians, like Christians today, worshipped Christ as God. God is a mystery beyond our understanding, but Jesus was someone people could see and touch. If Jesus is divine, then learning about Jesus shows us who God is. What is it that we learn about God through Jesus? That is the topic of chapter 1. When we learn about God by learning about Jesus, however, we discover that it is simplistic just to say, "Jesus is God." For a start, Jesus prays to someone he calls his "Father." Chapter 2, "Wisdom, Word, Son," will explore how Jesus, who is God incarnate, can pray to God if there is only one God.

The doctrine of the incarnation also implies that in Jesus we best learn what it means to be human. He is the one human being who got being human right. So how did he do it? That is the topic of chapter 3, "Truly Human." He was a *male* human being, a fact that raises enough awkward questions to deserve a chapter of its own, chapter 4, "The Man Jesus."

Jesus Christ united humanity with divinity, thereby transforming what it is to be human. We human beings turn away and separate ourselves from God, but in Christ divinity is reunited with humanity. In our culture, where many people are told, explicitly or implicitly, that they are worthless, Christian faith must declare all the more boldly that the humanity of every single human being has been united to God in Christ. Christian theology explains how divinity can unite with humanity, and the Bible gives us a story about it—the story of Christmas. The last two chapters of part 1 will consider first the explanation and then the story.

1

Truly God

Luke's Gospel tells how one day when Jesus was teaching, some people turned up with a paralyzed man on a stretcher. The crowd was so thick in the house where Jesus was that they couldn't get to him, so they climbed up on the roof, knocked a hole in it, and lowered the paralytic right into the midst of the astonished crowd in front of Jesus. Jesus told the man his sins were forgiven, and the religious leaders in the crowd reacted with horror: "Who is this who is speaking blasphemies?" they asked. "Who can forgive sins but God alone?" Jesus then told the paralyzed man to pick up his stretcher and go home—which he promptly did. "Which is easier," Jesus demanded, "to say, 'Your sins are forgiven you,' or to say, 'Stand up and walk'?" (Luke 5:23).

It's a good question—and its answer is far from clear—but even as we reflect on the end of the story, that initial objection still hovers unanswered in the air: Who can forgive sins but God alone?

So who then is this Jesus? Consider two brief answers from elsewhere in the New Testament. Colossians declares that Christ is "the image of the invisible God" (Col. 1:15). According to Hebrews, he is "the reflection of God's glory and the exact imprint of God's very being" (Heb. 1:3). An image, a reflection, the exact imprint—we see who God is by looking at Jesus Christ.

Theologians down through Christian history have explained what that means this way: if *we* try to reach toward God, using our intellects to understand God, then we're doomed to failure. God is utterly beyond anything we could imagine. If we are to know about God, *God* has to come to *us*. God, Calvin writes, "is *invisible* and that not merely to the eyes of the body, but also to human understanding."[1] Still, that does not mean our dreams of knowing God are hopeless: "It is not necessary for us to mount up on high to inquire about what must be hidden from us at this moment. For God lowers himself to us. He shows us only in his Son—as though he says, 'Here I am. Contemplate me.' "[2]

Apart from Jesus, our heads are full of all sorts of images of God: God as the powerful creator; God as the judge who makes us feel guilty; God as the moral force who establishes that we're right and those other people are wrong; the God who is on our side. Some of these images are partly right, some badly wrong, but we lack the ability to sort out truth from error, unless we turn to Jesus Christ. What we learn when we do that is that God comes to us in a kind of reckless love, but that even in so doing God does not cease to be a mystery beyond our comprehension. When we see this mystery and reckless love in Jesus, we recognize that these two categories are also key features in the Old Testament's picture of God.

Mystery

The Bible keeps reminding us that God is a mystery that lies utterly beyond our comprehension. All our images are inadequate; all our categories break down. All our efforts to fit God to our purposes or our values leave us worshipping an idol of our own manufacture. The ancient Israelites understood this, and, almost uniquely in history, insisted that one could not, must not, make images of God. A passage from the book of Isaiah ridicules anyone who chops down a tree, uses part of it to cook his food and warm himself, and then, "The rest of it he makes into a god, his idol, bows down to it and worships it; he prays to it and says, 'Save me, for you are my god!' " (Isa. 44:17). Anything we can make or manipulate, the prophet insists, isn't really God.

Instead, as Israel came to know in the course of its history, God is powerful, and God's actions are unexpected. God controls the storm, the flood, and the plague. Sometimes we can discern God's purposes, but they often remain inscrutable. God has no need to follow human rules.

God, the Bible says, is "holy," and "holy" does not mean just "very good"—it means awesome, wondrous, and more than a little terrifying. "Come no closer!" the Lord tells Moses. "Remove the sandals from your feet, for the place on which you are standing is holy ground" (Exod. 3:5). None of us would want to hang out with someone holy.

Similarly, when the prophet Isaiah sees a vision of this holy God, with the seraphim calling out,

> "Holy, holy, holy is the Lord of hosts;
> the whole earth is full of his glory,"

he can only respond, "Woe is me! I am lost, for I am a man of unclean lips, and I live among a people of unclean lips; yet my eyes have seen the King, the Lord of hosts" (Isa. 6:3, 5).[3]

Today, when we talk about the "mystery" of God, we're often thinking of the things in the universe that science hasn't yet explained. That seems to be where we still need God. But by that model, the more we learn about the universe, the less mysterious (and less important) God becomes, as if our ever-growing knowledge keeps pushing God into a corner.

The holy God we encounter in the Bible, however, is not just one piece of the universe's machinery, a gear we might no longer need. Instead, God lies behind all the forces that make any mechanism run at all, utterly beyond our categorizations.[4] So the more we learn of the ordered unity of things, and the sheer quirkiness of their details, the more astonishing this God becomes. As the fourth-century theologian Gregory of Nyssa wrote, the closer you get to seeing God, the more you realize that God is invisible.[5]

God's self-disclosure in Jesus doesn't dispel the mystery but deepens it. The Gospels tell how Jesus worked miracles and appeared unexpectedly in the midst of a lake. Even though the disciples travelled around with him, he often went off by himself to pray and regularly told them they hadn't understood anything he had been saying. One early Christian legend claims that Jesus looked different to everyone who saw him: a handsome boy to one, an old man to another, a cripple to a third.[6] Nothing in the Bible supports the story, and it's finally bad theology, for someone who lacks one particular shape isn't really human. Still, it does capture something right: Jesus' sheer *strangeness*, the ways in which even those closest to him didn't understand him and found themselves sometimes terrified of him.

Reckless Love

Yet in the midst of that strangeness, how loving he was—and, like the mystery, that love recalls the God of Israel. The people of Israel knew that the mysterious, holy God they worshipped had chosen Israel as a special people, had made promises to them, and would not forget them no matter what they did—because God *loved* Israel. In the writings of the prophet Hosea, God speaks of Israel (here called Ephraim) as if God were a sad, indeed angry, but still loving parent:

> When Israel was a child, I loved him,
>   and out of Egypt I called my son.
> The more I called them,
>   the more they went from me;
> they kept sacrificing to the Baals,
>   and offering incense to idols.
> Yet it was I who taught Ephraim to walk,
>   I took them up in my arms;
>   but they did not know that I healed them.
> I led them with cords of human kindness,
>   with bands of love.
> I was to them like those
>   who lift infants to their cheeks.
> (Hos. 11:1–4)

Elsewhere, even more boldly, Hosea compares God's experience of faithless Israel to his own experience of marriage to a wife who chased after other men. It was, he says, as if God had said to him, "Go, love a woman who has a lover and is an adulteress, just as the Lord loves the people of Israel, though they turn to other gods" (Hos. 3:1). Out of his own sad experience Hosea came to understand that the God of Israel knows all the pain that love can bring when the one you love proves faithless.[7]

Several centuries before Jesus' birth, the Greek philosopher Aristotle had insisted that God was unchanging and utterly indifferent to the affairs of the world. If God cared about the world, he argued, then God would be subject to shifts of mood from every passing change in the world's affairs. Having passions would destroy God's perfection, for God would bend to the world's every joy and pain.[8]

Many Christians have accepted Aristotle's conclusions, but I find myself agreeing with others, like the fourth-century poet and theologian Gregory of Nyssa, who disagreed with Aristotle. Gregory denied that getting involved with the world would be a weakness in God. "God's transcendent power," he wrote, "is not so much displayed in the vastness of the heavens or the luster of the stars or the orderly arrangement of the universe or his perpetual oversight of it, as in his condescension to our weak nature."[9] God is, oddly, most powerful in stooping to our weakness.

Loving in this way, after all, is not a form of weakness but a manifestation of strength. Really loving involves taking risks—the risk of rejection, the risk of having to give of yourself to help the one you love—and real love takes those risks recklessly. That takes strength. Indeed, it shows our weakness that we human beings dare not love with utter recklessness. I cannot care as much as I might about every needy person I meet. When a friend or a spouse or a child falls into addiction or crime or madness, I cannot commit myself to them utterly without the risk of destroying myself in trying to help—thereby probably adding to their misery if they feel guilty for what I have suffered in trying to help them.

But God can bear any burden. No risk is too great for God; God's love knows no limits, and therefore we can never sink so low as to be beyond God's reach. When we learn in the stories about Jesus that this mysterious God loves humankind, is committed to us, and will make sacrifices for us, we should not therefore think less of God. On the contrary, as the twentieth-century theologian Karl Barth wrote, "God does not forfeit anything by doing this," but precisely in showing willingness and readiness "for this condescension, this act of extravagance, this far journey," God is different from all the idols we imagine. We imagine gods who reflect the human pride that will not bend, will not stoop to that which is beneath it. But God, as we come to know God in Jesus, loves—recklessly.[10]

What then about Aristotle's worry? Is such a God changing, altered by the changing circumstances of the objects of divine love, and therefore imperfect, even unreliable? It depends, from a Christian standpoint, on what you mean by "not changing." Love, after all, manifests its utter *consistency* precisely *by* changing. If I love you, and I do not change (grow sad, seek to help) when you fall ill or get into trouble, then my love has changed. True love stays the same by adapting to the changing situation of the loved one. We can be constant in love only by altering our moods and responses according to the circumstances of the object of our love. In that sense the loving God remains ever the same.

I have described God's love as reckless. What we read of Jesus in the Bible seems to justify that term. "The exact imprint of God's very nature" (Heb. 1:3) is beaten and ridiculed by bored soldiers, abandoned by his friends, stripped nearly naked and left to die in agony near the city dump. It is just as a prophet had written centuries before:

> [H]e had no form or majesty that we should look at him,
> nothing in his appearance that we should desire him.
> He was despised and rejected by others;
> a man of suffering and acquainted with infirmity;
> and as one from whom others hide their faces
> he was despised, and we held him of no account. . . .
> He was oppressed, and he was afflicted,
> yet he did not open his mouth;
> like a lamb that is led to the slaughter,
> and like a sheep that before its shearers is silent,
> so he did not open his mouth.
> (Isa. 53:2–3, 7–8)

Yet who is this rabbi who so reminds us of Isaiah's account of God's "suffering servant"? He is "our Lord Jesus Christ . . . he who is the blessed and only Sovereign, the King of kings and Lord of lords. It is he alone who has immortality and dwells in unapproachable light, whom no one has ever seen or can see." (1 Tim. 6:14–16). His suffering does not mean that he is not really God, but shows the limitlessness of God's love.

Considering the meaning of the cross leads in part 3 to the question of *how* Christ's suffering saves us. However it might be done, God in Christ will do it. If this is the darkness into which love leads him, then this is where he will go. Whatever it takes.

The Scottish theologian Thomas Torrance tells how, as a young army chaplain, he held the hand of a dying nineteen-year-old soldier, and then, back in Aberdeen as a pastor, visited one of the oldest women in his congregation—and that they both asked exactly the same question: "Is God really like Jesus?" And he assured them both, Torrance writes, "that God is indeed really like Jesus, and that there is no unknown God behind the back of Jesus for us to fear; to see the Lord Jesus is to see the very face of God."[11]

2

Wisdom, Word, Son

To see the Lord Jesus is to see the very face of God. It won't do, however, simply to say that Jesus "is God." As we read the stories of Jesus in the Gospels, he regularly prays to and talks about someone he calls his "Father." When he is about to face death, indeed, he prays, "Father, if you are willing, remove this cup from me; yet, not my will but yours be done" (Luke 22:42). Dying on a cross, he cries out, "My God, my God, why have you forsaken me?" (Mark 15:34). He has a relation to a divine figure other than himself.

But that creates a problem. Nothing was more basic to Jesus' Jewish heritage than the belief that there is only one God. If Christ is truly God, and there is only one God, how can Christ be "talking to someone else" who is also God?

The New Testament writers were already struggling with this question. They used terms like "Wisdom of God," "Word of God," "Son of Man," and "Son of God" to try to express the way in which Christ was really God even while he was still able to pray to the one he called his Father. Over the following several centuries, Christian thinkers kept working on these issues, and one result of their efforts was the doctrine of the Trinity.

Any serious discussion of the Trinity would take up another book, probably larger than this one. In what follows, after discussing the "titles" the New Testament uses for Jesus, I will say only enough about the Trinity to explain how this doctrine enables Christians to preserve a belief in only one God while still affirming that in Christ it is *God* who saves us, not just a human being or even a lesser divine being. The idea of the Trinity emerged only gradually over several centuries in the early church, however, so the story needs to begin at an earlier stage.

Wisdom

We begin with "Wisdom," for it has some claim to be the earliest term Christians used for the relation of Jesus Christ to the one he called "Father."[1] The

Old Testament sometimes talks about various attributes of God—God's Power, or Wisdom, or Majesty—as if they had a kind of distinctness from God's own being. In some of the later Old Testament books and some Jewish works written even closer to the time of Jesus, God's Wisdom emerged as particularly significant. In a poetic work called the Wisdom of Solomon, probably written a century or so before the time of Jesus, King Solomon is imagined describing his love of Wisdom:

> I loved her and sought her from my youth . . .
> She glorifies her noble birth by living with God,
>   and the Lord of all loves her.
> For she is an initiate in the knowledge of God,
>   and an associate in his works. (Wis. 8:2–4)

Wisdom exists from eternity to eternity. God made the earth through this divine Wisdom; Wisdom is the radiance or image of God, the mother of all good things. By Wisdom "monarchs reign, and rulers decree what is just." Wisdom functions as the means by which God works salvation.[2]

Chapter 8 of the book of Proverbs sums up Israel's picture of Wisdom quite beautifully:

> The Lord created me at the beginning of his work,
>   the first of his acts of long ago. . . .
> When he established the heavens, I was there,
>   when he drew a circle on the face of the deep,
> when he made firm the skies above,
>   when he established the fountains of the deep,
> when he assigned to the sea its limit,
>   so that the waters might not transgress his command,
> when he marked out the foundations of the earth,
>   then I was beside him, like a master worker;
> and I was daily his delight,
>   rejoicing before him always,
> rejoicing in his inhabited world
>   and delighting in the human race.
> (Prov. 8:22, 27–31)

Scholars argue with some passion over what to make of all this. Wisdom helped God create the world; Wisdom orders things; those who listen to Wisdom will lead virtuous and prosperous lives. But are we dealing here with an extended metaphor for one of God's attributes or activities, a way of talking more colorfully about what God does? Or did these authors really conceive of a separate being called "Wisdom" who collaborated with God? One can find distinguished scholars arguing both sides and every position in between.[3]

What is undisputed is Wisdom's feminine gender. The words we translate "Wisdom" are grammatically feminine in both Hebrew and Greek, but "her" femininity goes beyond matters of grammar. Where most accounts of God's actions in Hebrew texts focus on the grand events of monarchs, patriarchs, and battles, the texts that talk about Wisdom tend to see God at work, through Wisdom, in the ordinary affairs of everyday life, which in a patriarchal society would have been more the realm of "women's work."[4] Wisdom herself is a distinctly feminine figure. Sometimes she even appears as a seductress standing by the city gates, seeking to win over passersby to a life of intelligence and prudence (Prov. 8:9).

For Christians looking for a way to talk about the divine Christ who was distinct from the one he called Father without betraying Jewish monotheism, Wisdom offered an already available category. Paul called Christ "the wisdom of God" (1 Cor. 1:24). Just as Jews had earlier done with Wisdom, Paul and other New Testament writers identified Christ as the one through whom all things were made, the image of the invisible God, the firstborn of all creation, and the radiance of God's glory (1 Cor. 8:6; Col. 1:15; Heb. 1:3). Matthew and Luke both identify Christ with Wisdom (Matt. 11:18–19; Luke 11:49). About two hundred years before the time of Jesus, a Jewish writer urged his readers:

> Put your feet into her [Wisdom's] fetters,
> and your neck into her collar . . .
> For at last you will find the rest she gives.
> (Sir. 6:24, 28)

Matthew, similarly, tells how Jesus proclaimed, "Come to me, all you that are weary and are carrying heavy burdens, and I will give you rest. Take my yoke upon you, and learn from me" (Matt. 11:28–29). Whether the text refers to Wisdom or Christ, it's the same image of taking on a yoke and finding the burden light.

Where the Jewish tradition speaks of Wisdom as "a reflection of eternal light, the spotless mirror of the working God, and an image of his goodness" (Wis. 7:26), Paul could say of Christ, "He is the image of the invisible God, the firstborn of all creation" (Col. 1:15). Jews said that God would be incomprehensible without the guidance of Wisdom,[5] or that even Wisdom would be elusive if it were not incarnated in the Law.[6] Paul and other early Christians said it was not in the Law but in a person, Jesus, that we could encounter God's Wisdom and thus come to know God.[7]

Word

Consider now one of the most famous of New Testament passages, the prologue to the Gospel of John:

> In the beginning was the Word, and the Word was with God,
> and the Word was God. He was in the beginning with God.
> All things came into being through him, and without him
> not one thing came into being. . . . He was in the world, and
> the world came into being through him; yet the world did
> not know him. . . . And the Word became flesh and lived among

> us, and we have seen his glory, the glory as of a
> father's only son, full of grace and truth.
> (John 1:1–3, 10, 14)

We could replace "Word" with "Wisdom" and this would sound like the Wisdom language used to talk about Christ. Indeed, a number of scholars think that this passage, or part of it, was originally a hymn to Wisdom, and "Word" was dropped in, an editorial revision.[8]

But "Word" didn't suddenly appear in that editor's imagination out of the blue. "The Word of the Lord" appears well over two hundred times in the Hebrew Scriptures, usually to describe a word of prophecy. We know about God because God's Word speaks through the prophets. But also, in Genesis, God *creates* by speaking a word. As the Psalmist declares,

> By the word of the Lord the heavens were made,
> and all their hosts by the breath of his mouth. . . .
> For he spoke, and it came to be;
> he commanded, and it stood firm.
> (Ps. 33:6, 9)

The Word acts in history:

> my word . . . shall not return to me empty,
> but it shall accomplish that which I purpose,
> and succeed in the thing for which I sent it.
> (Isa. 55:11)

But the Word endures long beyond particular historical events:

> The grass withers, the flower fades;
> but the word of our God will stand forever.
> (Isa. 40:8)

It is not surprising then that in a number of texts from shortly before the time of Jesus, "Word" and "Wisdom" are used more or less interchangeably.[9]

The "word" of God, then, already had a rich history of meaning in Hebrew. In Greek, *Logos* ("word") can also mean "story," "rational account," or "rational principle." It was a term that served to connect Jewish thought with Greek philosophy.

No one did more to develop that connection than Philo, an Alexandrian Jew who was born about thirty years before Jesus, and who used *Logos* as a key element in his philosophy. Greek thinkers had by then long used *Logos* as an important philosophical category. As early as 500 B.C. the Greek philosopher Heraclitus had talked about the *Logos* as the organizing principle behind a universe of constant change,[10] and talk of the *Logos* had become commonplace among Stoic philosophers.[11] The *Logos* represented the rational order of the universe, and the Stoics believed that each of us, if we developed our own reason, could put ourselves in relation with that order, for each of us had a small seed of the *Logos* within us.

Philo could thus say to his Greek friends, "Ah, yes, we Jews have this idea of *Logos* too—the Word that created the universe and spoke through the prophets." The word "*Logos*" appears over 1,400 times in his surviving works, where it refers to an eternal being closely related to God and through whom God created all things, "God's firstborn, the Word, who holds the eldership among the angels, their ruler as it were."[12]

In Hebrew texts about Wisdom and in the writings of earlier authors who talk about God's Word, there's usually an ambiguity as to whether they're talking about an attribute or activity of God or a separate being. Philo unambiguously gives a distinct existence to the *Logos*; he even contrasts the "Father of the universe" with "the second God, who is His Word."[13] In Philo's combination of Greek philosophy and Jewish theology, what we know of God is always only indirect and through the Word.[14] But the Word is the way God reaches out to us—at one point, Philo even identified the Word with the Messiah or Christ.[15]

The New Testament rarely picks up on this philosophical idea of the Word, which others were using in ways like Philo's. When *Logos* appears in the New Testament text, it usually refers just to an ordinary word spoken by someone or other. Occasionally, references to "the Word of the Lord" refer back to the prophets, and "the word" is sometimes a synonym for Christian preaching. Only in the few verses at the beginning of John's Gospel, and in some passing references in the First Letter of John, is the Word identified with Christ. Many scholars think that the "prologue" to John had a separate origin from the rest of the Gospel (after all, we don't know who wrote it, and the later chapters never pick up on this idea of the *Logos* made flesh).

But those few verses have had extraordinary influence in the history of Christian thought. Throughout the early church, Word (more often than Wisdom) became a crucial and common term for the divine being who became human in Christ. Irenaeus, perhaps the first great Christian theologian after the New Testament period, writing in France in the second century, offers a good example:

> The Word, who existed in the beginning with God, by whom all things were made, who was also always present with humankind, was in these last days . . . united to His own workmanship, inasmuch as He became a human being liable to suffering.[16]

The Word of God was eternal, and through the Word God created the universe and spoke through the prophets, so that what we know of the invisible God comes through God's Word—and now, so that we can really know God, that Word has become a human being in Jesus Christ. This theme appears in the work of nearly every writer in the early church, as a way of affirming Christ's divinity while avoiding polytheism and preserving a distinction between him and the one to whom he prayed.[17]

"Wisdom" was often used interchangeably with "Word,"[18] but most of the time "Wisdom" functioned just as a passing image, while "Word" became the technical theological term. Why? Two reasons. First, Word was the more accessible category to Greek culture, and, as Christians moved increasingly into the Greek world, the Hebrew meaning of Wisdom became less important. Second, in a male-dominated culture, the female gender of Wisdom probably made the men writing theology nervous, and they felt a good bit safer with the male term *Logos* as the key category for thinking about how they knew about God.[19]

Some contemporary theologians, particularly feminists, have rediscovered the importance of Wisdom as a category for talking about Christ,[20] and on occasion their efforts have aroused horrified denunciations of "worshipping the goddess Wisdom." Of course almost any theological terminology can be used in ways that would distort Christian faith, and it *is* dangerous if "Wisdom" (or "Word" or anything else) becomes the name for a second, separate divine being. But there is no reason in principle why Wisdom should be more open to such dangers than Word. It has solid biblical grounding, and it introduces a helpful female note into the predominantly masculine imagery of the Bible.

Son of Man

By contrast, both "Son of God" and "Son of Man" obviously involve male language. That male language seems to me unnecessary—we could talk about "Child of God" and "Child of a Human Being." Jesus of Nazareth was a male human being, but that need not imply some intrinsic maleness in the divine Person who became incarnate in him. Finding a way to use inclusive language, respect tradition, and avoid awkwardness is here particularly difficult (see my note on language at the end of this book). At this point, because I'm doing history—explaining how different terms came to be applied to Jesus—it seems most appropriate to use the traditional phrases.

Like "Wisdom," the term "Son of Man" played a crucial early role in Christian thinking about Jesus and then rapidly faded in importance.[21] With that marginalization, Christian theology lost an important concept, since "Son of Man" language tied claims about Jesus concretely to Israel's historical hopes for justice and freedom.

The phrase "Son of Man," to be sure, had diverse meanings for ancient Jews. One meaning is simply "human being." When God speaks to Ezekiel, he usually addresses him as "Son of Man":

> The word of the Lord came to me: Son of Man propound a riddle and speak an allegory to the house of Israel.
> (Ezek. 17:1–2, NRSV, revised)

Here the term just means something like, "You human being," or even, "Hey, you." The New Revised Standard Version translates it as "O mortal." Similarly, in Psalm 8, the NRSV has appropriately dropped the old version:

> What is man that you are mindful of him,
> and the Son of Man that you care for him?

and retranslated it so that it now reads:

> What are human beings that you are mindful of them,
> human offspring that you care for them?
>
> (Ps. 8:4)

Though "Son of Man" is singular in the original, here it really does just mean "human beings."

In chapter 7 of Daniel, however, the term seems to have a very different meaning. The prophet sees a vision:

> I saw one like a Son of Man
> coming with the clouds of heaven.
> And he came to the Ancient One
> and was presented before him.
> To him was given dominion and glory and monarchy,
> that all peoples, nations, and languages
> should serve him.
> His dominion is an everlasting dominion
> that shall not pass away,
> and his monarchy is one that shall never be destroyed.
>
> (Dan. 7:13–14, NRSV, revised)

Daniel was probably written about 160 years before the birth of Christ, in a time when Jews had been conquered by a kingdom based in what is now Syria, and were being persecuted for their faith. The prophet describes a series of visions that give hope to the people. He has pictured a series of beasts, which represent the various empires that had attacked Israel, and now he sees this heavenly Son of Man who will defeat all the beasts and establish liberty and justice. Because the beasts represent various other nations, one natural interpretation sees "the Son of Man" as Israel, but the figure seems individualized in a way that doesn't quite fit reference to the whole nation and might be an angel, or the Messiah, or even Wisdom.

Of course, symbols need not have just one meaning. Daniel uses the vivid symbolism of "apocalyptic," the literature written in the several centuries before Jesus in which, despairing of independence for Israel through normal political means, Jews turned to secret prophecies and dreams of cosmic battles. Although apocalyptic writings are full of imagery that seems to us bizarre and utterly unrelated to the practical world, their context then was political. "First-century Jews," the contemporary scholar N. T. Wright observes, "reading a passage like Daniel 7, would think of being oppressed, not by mythical monsters, but by real Romans."[22] The Jewish historian Josephus, writing of the Jewish war of rebellion against Rome, remarked that it was these prophecies in Daniel that, "more than all else, incited them to the war."[23]

It's hard to find the right language today to describe the meaning apocalyptic had at that time. It certainly wasn't taken "literally," but "metaphor" is too weak, and "secret code" sounds a bit silly. Apocalyptic writers believed that the world is in the hands of evil forces, but that, after struggle and suffering, thanks to the help of God, justice and freedom will triumph. In the face of God's mystery, however, they knew they literally could not imagine how God would intervene, and so they used every possible image and device to try to convey the awesomeness and wonder of the divine action they anticipated. People today often misunderstand their language—taken literally it leads either to very odd conclusions or to utter bewilderment—because we do not understand the style in which they were writing.

All this matters for Christians because, in all four Gospels, Jesus uses the phrase "Son of Man," with its apocalyptic resonances, more than any other term to refer to himself. It is particularly intriguing that this term always appears in the Gospels in Jesus' own words (the one New Testament exception comes in Acts 7:56, where Stephen, facing death as a martyr, sees a vision of "the heavens opened and the Son of Man [Jesus] standing at the right hand of God"), and within a generation after Jesus' death it dropped out of prominence in the life of the church. This adds up to good evidence that the church had mostly lost interest in talking about Jesus as "the Son of Man" but could not quite forget how often he had used the term himself.[24]

The Son of Man, to summarize a range of sayings in the Gospels, comes to earth to save those who are lost (Luke 19:10). He has nowhere to lay his head (Matt. 8:20). He "must undergo great suffering, and be rejected by the elders, the chief priests, and the scribes, and be killed, and after three days rise again" (Mark 8:31). He will be seated at the right hand of God and come in judgment (Mark 13:26; 14:62). The story of Jesus as the Son of Man presents a pattern of exchange. The Son of Man is the heavenly judge; but in earthly terms, he is the condemned defendent. The roles are all reversed as the story moves to its climax, where Jesus, who has condemned the evil in this world, stands himself as condemned—and quotes Daniel's prophecy to his judges at the culmination of his trial (Mark 14:62).

So here is a powerful image—the Son of Man, a cosmic, victorious figure from God who will bring liberty and justice to Israel—that nevertheless soon fell into general disuse—and misinterpretation. As early as the second century, Irenaeus could write, "The Word of God was made human, and the Son of God became the Son of Man,"[25] meaning by "Son of Man" just "a human being." With that shift, Christians lost a way of talking about Christ that kept his significance rooted in Israel's struggles for freedom. However odd its imagery can sometimes seem to us, apocalyptic did keep alive a vision of justice for the oppressed that went beyond mere hope for political reform or revolution.

Son of God

"Son of God," in contrast, became the more important category for Christian theologians. In the first century, it could mean all sorts of things. In the Greek world, a great hero, a ruler, or a famous philosopher could be called a "Son of God"; the Stoic philosophers applied the term to every human being. In the Hebrew Scriptures, the phrase is used of angels (Job 1:6), the nation Israel (Hos. 11:1), and the monarch (Ps. 2:7). Jewish works closer to Jesus' time use the term to speak of particularly righteous people, of martyrs for their faith, and of people who could work healings.[26] In a way, we have reversed the meanings—we tend to think of "Son of God" as referring to Jesus' divinity and "Son of Man" to his humanity, while in Jesus' time the Son of Man was the grand cosmic figure, and any sufficiently remarkable human being could be described as a Son of God.

The four Gospels all use the term "Son of God," but in very different ways. Mark and John make the most dramatic contrast. Mark refers to Jesus as "Son of God" six times (as opposed to many more references to "Son of Man"), but each one comes at a crucial point in the story. The Gospel begins by declaring itself, "the gospel [good news] of Jesus Christ, the Son of God," and a few verses later, at Jesus' baptism, a voice from heaven proclaims him, "my Son, the Beloved" (Mark 1:1, 11). Twice, demons cry out identifying him as the Son of God (3:11; 5:7).

Then, at the crucial turning point in the story, Peter identifies Jesus as the Messiah, Jesus warns his disciples that he ("the Son of Man") will have to undergo suffering, and they reject this idea. Six days later, on a mountaintop, Jesus is transfigured into a vision of dazzling white, Moses and Elijah appear beside him, and a voice from heaven proclaims him, "My Son, the Beloved" (9:7). Finally, at the moment of his death on the cross, a Roman centurion declares, "Truly this man was God's Son!" (15:39)—the first human voice to use the term.

So the pattern seems to run like this: We readers are let in on the secret from the start: Jesus is the Son of God. But in the story, that identity remains known only outside the human world—spoken only by voices from heaven and demons—until, at the end, the paradoxical identification comes just as Jesus might seem least Godlike, hanging dead on a cross.

By contrast, from the beginning there are no secrets about Jesus' identity in the Gospel of John. In the first chapter, John the Baptist and a fellow named Nathanael, who is invited to become a disciple, identify him as the Son of God. His claims to equality and intimacy with his "Father" generate public controversy in a way that makes sense only if people in general already know about those claims. The main body of the book (chapter 21 seems to be a later addition) concludes by explaining that all this has been written "so that you may come to believe that Jesus is the Messiah, the Son of God" (20:31). It is as if

Mark imagines the outsider's perspective, from which it is not clear who Jesus is, while John confronts everyone with the insider's point of view from the start.

For both Mark and John, however, "Son of God" seems crucial to Jesus' identity. But what does it mean? John uses the term most often, and his usages seem at first glance inconsistent. Jesus says, "The Father and I are one" (10:30), but also, "The Father is greater than I" (14:28). But how can the Son of God be one with the "Father" if the "Father" is greater? Such questions came to preoccupy many early Christian theologians.

On the one hand, when Christians talked about Wisdom or Word, Son of Man or Son of God, they wanted to say that Jesus Christ was not just a messenger or prophet of God, but that in him *God* is revealing God's own self to the world, and that, when Christ dies on the cross for our salvation, it isn't just someone God has *sent* to do the tough work for him, but it is *God* accomplishing our salvation.

On the other hand, whether we talk of God's Wisdom or God's Word or the Son of Man sent from God, or the Son of the Father, if we are really talking about someone independent from the one Jesus calls his Father (and if not, then to whom did he pray?), then it seems that either Christ is not God or there is more than one God.

Jesus did apparently talk about, pray to, and claim a relation with the one he called his Father. Lots of Jews would have prayed to God their Father, but Jesus claimed something more. As I noted earlier (and as I discuss again in part 2), the Gospels report that he taught, not like the scribes but as one having authority. That is, in fact, the very first thing Mark tells us about Jesus' teaching (Mark 1:22). More specifically, Jesus sometimes challenged or modified the Law that Jews took to be God's word for the direction of their lives. "You have heard it said . . . " he would say, "But I say to you . . . " To claim an authority higher than the Law was to claim a very special relation with God.

In the Gospels, this claim does not seem prideful, for at least two reasons. First, Jesus' special relationship with God manifests itself in utter obedience: "I can do nothing on my own," he says in John. "As I hear, I judge; and my judgment is just, because I seek to do not my own will but the will of [the one] who sent me" (5:30). "For I have come down from heaven, not to do my own will, but the will of [the one] who sent me" (6:38). Second, Jesus' sense of his own identity is one that calls him to suffering: "Then he began to teach them that the Son of Man must undergo great suffering, and be rejected by the elders, the chief priests, and the scribes, and be killed, and after three days rise again" (Mark 8:31).

Who knows whether Jesus actually spoke any of these words? But unless the Gospels have him entirely wrong, Jesus' special relationship with the one he called his Father meant obediently following a path of suffering; this idea was central to Jesus' own understanding of who he was. He was enacting God's work in the world.

In the early fourth century, an Alexandrian Christian named Arius tried to make the relation of "Son" and "Father" clear. (Trying to make things clear is often a mistake in theology.) The Son, or Word, he said, is a kind of lesser divine being, created before anything else, greater than any other creature, but still *created*, *like* God in many respects, and even in some sense "divine," but not really *God*.[27] As controversy about "Arianism" began to divide the church, Athanasius, a monk who became Bishop of Alexandria, eventually led the opposition to Arius.

Arius's position, Athanasius said, wouldn't do. Christ died for our salvation. If Christ is fundamentally different from "the Father," then either we owe our salvation to a creature and not to God, or there are two Gods.[28] To avoid such mistakes, Athanasius argued, Christians need to affirm two things: (1) the Word or Son is "begotten, not made"—in other words, comes from God's own being, and is not a creature; and (2) this Word or Wisdom or Son of God is of the very same substance (the Greek word was *homo-ousios*) with the one he called Father, and not just the same *sort* of thing (*homoi-ousios*, of similar substance). Whatever "Son of God" had meant in earlier contexts, it now meant not a created object, but one who is given birth from God's own substance.

When the Arian controversy first divided the church, the Emperor Constantine was a recent convert to Christianity, hopeful that this rapidly growing church would help him unite his fragile empire. He soon found Christians bitterly split over the beliefs of Arius. So he gathered a council at Nicaea, and the "Nicene Creed" they adopted, the first great creed of the Christian church, condemned Arius, affirming that the "Lord Jesus Christ, the Son of God" was "God from God, Light from Light, true God from true God, begotten not created, of the same substance as the Father."[29]

It was the genius of the Nicene Creed to say what needed to be said in order to show that Arius was wrong without offering too many explanations. The "Son" was not the "Father"—those prayers Jesus offered in the Gospels were not fake but real pleas from one to another. At the same time, the "Son" was really God—not created, not merely of similar substance to the "Father"—so that there is only one God. It is to that one God, and not to some lesser divine being, that we owe our salvation. Nevertheless, the interplay between Jesus and the one he calls Father is not just an appearance but mirrors something real within God. Even before God's love for the world, there is eternally a mutual love and conversation within God. Christian theologians realized that what they wanted to say about the love between Wisdom or Word or Son of God and the one Jesus called Father also applied to the Holy Spirit, and the doctrine of the Trinity emerged. There were three within the one God, in eternal mutual love.

The wonder of God's love is that one party in that perfect mutual love should be willing to come among us as a human being, and that the "Father" who so loved the Son should be willing to permit the pain and suffering that followed, for the sake of our salvation. When, with the help of the Holy Spirit, we learn about God in the Incarnation, we learn most of all that God is love.

3

Truly Human

It seems surprising that the best way to learn about God involves starting with this rabbi Jesus, who lived nearly two thousand years ago. It is equally unexpected that looking at Jesus is the best place to start in learning what it really means to be human. After all, there are human beings all around us; each of us is a human being. Why not engage in introspection, or research in social psychology, and thereby find out what "human nature" is?

Why not? Because what we discover, either by looking at ourselves or by looking at our neighbors, is only human nature as distorted by sin. We see aggression and selfishness, tendencies to violence and bigotry, and we say, "Well, too bad, but I guess that's just what it means to be human." Many anthropologists have reached just that conclusion; so did the great Sigmund Freud.

Christianity, however, teaches that, although we human beings have fallen into such attitudes and behaviors, we were not made that way by God. Looking at ourselves and trying to understand human nature is like trying to see how a machine is supposed to work after it has broken. Someone might say, "Well, why not look at sinners, and factor out the sin part and see what's left." But we are ourselves sinners, and, too often, we don't recognize sin in others when it corresponds to the sin in us. If I'm a bigot, I'll recognize greed or lechery in others, but bigotry will seem like reasonable judgment to me. Therefore, as odd as it seems, the best way to understand what it really means to be human is to start with Jesus, the person who got it right, who lived as we are supposed to live.

Obviously this does not mean that we should seek to resemble or imitate Jesus in every way. He was a Middle Eastern Jewish male who never used a telephone or spoke English, almost certainly grew a beard, and died in his early thirties. The rest of us cannot be like him in some respects and need not try to be in others. None of his qualities are sinful and, if we can identify the qualities at the core of what made him perfectly human, they will be qualities we ought to cultivate in ourselves.

First, like the rest of us, Jesus had a body, lived in (and was shaped by) a particular context, developed his character over time, and experienced conflict within himself. All of these are elements of authentic humanity and nothing to be ashamed of.

Second, like every other human being, he was in part defined by his relationships. In his case, obedience to God, love of neighbors, and imagination, in both the obedience and the love, shaped those relationships. Understanding these aspects of Jesus' humanity helps us see what humanity without sin could be.

Having a Body

Jesus had a body. When he had been walking most of the day, the Gospels tell us, he was tired (John 4:6). When he thought about the evils of the world, or heard that a friend had died, he wept (Luke 19:41; John 11:35). He could enjoy a good meal and admire the beauties of nature around him. He could get beaten and killed. Indeed, it's not enough to say of him (or of any human being) that he *had* a body, as if it were like having a new dress or a new car. Our bodies are *us*, not merely something we possess, and it was the same for Christ, "for in him the whole fullness of deity dwells bodily" (Col. 2:9).

Some early Christians denied that Jesus had a true physical body. Historians call them "Docetists," from a Greek word meaning "to seem," because they believed that Jesus only *seemed* to have a body. God is spiritual, they said. Some Docetists, influenced by philosophers like Plato, thought that the physical world is evil and that the body is a tomb in which the soul is entrapped. They thought the whole point of philosophy (or any kind of spiritual discipline) was to deny bodily desires so as to free the soul.

If humanity's goal is to free the soul from the body, however, then surely God would not get involved in anything so vulgar as having a body. Christ may have appeared in the guise of a human being, and pretended to suffer, the Docetists argued, but he certainly didn't die. Various Docetists proposed that someone else had died in his place, or that at the last minute the real Christ fled the body he had been inhabiting.[1]

But most Christian theologians refused to accept these arguments. The brief Second Letter of John, perhaps one of the latest works in the New Testament, already warned against "those who do not confess Jesus Christ as come in the flesh" (2 John 7). Christ came to be one of us in order to achieve our salvation, most Christians said. Thus, if he only *seemed* to be fully human, we only *seem* to be saved. Docetism turns the incarnation into a fake.

Writing at the beginning of the second century, Ignatius, Bishop of Antioch, stated this point with considerable passion. He had been arrested for being a Christian and was being led in chains to Rome where he would be killed. He knew he was going to die, but he had confidence that he was following the path pioneered by Christ. But if Christ had only *appeared* to die, Ignatius believed, then he had suddenly lost the ground of his hope: "If what our Lord did is a sham, so is my being in chains. Why, then, have I given myself up completely to death, fire, sword, and wild beasts?"[2]

He wrote a letter to some fellow Christians, urging them to "be deaf, then, to any talk that ignores Jesus Christ . . . who was really born, ate, and drank; was really persecuted under Pontius Pilate; was really crucified and died."[3] Martin Luther made the same point centuries later:

> [Christ] became a mortal like any other human being of flesh and blood. He did not flutter about like a spirit, but he dwelt among human beings. He had eyes, ears, mouth, nose, chest, stomach, hands and feet, just as you and I do. He took the breast. His mother nursed him as any other child is nursed.[4]

After all, if God created *all* the world and pronounced it good, as Genesis declared, then why believe there's something shameful about bodies?

Yet there are Docetists still among us. There is rarely a systematic philosophy behind the idea nowadays, but many people still feel that bodily needs and desires are somehow shameful, and surely Jesus wasn't involved in that sort of thing. These ideas are often heard when a movie about the life of Jesus seems to some Christians to make him "too human." A film may picture Jesus differently than Christianity would on any number of counts—but not on that one. Jesus could not have been any more human than Christian faith claims he is.

So, if we're thinking about what it means to be *truly* human and looking at Jesus, we have at least one negative answer: it *doesn't* mean somehow escaping from the "evil and corruption" of bodiliness. Christians should rejoice that we, like Jesus, have bodies, part of the good world created by God.

Being Someone in Particular

Being fully human, however, means more than having a body. Human beings are born into a particular culture, which shapes the way they think and behave. They grow up, developing over time intellectually as well as physically. If we were to imagine a being with a human body who was unaffected by being Chinese or French, by being born in the first century or the twenty-first, or who understood everything from the moment of birth, we would not be imagining someone truly human.

The New Testament assures us that Jesus *was* in these respects fully human. As he grew from childhood to adulthood, he "increased in wisdom" (Luke 2:52). The great nineteenth-century German theologian Friedrich Schleiermacher agreed that Jesus developed over the course of his life. But, Schleiermacher said, "His development must be thought of as wholly free from everything which we have to conceive as conflict."[5] Schleiermacher thought that Jesus grew in wisdom and developed in other character traits, but it seemed to him that, if that development involved *conflict*, then Jesus was caught up in sin.

That conclusion seems wrong in terms of both development and conflict. We grow in wisdom by testing ideas. We develop in courage by facing our fears. It is in the face of fear and doubt that we find faith. The Gospels tell how, at the beginning of his ministry, Jesus was tempted. As he faced death, he sweat blood in fear (Luke 22:44) and cried out, "My God, my God, why have you forsaken me" (Mark 15:34). Courage that has overcome real conflict with fear, or faith that has been tested by genuine doubt, are not somehow tainted with sin on that account but are all the more admirable human virtues.

Jesus developed, and his development involved conflict. He also developed in the context of a particular time and place. Every report we have portrays him as thinking like a first century Jew; the Bible never suggests that he miraculously knew Japanese, or Einstein's theory of relativity, or the role of DNA in genetics. Because he came to help human beings, "he had to become like his brothers and sisters in every respect" (Heb. 2:17). Some Christians' first reaction is understandably, "But he is not like *me*, for I am female/ Asian/European/African, and he was a male, middle eastern Jew." The next chapter will say more about that issue. For the moment, suffice it to note that he would be *totally* unlike us if he were not something or other in particular as to race, sex, nationality, and so on. Particularity is part of being human.

Being a particular kind of human being is thus not somehow an imperfection. For instance, even the most brilliant artists or musicians work, at least to some extent, within the conventions of a particular time and place. Indian composers write ragas and write for the sitar; Mozart wrote concertos for violin and orchestra. Part of what it means to be a genius is to work with culturally available materials in a way that perfects and thereby transcends them.[6] Jesus, who was something far more than a genius, perfectly manifested humanity in his own particular human context.

But could he then also be God? We think of God as *not* culturally limited, as knowing everything. So how could the Galilean rabbi, or the baby in the cradle, be God incarnate? Some theologians have argued that Jesus did not really give up divine attributes like knowing everything, but merely pretended to do so. But that gets us back to Docetism again—an all-knowing person peering through the eyes of an infant isn't really human. Others have claimed that the Word of God, the second person of the Trinity, gave up divinity in becoming incarnate in Jesus. But that won't do either, because if Christ wasn't God, then either God didn't save us or Christ didn't save us. Christians want to say that *God in Christ* saved us, so Christ's humanity cannot involve a surrender of divinity.[7]

Remember, however, that Christians understand "divinity" in terms of what we learn from Christ about mystery and reckless love. Self-limitation therefore need not involve "giving up" divinity. When the Word of God becomes a human being, it happens without reservation, truly and fully. Since having particular limitations is part of being human, Jesus thought in Aramaic rather than English or Chinese; he understood scientific questions in terms of the science of his time and place, and so on. But in taking on such limitations, the Word was being *most divine*, reaching out to sinful human beings in love and doing whatever it took to reach them.

A friend of mine works helping blind people. When he started his job, he spent some time walking around his city wearing a blindfold, learning something about what blindness means, lived minute to minute. (He tells the story of accidentally bumping into someone and apologizing, only to hear the impatient response, "Well, it wouldn't happen if you'd take off that stupid blindfold.") I wouldn't want to push the analogy too far—for one thing, it wouldn't be right to say that God needs to become human in order to understand what it's really like. But I would say that my friend was not *giving up* the qualities that make him so good at his job in this experiment. Rather, in his effort to identify more completely with those he seeks to help, he was precisely manifesting the compassion and wisdom that make him so good at his work, even if, in the immediate context, that "weakened" his abilities.

So the God who becomes a particular, limited human being is acting out just what it means to be a God of love. It would be a *limit* on God's love if God could not engage in such self-limitation in the service of love—and a limit on God's mystery if we could understand what that means for the relation of the Word made flesh to the whole of the Triune God.

Granted, then, that Jesus Christ didn't know everything—did he at least know that he was the Word of God incarnate? Did he understand his own identity? Did he know that from the start? Well, yes and no, I think. There's more than one way of knowing things. A little child knows that her parents love her unconditionally without knowing terms like "unconditional love" or even having thought about the matter explicitly. A skilled athlete knows the right techniques, perhaps without being able to articulate or explain them, even to herself. So, as the twentieth-century Catholic theologian Karl Rahner has argued, Jesus *implicitly* knew his unique relation with God. That connection with God was always part of who he was. Saying that need not imply any particular claims about how much he had thought through the issues or what language he might have used in describing them.[8] In those matters, as in others, he was a particular, limited human being.

Thus in having a body and developing through internal conflict and in the context of a particular culture, Jesus was like us. But if he had been *exactly* like us, he would have been just one more human sinner. Christians, therefore, also have to consider how he was *different* in his humanity.

Being in Relation

Like every other human being, Jesus was human by being in relation with others. This is a point we could learn from many schools of contemporary philosophy and psychology. Human beings do not have a basic core identity, and then develop relations with other people. Rather, their relations help shape their core identities. If I grow up in a family where my parents constantly demean and insult me, then I will probably become emotionally stunted and have no self-confidence. That would not be a secondary modification of my real identity; it would be, alas, a crucial aspect of the person I have really become. Similarly, falling in love doesn't leave me the same person with now a different external relationship; it changes who I am.[9]

The New Testament likewise does not offer us a picture of Jesus apart from relationships, the inner core of who he was apart from his interactions. Shakespearean characters speak soliloquies, in which we seem to overhear them speaking to themselves. But Jesus is always talking to someone else. "Of course the story does not give his inner thoughts," some might protest. "The narrator could not claim to know them." But the Gospel narrators *do* recount prayers Jesus spoke to God, which no one could have overheard. So the absence of monologues is not only because no one heard Jesus talking to himself; it is a way of deliberately presenting Jesus as never just engaged with himself, but always in relation to someone else, whether that someone else is his divine "Father" or other human beings.[10]

The most important of his relationships, of course, is with the one he called his Father, and the basic character of that relationship is his obedience. In Luke's Gospel, the first words Jesus speaks come when his parents find him, a boy of twelve, talking with the elders in the Temple. Why did he wander off, they demand, and he replies, "Did you not know that I must be in my Father's house?" (Luke 2:49). The last words he speaks, dying on a cross, are "Father, into your hands I commend my spirit" (23:46). Beginning to end, it is a story of obedience to God.

The theme of obedience echoes through the New Testament. Consider first some passages from John:

> Whatever the Father does, the Son does likewise. (John 5:19)
> I seek to do not my own will but the will of [the one] who sent me. (5:30)
> The words that I say to you I do not speak on my own; but the Father who dwells in me does his works. (14:10)

The letter to the Hebrews talks about how, "although he was a Son, he learned obedience through what he suffered" (Heb. 5:8).

Paul understood Jesus as a "second Adam" whose life of obedience undid what the first Adam had done: "For just as by the one man's disobedience the many were made sinners, so by the one man's obedience the many will be made righteous" (Rom. 5:19). The second-century theologian Irenaeus developed this idea into a theory of "recapitulation": just as Adam's descendants live out the consequences of his original *disobedience*, so Christ, by becoming human, redefines what it means to be human by recapitulating the story of human life, this time as a narrative of *obedience* to God.[11]

Obedience might strike us as a stuffy, boring virtue, "just following the rules." But not when we look at Jesus; his obedience is consistently *imaginative*. The Broadway musical *Godspell* portrayed Jesus as a kind of vaudeville clown, acting out crazy stories, always coming up with the unexpected punchline. There were aspects of the Gospel it got wrong or just missed, but remarkably, the vast majority of the words in the script came straight from the Gospel according to Matthew. Jesus has the kind of imagination we see in brilliant comedians. In what he says and does, as we meet him in these stories, he is full of unexpected twists and turns. He touches ritually unclean people. He spends his time with the poor and despised folk, but then he sits down to dinner with a wealthy and corrupt tax collector. He admits that the Law says one thing, but he himself says something else. He tells crazy stories about how people who worked only the last hour of the day get paid as much as those who worked the whole day long.

And yet he makes all this strangeness seem *right*. The unclean people don't pollute him; *he* cures *them*. The tax collector reforms and gives away most of his wealth. The new things he says about the Law, and the crazy stories he tells, seem to fit the picture of a God who would come down among us in reckless love. If one were obedient to such a God, this is what it would look like—and it doesn't look boring at all.

The best analogy may come from the arts. What's amazing about a Mozart symphony or a Shakespearean sonnet is that it keeps surprising us, yet every surprise seems just the right answer in a way that makes it feel retrospectively inevitable. The music or words seem to do just the right thing, but in a way we never would have thought of. So it is with Jesus' way of being human.

This obedience to God doesn't distract Jesus from other relations. We might expect that in a life of perfect obedience to God there wouldn't be time for anyone else. Again, not so. Jesus heals the sick and preaches to the poor. He teaches his disciples and holds small children in his arms. One senses he's the sort of person who can change people's lives in a brief meeting because he is so completely engaged with them. When asked to identify the most important of all the commandments, he *refuses* and insists on citing two—not only loving "the Lord your God with all your heart, and with all your soul, and with all your mind, and with all your strength," but also loving "your neighbor as yourself" (Mark 12:30–31).

Love, like Jesus' kind of obedience, flourishes when manifested imaginatively. Imagination helps us show our love in ways that do some good. "I wish there was something I could do," we often say to a friend in grief or pain. But often there *is* something we could do, had we the wit to think of it. So Jesus loves the woman taken in adultery (John 8:1–11). But she is about to be stoned to death—what can he do? Should he argue her innocence? She is guilty. Should he try to fight off her attackers? They outnumber him. So he responds imaginatively: "Let anyone among you who is without sin be the first to throw a stone at her," he says (John 8:7). And, one by one, her accusers depart.

In part 4, I will return to the ways in which imagination can offer alternatives to violence and confrontation. My point here is simply that Jesus' love, like his obedience, draws power from his imagination, and that love is not in conflict with obedience.

But why should this really be surprising? If Jesus is revealing how much God loves us by enacting that love, then why would there be any contradiction between obedience to God and love to human beings? Indeed, wouldn't such obedience manifest itself most naturally precisely in such love? If Jesus shows us the recklessness of God's love, are the forms it takes not likely often to be surprising?

The Firstborn of All Creation

To talk only about Jesus' relations to the one he called his Father and to human beings, however, is to narrow the picture of his relatedness far too much. Jesus the Christ is not just the pioneer of salvation for human beings, but "the firstborn of all creation, for . . . all things have been created through him and for him" (Col. 1:15–16). After all, the whole creation needs redemption.

The prophet Hosea described how, as a result of the faithlessness of the people of Israel,

. . . the land mourns,
  and all who live in it languish;
together with the wild animals
  and the birds of the air,
  even the fish of the sea are perishing.
      (Hos. 4:3)

In Hosea's time, such language functioned for the most part as metaphor—things were so bad among humankind that it was *as if* the land mourned. But in our age, human sin really can devastate ecosystems and cause whole species to perish. Any righting of the wrongs caused by sin has to address such issues.

Christian hope therefore involves not just hope for human beings but, as Paul wrote to the Romans, hope "that the creation itself will be set free from its bondage to decay and will obtain the freedom of the glory of the children of God" (Rom. 8:21). At one level, that could imply practical improvements: if Christ inspired human beings to be less selfish, we could improve the state of the world's environment. But the Christian tradition has also envisioned a deeper relationship between humankind and the rest of creation. In human beings, creation reaches a point where creatures can *consciously* enter into relation with God's love, so that, if Christ's obedience begins a process of transforming humanity, we can in turn serve as representatives to begin a cosmic process of enfolding all creatures into the embrace of God's love.[12]

4

The Man Jesus

Jesus was not just a generic human creature, but a male. Among all the ways in which Jesus was a *particular* human being, his maleness has become, for many Christians, the most problematic. Women who encounter the stories of Jesus, presented as the good news that God came to be a human being like us, may understandably say, "Well, he came to be like a *man*; he didn't come to be like *me*." Women who have fought for the right to make their own decisions about their own lives, presented with this male savior, may understandably say, "Here we go again. Once more I'm being asked to save myself by throwing myself helplessly into the arms of some *man*."[1]

But the awkwardness isn't easy to fix. Jesus wasn't a woman—the stories make that clear enough. And human beings do come with one sexual identity or another. If we try to deny the maleness of this person who shows us what it is to be truly human, we end up implying that sexuality is an evil thing that isn't part of true humanity.

The Bible generally takes it for granted that our sexuality is a part of who we are, natural and therefore as good (though also as subject to misuse) as any other aspect of our humanity. Too many Christians down the centuries have taken the path of hating or fearing sexuality, in defiance of biblical claims and to the great detriment of psychological health. The Renaissance artists had it right: they deliberately painted the baby Jesus, naked, penis and all, leaving true humanity indisputable.[2]

But what do we do about the fact that women may therefore feel that these stories leave them out? First of all, it is worth pointing out again that Jesus was a particular human being in all sorts of ways: a man rather than a woman, a Middle Easterner rather than a northern European or an East Asian, the son of a young girl rather than of an older woman, and so on. To many of his contemporaries, perhaps his most important particularity was that he was a Jew rather than a Gentile.[3]

The Vatican recently argued that priests must be male on the grounds that "there must be a natural resemblance between the priest and Christ."[4] What does that mean? Does that mean that all priests also need to be, just for a start, Middle Eastern Jews? We are all like Jesus in some ways and unlike him in others. None of us is in a position to feel privileged in being altogether like him (as men often have); none of us should feel (as women sometimes do) left out because of our difference.

Moreover, given that Jesus grew up and lived in a patriarchal culture where women's subordination in a great many ways was taken for granted, he said and did some surprising things. In the Gospel stories, he never says anything demeaning about women or praises them for some "distinctively feminine" gift. On the contrary, he praises Mary of Bethany for "neglecting" her household tasks to listen to his teaching (Luke 10:42). Normally in that culture the men would have listened while the women tended the kitchen. In defiance of his culture's sense of propriety, women seem to travel about with him, all the way from Galilee to Jerusalem.[5] He uses female imagery to describe both himself and God, imagining himself as a hen who gathers her brood of chicks under her wings (Matt. 23:37). His "masculinity," in any stereotyped sense of the word, does not form a central element of his character. For macho Samson or Father Abraham, masculinity seems critical to who they are. Jesus' maleness seems almost irrelevant to his identity.

From time to time in Christian history, particularly from the twelfth to the fourteenth centuries, indeed, some Christians have spoken of Jesus as "Mother." Listen to the great theologian Anselm, writing in about 1100:

> And you, Jesus, are you not also like a mother?
> Are you not the mother who, like a hen,
> gathers her chickens under her wings? . . .
> And you, my soul, dead in yourself,
> run under the wings of Jesus your mother
> and lament your griefs under his feathers. . . .
> Mother, know again your dead son,
> both by the sign of your cross and the voice of his confession.
> Warm your chicken, give life to your dead man,
> justify your sinner.[6]

A couple of centuries later, the Englishwoman Julian of Norwich, a mystic and theologian, developed such language and connected it with the idea of Christ as Wisdom, pairing God the Father with Jesus our Mother:

> God almighty is our loving Father, and God all wisdom is our loving Mother, with the love and the goodness of the Holy Spirit, which is all one God, one Lord. . . . The high might of the Trinity is our Father, and the deep wisdom of the Trinity is our Mother, and the great love of the Trinity is our Lord. . . . And so . . . in our Mother Christ we profit and increase, and in mercy he reforms and restores us.[7]

In some medieval monasteries, the model of Jesus as mother even led abbots to think of themselves in more stereotypically maternal terms, and to provide a more nurturing and less hierarchical kind of leadership.[8]

Given that we ought to pay more attention to feminine images for Jesus' identity, he still was biologically male. Should we make anything of that theologically? It's tempting to say that he was simply human, and none of the particularities of his humanity make any theological difference. But some of the ways in which he was particular do seem to matter. If he had been born a prince in the royal palace, his story would give us a very different picture of how he is the Lord who is a servant. If he had not been born a Jew, could we have understood him as the fulfillment of Israel's hopes concerning God's promises? Maybe—but in a very different way. So what about the fact that he was male?

One very old Christian answer is that Christ's maleness precisely encompasses all of humanity in the incarnation, since Mary, a woman, gave birth to Jesus, a boy. If Mary had given birth to a daughter savior, then men would have been left out of the story altogether. Yet Mary was still not God incarnate. Without her, there could have been no incarnation, and no purely human male had such a role. But it remains a supporting role, even if the most important one, and indeed too much emphasis on this line of argument risks *reinforcing* bad stereotypes—the woman as the passive one, the one whose most important role is to give birth to babies.[9]

A more challenging interpretation comes from another perspective. What we learn in the life of Jesus, after all, is that true power must manifest itself in servanthood. Given the way men's power has dominated history, having a *man* illustrate that point makes it all the clearer.[10] To have a woman manifest the lessons Jesus teaches us about the interplay between power, love, and suffering would have risked losing the moral of the story. We could have said, "Ah, yes, this is the way *women* influence history—through gentle love and suffering." If Jesus is a man, we are at least saved from the double mistake of reinforcing cultural stereotypes about women and ignoring the radical challenge Jesus poses to many stereotypically male forms of power.

Still, it seems risky to make quite so much of Jesus' maleness as is involved in trying to explain the point of it, particularly since this is a move the Bible itself doesn't make. Jesus had to be someone particular. That he was male raises one set of problems, but another set would have emerged had he been female. His being male risks reinforcing ideas of male superiority, but his being female might have reinforced stereotypes of feminine suffering servanthood. Perhaps it is best to leave it at that. What matters is that the loving and mysterious God became a human one among us.

Christ, then, was both human and divine. He showed us how to be human and showed us what it means to be divine. How is it possible to be both at once? And what difference does it make for us that human and divine natures are united in this one person?

5

Human *and* Divine

By uniting humanity with the divine, Christ changes what it is to be human. "Having become what we are," Gregory of Nyssa wrote, "He through Himself again united humanity to God."[1] Christian theologians of the third and fourth centuries used a variety of images to explain this transformation. Cyril of Alexandria said that Christ had dyed the human soul with the divine nature.[2] Athanasius and Hilary both compared humanity to a whole city which is honored and given special care because the king lives there.[3] Just as all the other inhabitants of the city get special attention because of the identity of one of their fellow citizens, so we are different because divinity was united with humanity in one of our fellow human beings. Gregory of Nazianzus compared it to how the sun's rays burn off the fog in the morning—the quality of all the air changes as the sun's light fills it.[4]

In the Eastern churches, the dominant idea was *deification*. The divine Word became human so that humanity might become divine.[5] Other theologians usually preferred to think that, even in our transformed state, we remain creatures and therefore not divine. They often talked about *adoption*—the Word, the *natural* child of God, became human so that we might all become *adopted* children of God.

Either way, the idea was that, once Christ has become human, what it is to be human changes for everyone else. Most early theologians did not think of this transformation as an event that happened in the instant of the incarnation. It was only through the "whole course of his obedience" that Christ transformed humanity.[6] But the incarnation provides the starting point: our sin had so cut us off from God that, before anything else could happen, God had to reestablish contact, and that meant changing wayward, lost, sinful humanity into something open to connection with God.

The incarnation reestablished that contact in the most dramatic way imaginable. When the word became flesh, what it means to be human changed for each of us—you, me, Hitler, the bag lady, and the heroin addict huddled on a street corner on a winter night—because in one human being humanity was united with divinity. "For you know the generous act of our Lord Jesus Christ, that though he was rich, yet for your sakes he became poor, so that by his poverty you might become rich" (2 Cor. 8:9). That transformation implies both a factual claim—humanity really has been changed—and an ethical injunction—therefore we ought to try to live lives worthy of what we have become.[7]

But what does it mean to say that humanity and divinity were united in Christ? An ongoing debate on such matters in the early church reached one level of resolution at the Council of Chalcedon in 451. But as with many agreements, the document produced at Chalcedon then raised another set of questions about exactly what it meant, and debates continued for several centuries.

Alexandria and Antioch

Historians often identify the two most prominent parties in the debate with two of the great cities of the eastern Mediterranean—Alexandria in Egypt and Antioch in Syria. The Alexandrians began with the Word or *Logos* as it was described in the first chapter of John: "The Word became flesh and lived among us." "The Word of God," as Athanasius, the greatest of Alexandrian theologians, put it, "took a human body to save and help human beings, so that having shared our human birth, he might make human beings partakers of the divine and spiritual nature."[8]

This approach embodied both a strength and a danger. The strength was that it portrayed, as the New Testament does, one agent, the Word made flesh, doing what Jesus Christ does.[9] Who took on human flesh? Who died on the cross? Who accomplished our salvation? The Word of God, none other.[10]

The danger came when you asked what then was human about Christ. Athanasius seemed unaware of the importance of this question and made inconsistent comments about it, but a younger friend of his named Apollinaris took an unambiguous position. Christ, he said, had a human *body*, but not a human mind or soul. The Word took the place in him that would normally have been occupied by a human mind. In Apollinaris' words, "The Word became flesh without assuming a human mind; a human mind is subject to change and is the captive of filthy imaginations; but he was a divine mind, changeless and heavenly."[11]

What was wrong with that? Well, two things at least. First, the Gospels tell us things about Jesus Christ that seem to imply that he had a human mind as well as body. He got tired and thirsty; he was afraid sometimes; he was tempted. These aren't things we would say of God—yet they seem to be, at least in part, mental as well as physical.[12]

Second, the whole argument about the saving power of the incarnation rests on the idea that sinners like us can be saved because humanity has been united with divinity in Christ. But suppose, as Apollinaris seemed to claim, only a human *body* has been united with divinity. Our minds seem to be the part of us that principally sins—yet on Apollinaris' model, no human mind was united with anything in Christ.[13] Gregory of Nazianzus objected that uniting divinity only with human flesh when sin lies principally in the soul would be as if, noticing someone's eye had been injured, "you were to tend to the foot and leave the eye uncared for."[14] Only what is united with God can be saved, and therefore, "that which he has not assumed he has not healed"[15]—so, their critics said, for the Apollinarians our mind or soul is not healed.

Thus from the wrong turn some Alexandrian theology took, Christians learned a lesson: however humanity and divinity were united in Christ, *all* of human nature had to be involved in that unity.

The theologians of Antioch understood that principle from the start, but some of them made their own wrong turn. They taught that Christ had a human *nature* and a divine *nature*, and the two were united in one *person*. That seemed safe enough—a "human nature" would include everything human, mind as well as body—until one started to ask what kind of unity they meant. Not much of a unity, it sometimes turned out. Theodore of Mopsuestia, maybe the greatest of the Antiochene theologians, said that the divine nature didn't "taste the trial of death" on the cross but only hung around "near enough to do the needful and necessary things for the [human] nature that was assumed by it."[16] The divine nature itself wasn't directly involved in suffering. Theodore even called each of the natures "he," which made it sound as if he was really talking about two *persons*,[17] and a later theologian in the Antiochene tradition named Nestorius pushed the distinctions even harder. As one historian put it, it's as if the "Nestorians" thought of the human and divine as two people in a sort of business partnership.[18]

For Antiochene theology in its more extreme forms, the two natures seemed so separate that they lost that unity of agency which is one of the most obvious characteristics of the Gospels, where we never sense that Jesus is some sort of two-member committee. In particular, if Nestorius and others assigned things like "suffering on the cross" to the human nature, then it seemed as if the human nature really saved us—the human nature did the heavy lifting while the divine nature looked on.

So from the wrong turn taken by Antioch, Christian theologians realized (1) that the unity of human and divine in Christ had to be strong enough so that Christ was one agent, yet, (2) if one was to avoid falling into the Alexandrian trap, that one agent had to include a human mind as well as a human body.

The Council of Chalcedon

When the leaders of the church gathered at Chalcedon in 451, they therefore affirmed:

> We all with one voice confess our Lord Jesus Christ . . . truly God and truly human, the same consisting of a reasonable soul and a body, of one substance with the Father as touching the Godhead, of one substance with us as touching the humanity . . . to be acknowledged in two natures, without confusion, without change, without division, without separation.[19]

Against Alexandrian extremes, Christ had not only a human body but a "reasonable soul." Against Antiochene extremes, Christ's "two natures" were joined without "division" or "separation."

In reaching this conclusion, the members of the Council of Chalcedon followed at least three principles.

1. Like the Council of Nicaea, they stated what Christians needed to affirm, but they didn't offer a lot of explanations about *how* that could be the case. Notice that the crucial section consists of four negatives: the two natures are *without* confusion, change, division, or separation. Those negatives draw the line against potential errors. They do not claim to penetrate the mystery of God far enough to understand how the relevant mechanisms work.[20]

2. Without getting into the details of the Greek terminology, the basic argument, particularly as Chalcedon was interpreted in subsequent generations, was that in Christ there were two *whats* and one *who*.[21] That is, if we ask *what* Jesus Christ was, there are two answers: he was God, and he was a human being. He did things—forgiving sins and accomplishing our salvation, for example—that only God can do. He did other things—growing tired or eating a meal—that human beings do. But if we ask *who* did these things, there is just one answer—Jesus Christ did them.

Instead of an explanation of how that could be possible, the Bible gives us stories that *show* it. Christ cures a blind man—but he does it by applying his own spit. He thus does a divine thing in a very human way. He dies on a cross, but he does it in a way that wins our salvation, thus doing the most human of things in a divine way. The story thus keeps both the "whats" always before us, but we never get a sense of two agents at work, much less of first one and then another, like some weird story of multiple personalities. Jesus Christ is the one "who" that he is, even as he is both divine and human.[22]

An inadequate analogy: In the Broadway musical *Camelot*, King Arthur gives a speech after he discovers that his queen and Sir Lancelot have fallen in love. "I am a man," he says, and therefore angry and jealous, and ready to go out and challenge Lancelot to the death. But "I am a king," he says, and therefore he needs the help of his finest knight to defend the land, and he can't afford the risk of dividing the knights of the round table. His problem is that he is both a king and a man, yet there is never any doubt that he is just one Arthur. One who, two whats. In Christ, the whats—being a human and being God—are much more radically different than in any other example, and so understanding how they could be united is more difficult. But Christ doesn't have Arthur's problem, and the reason goes back to one of the categories that defines his humanity—obedience. Christ's humanity manifests itself in his full obedience to God, so that, while the differences between humanity and divinity are immeasurably greater than those between Arthur's manhood and kingship, they never come into conflict. We do not have a way of *imagining how* the unity operates, but we *see it enacted* in what this one person does.

3. In the relation of human and divine in Christ, however, there is always a kind of asymmetry. He acts both humanly and divinely, but the human in him is always obedient to the divine. The divine takes priority. That's what Chalcedon kept from the Alexandrian tradition, where the divine Word was always the agent in Christ.[23] In the incarnation of the divine Word, however, humanity is transformed—not just for Jesus but for all of us. It has become a different thing to be a human being.

Our society, like many others, tends to tell lots of people that they are not very important. We celebrate the "rich and famous," but few of us are famous, and a shrinking number of people holds a larger and larger percentage of the wealth. The power that emerges when a group of people follows Jesse Jackson in chanting, "I am somebody," makes it vivid how people can begin to doubt that they are anybody, and how much pain that doubt can cause them.

I remember some years ago visiting Washington, D.C., noticing how many people defined themselves by their connections. "I went to prep school with the vice president's son." "That cabinet secretary used to be my boss, and she still remembers me." Hearing such comments in Washington, I noticed them particularly, but don't we all say similar things? "I studied in graduate school with the famous professor." "My office is right next to the boss's." "I used to play basketball with the famous star." And yet, these claims are trivial compared with the one available to us all: "I share the same humanity assumed by the Word of God." If we really understand that, then all our doubts about our own worth, all our compulsive needs to prove the significance of our particular connections, ought to dissolve, and at the same time so should our sense of who the "important people" are. Compared with this qualification that *every-body* has, all our usual criteria of importance seem singularly *un*important.

In our society, it seems hard to grasp the importance of every human life. Pope John Paul II has denounced the "culture of death" which pervades the contemporary world. He condemns abortion, the death penalty, and war as among its manifestations. Yet a recent survey of the United States Congress (which includes many Catholics) could find only one member who opposed both abortion and capital punishment. Political values rather than religious ones usually shape our views: liberals favor abortion on demand, conservatives applaud executions, and very few consistently begin their thinking with the inestimable value of each human life.

I know that these are complicated issues. I will consider some of the complexities of criminal justice and war in later chapters. With respect to abortion, I acknowledge that the moment when human life begins continues to be debated (even Thomas Aquinas thought that it occurred at "quickening" rather than conception) and that in some painful circumstances abortion might be a lesser evil than other options. But if we value every human life, then abortion seems a tragedy, even if what it ends is only a potential human life and even if the tragedy lies most of all in the events and oppressive social structures that led to the abortion. Christians, moreover, should be cautious about trying to legislate our own moral views in a pluralistic society. But that doesn't mean we should abandon the right to have moral views. If the Word of God, through whom all the universe came into being, became incarnate in one human being, then we cannot treat even a potential human life cavalierly.

Matthew tells how Jesus described the final judgment in which he will tell those at his right hand, "I was hungry and you gave me food, I was thirsty and you gave me something to drink, I was a stranger and you welcomed me, I was naked and you gave me clothing, I was sick and you took care of me, I was in prison and you visited me." Then he will tell those on his left, "I was hungry and you gave me no food, I was thirsty and you gave me nothing to drink, I was a stranger and you did not welcome me, naked and you did not give me clothing, sick and in prison and you did not visit me" (Matt. 25:35–36, 42–43). Neither group can remember such events, and Jesus has to explain that, when they did or failed to do these things for the least of human beings, they were doing it or failing to do it for him, Jesus Christ, the Word of God made flesh. Just so: for the humanity in each of us is united with divinity in Christ.[23]

6

Christmas

When most Christians reflect on God becoming human in Jesus Christ, they think not about theories about the incarnation but about the Christmas stories. We may not understand the relation of natures and person, but we remember Mary and Joseph and the baby, the shepherds and the wise men. St. Francis showed his characteristic genius when, at Christmas in 1223, he set up, for the first time we know of in history, an image of the baby in the manger, and invited the people in the neighborhood to come see this representation of the Christmas story. Here as much as anywhere, stories and images may convey meaning better than theological concepts. "Look upon the Baby Jesus," Martin Luther once wrote. "Divinity may terrify us. Inexpressible majesty will crush us. That is why Christ took on our humanity, except for sin, that he should not terrify us but rather that with love and favor he should console and confirm."[1]

The danger is always to sentimentalize the Christmas stories, and focus on the cuteness of the newborn child rather than the awesome mystery of the Incarnation. If we can get behind all the bad Christmas card art to the biblical stories themselves, however, we will find that they are remarkable in their resistance to sentimentality.

Before looking at these stories of Jesus' birth, however, it is worth noting that they have an odd relation to the rest of the Gospel narratives. Of the four Gospels, Mark and John tell us nothing about the events surrounding Jesus' birth. Both Matthew and Luke trace his genealogy (though differently), and both tell of his birth from a virgin. Matthew has the story of the three Magi (the astrologers or "wise men") and an angel appearing to Joseph, while in Luke there are shepherds, and the angel appears to Mary—and there's a whole account of the birth of John the Baptist besides. These birth stories seem unconnected to the rest of the Gospels—after them there is a big jump forward in time to Jesus' adulthood, and no one in the rest of the story seems to remember these strange events surrounding Jesus' birth.

None of this need imply skepticism, but it does invite us to reflect on the character of these particular stories. One cannot imagine two of the Gospels leaving out the cross or the resurrection or expressing them in some other way. But Mark and John find different ways of indicating that Jesus was the Son of God. To my reading, the birth narratives in Matthew and Luke just feel different—more abrupt, more mysterious, a bit less like history and more like fairy tale—than the accounts of Jesus' ministry which follow them. The 1964 Roman Catholic Pontifical Biblical Commission on "The Historical Truth of the Gospels" may have been wise in making claims of historical accuracy only for the stories of Jesus' ministry, when his disciples were following him.[2] Matthew and Luke may have been struggling to find ways to convey a mystery in a form as much poetry as history. This is all the more reason to read their stories with care.

Unfamiliar Readings of Familiar Stories

At the core of the stories is this: a young virgin named Mary came to be with child by the Holy Spirit. The first result was scandal—her fiancé wanted to disown her. "This holy virgin," in Luther's words, "celebrated by all the prophets, was judged by her own husband to be a loose woman."[3] The story of the Virgin Birth emphasizes that Jesus Christ does not somehow emerge from gradual human advances but from the pure grace of God. It is not, Karl Barth once wrote, meant to *explain* Jesus' birth. "Rather it brought to light essentially and purposefully its very inexplicability, its character of mystery."[4]

Matthew's version of the story begins with a genealogy of "Jesus the Messiah, the son of David, the son of Abraham." That locates Jesus in the context of Israel's history, from the first patriach through the greatest king. In general, the genealogy traces (as we might expect in a patriarchal culture) the male lineage, but five women do appear in this list of Jesus' ancestors. What an odd group they are! Tamar's story comes from Genesis 38: Judah had promised her that she would marry his son, and then broke his promise. So she disguised herself as a prostitute and tricked Judah into fathering twins by her. Perhaps to the surprise of most modern readers, she is judged to be in the right, and her twins become the ancestors of two tribal lines in Israel.

Rahab was a prostitute who hid Joshua's first spies in Israel. Ruth was a despised foreigner who married into the Israelite people but became the great grandmother of King David. Bathsheba became the wife of David only after he had her husband killed in battle, but she gave birth to Solomon. And Mary, Jesus' mother—she's engaged to Joseph but hasn't slept with him, and now she's pregnant: "Joseph, being a righteous man and unwilling to expose her to public disgrace, planned to dismiss her quietly" (Matt. 1:19).

In a world convinced that, with rare exceptions, men made history, not women—and certainly not such an odd collection of women as these, who violate all sorts of social norms of respectability—the stories tell us that they are part of the way in which God was at work to bring about the Incarnation.[5]

Matthew's story shifts abruptly from Mary, the poor woman under suspicion, to the Magi. They are mysterious figures—wise men, magicians, astrologers—but it is clear that they move comfortably in the world of power. They go to the king's palace, and Herod meets with them. In that respect, they stand in radical contrast to Mary. Yet they too are outsiders. Garrison Keillor tells of the Lutheran pastor in Minnesota who singled out the Magi as particularly relevant to his congregation: because they were the only people in the Gospel not identified as either Jews or Romans, they were the only ones who might, just might, have been Norwegians. At any rate, they were foreigners. Matthew is the most Jewish-oriented of the Gospel authors, yet right at the start he presents these mysterious Gentiles from who knows where as the first to pay Jesus honor.

They had followed a star, the story says, and Christians with a bent for astronomy have often speculated about various comets, supernovae, or particular juxtapositions of planets in the night sky, which might explain the bright star. In Jesus' time, any of these might have served for a portent in the sky, and people took such phenomena seriously. During the Jewish rebellion against the Romans a generation or so after the time of Jesus, the historian Josephus reports, the Jews held out as long as they did when Jerusalem was under seige in part because "a star resembling a sword, stood over the city, and a comet . . . continued for a year."[6] But we know no more about the astronomical details of the Magi's star than we do of the one reported by Josephus.

What we have is a story. In search of a newborn king, the Magi naturally enough went to the royal palace. But the scribes and priests consulted the Scripture and referred them instead to the little town of Bethlehem. King Herod, the villain of the story, feared a rival in this "new king" for whom they were searching, so he asked the Magi to report to him once they had found the child. But a dream warned them to go home another way, and we never hear of them again. Herod, however, takes no chances, and kills all the children he can find around Bethlehem under the age of two.

> "A voice was heard in Ramah,
> wailing and loud lamentation,
> Rachel weeping for her children."
> (Matt. 2:18, quoting Jeremiah)

Another dream had warned Joseph, however, and he had taken his family and fled to Egypt.

It is a brutally realistic way of looking at God's work in history, with the birth of God's Son so closely connected to all those murdered babies. But history *is* brutal. From other historical sources we know that Herod killed two of his own children, and ordered prominent citizens from all the villages of Judea murdered when he died, so that people would treat the occasion as one of mourning.[7] If anyone thinks of the Christmas stories as piously cute and therefore irrelevant to the lives of real, suffering people, they have not read them carefully.

Immersed as he is in the Hebrew Scriptures, Matthew makes all sorts of connections—with Jeremiah's lamentations for Rachel and her children, and even more with Moses. His Gospel presents Jesus as a new Moses bringing a kind of new law, and here already he connects the two stories: just as Moses was floated in a basket in the bulrushes when Pharaoh sought to kill all the Hebrew babies, so Jesus is rescued from the murderous plot of Herod. In case we missed the connection, Matthew notes that the family fled to Egypt.[8]

But the story also seems to contain more universal lessons. Human beings, even the wisest and most learned among them, we are reminded, assume that power lies in palaces, but that kind of power produces violence and horror. Stars and dreams and Scriptures point in a different direction—in this case, improbably enough, to a baby in a stable. The Magi bring him gifts: the gold that befits a monarch, the incense employed in the worship of a god, and myrrh, used in anointing a dead body. Here at its beginning, Matthew's story of Jesus anticipates monarchy and divinity, yet of such an odd sort that they come to glory only on the other side of death. Showing us what it means to be truly God and truly human, Jesus will show the power of vulnerable love, and the servanthood that is the most perfect kind of rule.

Luke draws some of the same lessons from a different set of stories. He also interrupts his account of Jesus' birth and surrounding events with three hymns or poems. In the "Magnificat" (Luke 1:46–55; these are the traditional names, derived from a Latin word or phrase at the beginning of each poem) Mary gives thanks for her miraculous pregnancy. In the "Benedictus" (Luke 1:67–79), Zechariah, the father of John the Baptist, prophesies concerning the Messiah about to be born. In the "Nunc Dimittis" (Luke 2:29–32) the aged Simeon, who had been promised in a vision that he would not die before he had seen the Messiah, gives thanks on seeing the infant Jesus.

Luke (or whoever wrote this Gospel) must have drawn on earlier material here. The poems fit abruptly into the narrative, and their imagery includes more Hebrew-like grammatical constructions than normally are found in Luke's elegant Greek.[9] They are filled with the traditional language in which Israel thanks the Lord for defending the nation against oppressors.

To a Jew, this would not be just pleasant poetic language about the birth of a baby. The Magnificat evokes the Song of Miriam, celebrating the triumph in which the Lord drowned the Egyptian army in the sea (Exod. 15), and the Song of Deborah, in which the prophetess Deborah rejoiced in a military victory by reviewing God's mighty acts through Israel's history (Jud. 5). The closest verbal parallel connects Mary to Jael, "the wife of Heber the Kenite," who had killed a general who had fought against Israel, after he fled the battle scene, by driving a tent peg through his skull (Judg. 5:26).

One cannot complain that the imagery related to Mary is too passive, gentle, and stereotypically female! Moreover, her words emphasize the radical implications of this child she carries. "My soul magnifies the Lord," Luke has her say,

> and my spirit rejoices in God my Savior,
> for [God] has looked with favor on
> the lowliness of [God's] servant. . . .
> [God] has scattered the proud in the thoughts of their hearts.
> [God] has brought down the powerful from their thrones,
> and lifted up the lowly;
> [God] has filled the hungry with good things,
> and sent the rich away empty.
> (1:46–48,51–53)

Though it is other things too, this is poetry about social revolution and victory over oppressors.

Some Lessons from the Stories

The radical priest Ernesto Cardenal, in the worst times under the Somoza dictatorship in Nicaragua, would invite his peasant congregation to discuss the Gospel texts. They quickly warmed to these stories of Jesus' birth: "It's as though someone here in Somoza's Nicaragua was announcing a liberator," one said. And others responded: "And Mary joins the ranks of the subversives, too, just by receiving that message." "That Jesus who was born in a manger, like a child is born here . . . in a farmhouse, is the liberation that's being born here, in a humble form."[10] Later, Cardenal proved indifferent to the oppression imposed by a Marxist government in which he and his brother played prominent roles. But as a pastor, before the Marxist revolution, he heard the voices of the peasants in his congregation as they heard the stories of Jesus' birth speak to their situation.

In our comfortable lives, we can lose sight of how much the context of the Gospel birth narratives concerns political oppression. Mary and Joseph set off to Bethlehem because it was the city of Joseph's ancestors, and the Roman governor had ordered everyone to go to their ancestral city so that a census could be taken.

Censuses have a bad reputation in Scripture. When David took a census of the people of Israel, he so angered the Lord that a great plague was sent to the nation as punishment (2 Sam. 24). One point of this odd story is that a census gives the king greater power over the people (who can be tracked for purposes of taxes and military drafts), and refuses simply to trust in God for the health of the nation. It may be even worse when the Romans conduct a census, given that they are foreign conquerors with a notoriously corrupt system of taxation. This Roman census, in fact, apparently produced a Jewish revolt led by Judas the Galilean.[11]

Real justice, the Greek historian Thucydides has one of his characters remark, exists only between equals, while "the strong do what they can, and the weak suffer what they must."[12] In this story imperial officers lay down their edicts, and an ordinary man and his pregnant wife accommodate themselves as best they can. In Thucydides, though, the interaction of political and military power is the *only* story; in the Gospels, it is only background for the story that really matters, and in that story human power does not have the last word.

The place of shepherds in the story reinforces the point. We are apt to romanticize the gentle shepherds and their sheep, but in Jesus' time most respectable people would not have recognized such portrayals. Shepherds were thoroughly disreputable. They were poor, and they were always trying to graze their sheep on someone else's property; the Babylonian Talmud even lists them among the categories of people who may not testify in court, because their word simply cannot be trusted.[13] Yet it is to them that angels appear with news of the Messiah's birth, they who will thus be God's witnesses.

"There are many of you," Luther scolded his congregation, "who think to yourselves: 'If only I had been there! How quick I would have been to help the baby!' . . . You say that because you know how great Christ is, but if you had been there at that time you would have done no better than the people of Bethlehem. . . . Why don't you do it now? You have Christ in your neighbor."[14] The doctrine of the incarnation gives us the principle that the humanity in the least of persons is now transformed. And the Christmas story gives that principle a human face, in the baby born in the stable because there was no room in the inn.

Even the stories of his birth make clear that Jesus is going to change the rules. He is a king born in a stable. He is God made flesh, but his birth occasions scandal and violence. Authorities appear in the story ordering people around and massacring children. It is an embarrassed woman, some strange foreigners, and some disreputable shepherds who seem to be those with whom and through whom God is working in the birth of this human being who is also God. Jesus' birth set the pattern for his ministry.

PART 2

Ministry

Ministry

This part of the book moves from Jesus' birth (discussed in part 1) to the time just before his death (discussed in part 3). I've entitled it "ministry" rather than "life" to emphasize the point that no one can write a biography of Jesus. The Gospels skip over most of his life, concentrating almost exclusively on his last year or few years, when he traveled about teaching and healing. We can make guesses about his life before then—an ordinary adolescence and young manhood as a carpenter's son in a small Galilean town, or perhaps something very different—but we have no way of knowing. Here as elsewhere the New Testament presents stories about what he said and did only when they are relevant to his role as Savior. I'm using "ministry" in that general sense: his activities as a preacher, teacher, healer, leader, and friend in those years or months before the last week of his life.

Much of Christian theology down the centuries has downplayed this part of Jesus' story, focusing on his incarnation, death, and resurrection. In his catechism for the children of Geneva, for instance, John Calvin turned directly from the questions about the incarnation and birth of Jesus to those on his suffering and death. "Why do you leap at once from his birth to his death, passing over the whole history of his life?" the questioner asks. Nothing relevant to our salvation, comes the answer, happened in between.[1]

It's one of the stupidest things Calvin ever said (and contrary to his more considered judgment that Christ saved "by the whole course of his obedience"), yet he was following much of the Christian tradition in saying it. The two most important creeds of the church—the Nicene and Apostles'—likewise jump straight from Jesus' birth to his death. The Sunday School Christianity of the last century or so, often treated condescendingly by sophisticated theologians, has here recovered something important from the Bible that was too often lost in earlier theology: the Gospel stories about Jesus.

When I was a little kid, we sang "Tell me the stories of Jesus" nearly every week in Sunday School. Well, why not? Stories of Jesus fill the Gospels. I have no doubt that many of those stories are altered in detail, simplified, or sometimes just invented, but they nonetheless show us the kinds of things Jesus did, the sorts of things he taught, and, in these and other ways, the human being he was. And in what he taught and did during the course of his ministry, he was also working for our salvation.

Gospel Stories

Without the Gospels, the New Testament would have offered little information even about the last period of Jesus' life. Paul reports a few sayings and a few incidents from Jesus' ministry, but all the emphasis in his account of who Jesus was falls on incarnation, death, and resurrection. Except for the Gospels, the same could be said of the rest of the New Testament. The Gospel of Thomas, an early Christian text not included in the New Testament, includes some sayings that sound authentic to many scholars, but it provides no narrative framework.

The Bible, however, includes four Gospels—combined, they make up about 40 percent of the New Testament. The word "Gospel" means "good news"; in Greek, it could refer to the proclamation of a new ruler or to the report of a victory in battle. None of the four Gospels is anything like a modern biography. Not only do the Gospels cover only a few months or years of Jesus' life, but their authors all have theological agendas, and we can assume that they choose, interpret, or invent their stories to drive home their messages. They are not disinterested reporters and never claim to be. Still, without their stories of how Jesus healed the sick, told parables, and interacted with such an amazing variety of people, we would miss a lot of what we now know about who Jesus was and why he matters for our salvation.

The Gospel we call Mark (though, as with the other three, we cannot be sure who wrote it), probably the first of the four to be written, begins by declaring itself, "The beginning of the gospel of Jesus Christ, the Son of God" (Mark 1:1). Its author invented a new literary form. In the ancient world, serious narratives, whether epics, tragedies, or histories, were concerned with kings and queens and other grand personages. The common folk appeared in literature, if at all, only in comedy or in walk-on roles. But the author of Mark, who couldn't even write Greek very well, did something entirely new. He told stories of ordinary people—fishermen, women from the villages, a wandering teacher named Jesus with a dozen or so followers and no money to speak of—and treated the stories as if, because they were about Jesus, they were the most important stories in the world.

The good news about Jesus offers better news, the author of Mark believed, more important to the history of the world, even than a coronation of some monarch or a victory in some battle.[2] The very form of the story is thus a challenge to the dominant standards, in his society or ours, of what is valuable.

Others followed Mark in writing this new kind of text, a "Gospel." Most scholars believe that Matthew and Luke both had Mark's Gospel as a resource when they sat down to write. Between them, they quote more than 90 percent of Mark, and when one varies from Mark, the other nearly always follows him. These early Christians, in other words, also wanted to tell about Jesus, and used Mark's framework, adding a good bit of other material. Scholars call these three Gospels together the "Synoptic" ("seeing together") Gospels because they see Jesus in so many ways from the same perspective.

The Gospel of John is another matter; John offers many very different stories, and his Jesus speaks in long discourses rather than short parables and sayings. In the Synoptics, Jesus discloses his identity slowly and cautiously; in John he proclaims himself Son of God from the start. It used to be generally agreed that John was by far the last of the four Gospels to be written, but new research keeps pushing it to an earlier date, so that we can no longer be confident of its chronological relation to the Synoptics. It does seem reasonably clear that all four Gospels were written between 25 and 70 years after Jesus' death.

The Symbolic Beginning of Jesus' Ministry

The story Luke uses to begin his account of Jesus' ministry sets the stage for much of what follows. Jesus is visiting his home town, Nazareth. After being baptized by John the Baptist, Luke tells us, he had retreated into the wilderness for forty days of fasting and spiritual testing—a period of withdrawal common to the lives of spiritual leaders in many different cultures. Then, "filled with the power of the Spirit," he began preaching in the synagogues of Galilee.

In the Sabbath service at a typical synagogue, the local rabbi (teacher) would read a passage from the Jewish scriptures and then explain its meaning. When Jesus was in Nazareth on the Sabbath, someone invited this wandering teacher, local boy maybe or maybe not made good, to lead the service. He began by reading from the Book of Isaiah:

> The Spirit of the Lord is upon me,
> because he has anointed me to bring good news to the poor.
> He has sent me to proclaim release to the captives
> and recovery of sight to the blind,
> to let the oppressed go free,
> to proclaim the year of the Lord's favor.
>
> (Luke 4:18–19)

Then he rolled up the scroll, looked his former neighbors in the eye, and declared, "Today this scripture has been fulfilled in your hearing" (4:21).

All hell promptly broke loose. It sounded as if Jesus was claiming to be the Messiah! "Is this not Joseph's son?" some of the people asked dismissively—the kid who used to work in his father's carpentry shop? (4:22). When they called on him to work a miracle, he replied that God doesn't work miracles on command and then admitted the hard reality: "No prophet is accepted in the prophet's hometown" (4:24). So they were filled with rage, dragged him out to the local cliff, and were ready to throw him over it.

Why had just reading a passage from Isaiah and proclaiming its fulfillment generated such controversy? The answer involves some complicated history. Luke doesn't precisely quote from Isaiah in this passage, but rather edits some passages from Isaiah 61:1–2 and throws in a bit of Isaiah 58:6. These passages were written by a follower of the eighth-century B.C. prophet Isaiah, but this follower was writing centuries later, slightly before 500 B.C.

Long before the time of this author, whom scholars call "Third Isaiah," the leaders of Israel had been led into exile in Babylon. They left behind a poor and devastated community in Palestine; the Temple was destroyed. But in 539 B.C. Babylon was in its turn conquered by the Persians. Jews in Babylon were hearing rumors that they could soon go home, rebuild the Temple, and recover a measure of independence. Excitement grew, and "Third Isaiah" seems to give God's endorsement to hopes then growing among the people.

His prophecies offer perhaps the most inclusive vision of hope to be found in the Old Testament.[3] He speaks of "the Lord God who gathers the outcasts of Israel" (Isa. 56:8) and says,

> Do not let the foreigner joined to the Lord say,
> "The Lord will surely separate me from his people";
> and do not let the eunuch say,
> "I am just a dry tree."
>
> (Isa. 56:3)

Let everyone join in the hoping, this prophet declares. Outcasts may think themselves abandoned, but the Lord gathers them. Eunuchs, who had no possibility of having children, lack that particular hope for the future, which sustained many in ancient Israel; they were also judged unclean in a way that excluded them from many religious rituals. But here, in these prophecies, the Lord promises them "a monument and a name better than sons and daughters" (56:5). Likewise, the text welcomes foreigners to be "joyful in my house of prayer . . . for my house shall be called a house of prayer for all peoples" (56:7).

The beginning of the story of Jesus' ministry thus identifies him not merely with the hopes of Israel in general, but with Third Isaiah's particular version of those hopes, a version especially inclusive of outsiders and the rejected. The passage had become identified with hopes for a Messiah. If Jesus read that particular Scripture and then announced its fulfillment, pious Jews would have recognized his claim as somehow "Messianic." That would have meant different things to different people, but in one way or another it implied at least, "Here I am, the herald of the long anticipated future in which God will bring the troubles of the present age to an end." It was bad enough that a new rabbi in town should make such a claim. But it was worse that, in a time when most Jews hated their Roman occupiers, he quoted a passage that extended Israel's hopes to foreigners. And it was even worse that the new rabbi was a local kid his neighbors could remember working in his father's carpentry shop. No wonder the crowd turned against him.

Luke used this scene to introduce key themes of Jesus' ministry, and I have used it to begin this part of the book, on Jesus' ministry, because it touches on the topics of the chapters that follow. (1) By quoting Third Isaiah, Jesus located himself in the tradition of Old Testament *prophets*. So I will begin by discussing the prophetic tradition. In his ministry of preaching and healing, Jesus acted as a prophet. (2) Jesus' sermon at Nazareth focused on a hope for the future which lies at the core of Jesus' *message*: he proclaimed the coming of the reign of God. (3) In proclaiming that that Scripture was being fulfilled in their midst, Jesus made it clear that his own identity as *messenger* is part of his message. (4) The angry responses to his comments show how often Jesus' message led to *controversy*. (5) The way Jesus dealt with controversies and the inclusiveness of the hope he offered provide a model for how Christians today might think about controversial issues like *homosexuality* (one of the three ethical issues I will consider in this and the next two chapters). (6) In the synagogue at Nazareth, Jesus was *preaching*, and what he did provides guidance for contemporary Christian preaching, thereby connecting Jesus' activity with an ongoing activity of the church.

7

Jesus and the Prophets

When various people in the Gospels tried to describe Jesus, their first tentative attempt was often, "He is a prophet." From the Christian point of view, that ends up being an inadequate answer, but it does put him in the right general territory. Christians could say of Jesus what in Matthew Jesus says of John the Baptist: "A prophet? Yes, I tell you, and more than a prophet" (Matt. 11:9). Thus the book of Hebrews begins: "In many and various ways God spoke of old to our ancestors by the prophets, but in these last days he has spoken to us by a Son" (Heb. 1:1). This passage identifies Jesus as the culmination of the tradition of the prophets of ancient Israel, just as in Luke Jesus began his ministry by placing himself in the prophetic tradition. To understand Jesus, therefore, we need to know something about prophets.

Prophets in Ancient Israel

Prophets had appeared in Israel and the countries around it for a very long time. They had claimed to speak on behalf of God: "Thus says the Lord . . . " they would proclaim. By the time of Jesus, however, prophets seemed a thing of the past. The last generally recognized prophets had been Haggai, Zechariah, and Malachi, all in the sixth century B.C. The Maccabean leaders, whose revolt briefly achieved Israel's independence in the century before Jesus, would sometimes indefinitely postpone religious decisions since there were no prophets around to settle them.[1] By Jesus' time a popular folk belief held that there would be no more prophets until the Messiah came.[2]

Some of the earliest Old Testament stories about prophets refer to the time of King Saul, slightly more than a thousand years before the time of Jesus (1 Sam. 10; 19). In one of them, the great prophet Samuel is persuading the young Saul that God really does have a plan for him. To do this, Samuel describes a series of events that are about to happen. His last prediction is: "You will meet a band of prophets coming down from the shrine with harp, tambourine, flute, and lyre playing in front of them; they will be in a prophetic frenzy. Then the spirit of the Lord will possess you, and you will be in a prophetic frenzy along with them" (1 Sam. 10:5–6).

The "prophets" Samuel speaks of were wild characters who wandered in bands in a kind of ecstasy that their contemporaries identified as a sign that "the spirit of the Lord" had "possessed" them. Samuel himself seems to have been a prophet of a different sort, a much more rational and articulate spokesperson for God, and later prophets were more like him. Yet the "prophetic frenzy" of those wandering bands never became entirely irrelevant to prophecy in Israel. Prophets always acted under some strange compulsion from God that seized them and led them to prophesy. Late in the history of prophecy, Jeremiah complained that God kept forcing him to give bad news that made people hate him. And yet:

> If I say, "I will not mention him,
>   or speak any more in his name,"
> then within me there is something like a burning fire
>   shut up in my bones;
> I am weary with holding it in,
>   and I cannot.
>
> (Jer. 20:9)

Prophets find themselves under the control of a force beyond themselves, impulses they can only explain as coming from God.

At the same time, being a prophet was sometimes a job or profession. Every king had a "prophet" who gave advice, presumably also under some sort of divine inspiration. Many courts of the ancient Middle East would have had prophets like that. But in Israel (and this seems to be different from the way prophets operated in other countries), the prophet didn't always tell the king what he wanted to hear.

Take the story of how King David fell in love with a woman named Bathsheba, who was inconveniently already married to a soldier named Uriah. David sent Uriah off to the front lines to die and added Bathsheba to his already extensive harem. Sometime later, the prophet Nathan told David the story of a rich man who had large flocks but who nevertheless stole a poor man's one and only lamb. Such a man ought to be killed! David responded, only to hear Nathan charge, "You are the man!" (2 Sam. 12:7). Nathan seems to have been a court official on the king's payroll, and yet he could deliver a denunciation like this and not lose his job (indeed David promptly repented).

As a prophet, Nathan was acknowledged to speak for the Lord with an authority greater than that of human institutions.

Indeed, a prophet did not even have to have that position officially in order to prophesy. Several generations after David, the prophet Amos, an ordinary shepherd, insisted, "I am no prophet, nor a prophet's son; but I am a herdsman, and a dresser of sycamore trees, and the Lord took me from following the flock, and the Lord said to me, 'Go, prophesy to my people Israel' " (Amos 7:14–15). So Amos went—and thoroughly denounced Israelite corruption

> because they sell the righteous for silver,
> and the needy for a pair of sandals—
> they who trample the head of the poor into the dust of the earth,
> and push the afflicted out of the way.
>
> (Amos 2:6–7)

Amos delivered his prophecies at a royal shrine, an official place of worship, and, although the local priest quickly told him to get out of town, he nonetheless proclaimed his message and walked away unharmed.

The role of a prophet thus embodied a paradox: prophets functioned as a part of Israel's religion and sometimes even as court officials, and yet they were often the subverters of religious or political institutions, "the figure outside the family, outside politics, outside culture."[3] Amos, for instance, could even imagine God condemning all the rituals of Israel's religion:

> I hate, I despise your festivals,
> and I take no delight in your solemn assemblies.
> Even though you offer me your burnt offerings and grain offerings,
> I will not accept them;
> and the offerings of well-being of your fatted animals
> I will not look upon.
> Take away from me the noise of your songs;
> I will not listen to the melody of your harps.
> But let justice roll down like waters,
> and righteousness like an ever-flowing stream.
>
> (Amos 5:21–24)

The prophets, the Jewish scholar Abraham Heschel wrote, were "some of the most disturbing people who ever lived."[4] "The prophet is an iconoclast, challenging the apparently holy, revered and awesome. Beliefs cherished as certainties, institutions endowed with supreme sanctity, he exposes as scandalous pretensions."[5] Prophets often came from peripheral groups in society—they were social outcasts, younger men[6]—or, surprisingly, women.[7] If "prophet" was one of Jesus' offices—that is, if part of his job was to stand in this tradition—then causing trouble and asking hard questions, especially to those in power, went with the territory.

Jeremiah, the Prophet Most Like Jesus

The prophet Jeremiah's story demonstrates the tough lot prophets faced. During his lifetime, in 586 B.C., the Babylonian Empire finally conquered Judah (the last remaining independent section of David's kingdom of Israel), destroyed the Jerusalem Temple, and led many of the leaders of the people off into exile. The problem Jeremiah faced was not simply the moral corruption Amos had attacked 150 years before. Even the people in Judah most committed to ethical reform believed that God would never abandon their central institutions, the monarchy and the Temple. But a prophet knows that *no* institution is the same thing as the will of God.

Thus in his early prophecies, before the fall of Jerusalem, Jeremiah warned people who were gearing up to fight for God's nation that they could not assume that the Lord was committed to protecting Israel. Indeed, he said, they should avoid further bloodshed and surrender to the Babylonians (Jer. 21:3–7; 27:12; 34:1–5). They thought he was a traitor, beat him up, and threw him in prison.

> I have become a laughingstock all day long;
> everyone mocks me.
> For whenever I speak, I must cry out,
> I must shout, "Violence and destruction!"
> (Jer. 20:7–8)

Earlier prophets like Amos had spoken their prophecies and, despite the danger and ridicule that might involve, had gone on with their lives. Isaiah had acted out his calling as a prophet: he gave his children symbolic names and walked around Jerusalem naked and barefoot (perhaps not really naked, but at least scantily clothed) to symbolize the fate that awaited the people of Israel (Isa. 20). But Jeremiah's vocation as a prophet became his whole life.[8]

His was a vocation filled with pain, inflicted by both his neighbors and his God. His neighbors subjected him to ridicule and hatred and very nearly killed him. Even worse, he did not feel that he was a righteous person standing on God's side and looking at Israel's problems from the outside, but knew, rather, that he was part of Israel, the people God was condemning for faithlessness.

> My joy is gone, grief is upon me, my heart is sick.
> Hark, the cry of my poor people from far and wide in the land:
> . . .
> "The harvest is past, the summer is ended, and we are not
> saved."
> For the hurt of my poor people I am hurt,
> I mourn, and dismay has taken hold of me.
> Is there no balm in Gilead? Is there no physician there?
> Why then has the health of my poor people not been restored?
> (Jer. 8:19–22)

In the story of Jeremiah the prophet, who challenges even the most admired of human institutions on behalf of God's sovereignty, and at the same time bears the pain of the judgment of his people when their sins have separated them from God, we come as close as any prophet's story to the pattern of the Gospel.

Even a quick review of the history of prophecy suggests that much of it anticipated characteristics of Jesus' ministry: the strange force of God's inbreaking into history that went all the way back to roving bands of ecstatic prophets; the moral judgment on human institutions, even religious ones, characteristic of Nathan or Amos; and the personal suffering of Jeremiah. Jesus was indeed "a prophet. Yes . . . and more than a prophet."

8

Message: The Surprising Reign of God

The immediate historical context of Jesus' preaching, however, was not the prophetic tradition (there hadn't been prophets around for some time) but *apocalyptic*. Most Hebrew prophets engaged themselves with history, but they urged reform here and now. They predicted punishments or rewards in the near future. They recommended governmental policies of one kind or another. When the Hebrew people had been conquered and no longer had a nation of their own, such short term hopes became increasingly implausible. I mentioned apocalyptic briefly in part 1, and it was to apocalyptic hopes that the Jewish people then increasingly turned. The apocalyptic tradition declared that a better day wasn't just around the corner. Instead, in the short run, things would get much worse, until they got *so* bad that God would intervene, bring an end to the present age, and establish a radically new kind of world in which God would reign.

Meanings of the Reign of God

Such apocalyptic ideas lie at the core of Jesus' message as the Gospels report it. Mark begins his account of Jesus' ministry with characteristic abruptness:

> Now after John was arrested, Jesus came to Galilee,
> proclaiming the good news of God, and saying, "The time is
> fulfilled, and the reign of God has come near; repent,
> and believe in the good news.
>
> (Mark 1:14–15)

This passage implies that the "gospel"—the "good news" of Jesus' message—concerns the "reign" (or "kingdom") of God. But what does that mean? This is a question scholars have found difficult to answer.

Talk of "reign" obviously reminded Jews of the monarchs of Israel, but by the time of Jesus there was no longer a Jewish king, or much hope for one. Indeed, no human force on the horizon seemed particularly likely to bring about freedom, justice, or lasting peace. Hope therefore turned to God as the one who might transform the future. Different people had different theories of how God would reign, but to many "the reign of God" meant at least this: *not* the rule of corrupt tyrants, *not* the rule of foreign oppressors, but the dream of a time when *God* would take charge.

The prophet Ezekiel had written centuries earlier:

> For thus says the Lord God: I myself will search for my sheep, and will seek them out. . . . I will seek the lost, and I will bring back the strayed, and I will bind up the injured, and I will strengthen the weak, but the fat and the strong I will destroy. I will feed them with justice. . . . They shall never again defile themselves with their idols and their detestable things, or with any of their transgressions. I will save them from all the apostasies into which they have fallen, and will cleanse them. Then they shall be my people, and I will be their God.
> (Ezek. 34:11, 16; 37:23)

Such prophecies promise a radical shaking up of the social order ("I will strengthen the weak, but the fat and the strong I will destroy"), a purification of the society, and a renewed relation between the people and their God.

How would Israel get from here to there? By Jesus' time, there were many proposed answers. The Zealots, a party of revolutionaries, hoped to defeat the Romans by guerrilla warfare. The Essenes, a small community whose members apparently wrote many of the Dead Sea Scrolls, had retreated into desert monasteries, where they planned to follow all the laws of Israel and thereby inaugurate God's reign, at least among themselves, and perhaps, by divine intervention, in the world at large.[1] Other groups had still other strategies. Some simply hoped and prayed.

The New Testament itself gives mixed signals about the reign of God. Sometimes it portrays a dramatic event of cosmic proportions:

> the sun will be darkened,
>   and the moon will not give its light,
> and the stars will be falling from heaven,
>   and the powers in the heavens will be shaken. . . .
> Then he will send out the angels, and gather his elect from the four winds, from the ends of the earth to the ends of heaven. . . . Beware, keep alert, for you do not know when the time will come.
> (Mark 13:24–25, 27, 33)

This sounds like a public event at some future date with spectacular fireworks and the rescue of those to be saved from some general cataclysm.

Other passages, however, describe God's reign as emerging quietly in Jesus' own activity:

> Once Jesus was asked by the Pharisees when the reign of God was coming, and he answered, "The reign of God is not coming with things that can be observed; nor will they say, 'Look, here it is!' or 'There it is!' For, in fact, the reign of God is among you."
>
> (Luke 17:20–21)

Again, when some of Jesus' critics charged that, if he could cast out demons, it must be because he was in league with the Prince of Demons, he replied that demons don't compete with each other. He must therefore be drawing on a different power, and "if it is by the Spirit of God that I cast out demons, then the reign of God has come among you" (Matt. 12:28).

So which is it? Is the reign of God a dramatic public event which we still await? Or is it an inner transformation of things already beginning in Jesus' ministry? Is one perspective Jesus' own and the other a later addition? Scholars have argued all sides of this debate.[2]

The Metaphor of the Seed

A number of texts, particularly in Jesus' parables, support an interpretation I find persuasive that includes both present and future elements in its image of the coming reign of God. Jesus' parables, it is worth noting, use imagery familiar to the common people. The frequency of their references to debts, to people standing in the marketplace most of the day looking for work, to occupying soldiers ordering ordinary folk to do work for them, to people beaten up by robbers and left for dead by the side of the road—all this reminds us of the tough world in which Jesus' audience lived. With respect to the reign of God, Luke describes Jesus as appealing to a familiar agricultural image:

> What is the reign of God like? And to what should I compare it? It is like a mustard seed that someone took and sowed in the garden; it grew and became a tree, and the birds of the air made nests in its branches.
>
> (Luke 13:18–19)

Jesus' contemporaries thought that the mustard seed was the smallest of all seeds. Jewish tradition, indeed, identified it as the very smallest thing the human eye can perceive.[3] Yet it turns into a large plant, and in a process that begins secretly, underground, and as if by miracle.

> The reign of God is as if someone would scatter seed on the ground, and would sleep and rise night and day, and the seed would sprout and grow, he does not know how. The earth produces of itself, first the stalk, then the head, then the full grain in the head.
>
> (Mark 4:26–28)[4]

So it is with the reign of God. Someday, the world really will be different—publicly, dramatically. Some of Jesus' stories identify that transformation with the time of his own return. In the meantime, the quiet work of gospel and love, which Jesus is beginning, already anticipates and begins that future. He gathers disparate groups together. The "people" who follow him (the Greek word means something like "the mob" or "the poor folk") always get enough to eat in his company. Many who would ordinarily be rejected are welcomed.

The image of the seed captures both sides of the picture: the radical difference of the future from anything present but also the *continuity* between present beginnings and future anticipations.[5] The attention to radical difference reminds us that human efforts can produce hints of this hoped-for future, but they cannot bring it about. *God* accomplishes God's reign.

Jesus' Rejection of Violence

In particular, Jesus believed, we must not try to bring it about by violence. Some of Jesus' contemporaries, especially the Zealots, believed that, if they only began a revolt against their Roman occupiers, God would come to their aid. A generation after Jesus, in 70 A.D., about the time some of the Gospels were being written, they tried such a violent revolution and suffered catastrophic defeat. In the Gospels Jesus keeps emphasizing that violence never offers the right answer. After all, God makes seeds grow in God's own time.

The Zealots wanted a revolution. Jesus did *not* oppose revolution—he did not say that things were pretty much all right the way they were, or propose a transformation in people's hearts that would leave the social order relatively unchanged. The revolution he proposed was *more* radical than anything the Zealots imagined. They wanted to change who was on top of the power structure. Jesus, in contrast, envisioned a structure in which leaders would be servants rather than lords. The Zealots hoped to accomplish their goals by violence; Jesus insisted that violence always leaves us trapped in a cycle of counter-violence. They insisted on excluding the impure and unfaithful from the armies and the reign of the Lord; Jesus welcomed everyone.[6]

In the Gospel parables, Jesus presupposes that God will, in some unimaginable future way, bring about God's reign. And yet, in Jesus' activity, which is God's activity, God's reign is already anticipated. If it has already begun, in however "seedlike" a fashion, then the question of when it will achieve fulfillment becomes less important.

Matthew, Mark, and Luke all report Jesus as saying, "Truly I tell you, there are some standing here who will not taste death until they see that the reign of God has come with power" (Mark 9:1, Matt. 16:28, Luke 9:27). Did Jesus really say that? Does it imply that he anticipated the public transformation of the world within thirty or forty years of when he spoke?

That didn't happen. A good many scholars have speculated about how the delay of the reign of God must have produced a great crisis in the history of the church. If the early Christians expected such a transformation of the world within a generation of Jesus' death, and it didn't occur, these scholars ask, must not their faith have been shattered? How did they rethink what they believed?[7]

Despite the passion of some of the scholarly debates, this great crisis of faith seems never to have happened. Many early Christians evidently assumed that, since the transformation of the world has already begun in the ministry of Jesus, we should live in excitement and tension and with the urgency of those who know that their own activities are beginning a great work—but not worry too much about dates and times for when the transformation will be completed: "About that day or hour no one knows, neither the angels in heaven, or the Son, but only the Father" (Mark 13:32). In Jesus' ministry and the community of Jesus' followers, we begin to see the first signs of the reign of God, but the transformation it brings may be very far indeed from fulfillment.

An Inclusive Community

What sort of transformation will it eventually be? For one thing, a radical transformation of the current order of things: "Many who are first will be last, and the last will be first" (Mark 10:31). A great reversal will come between those who are now powerful, wealthy, and respectable, and the poor, the powerless, and the despised.

> Blessed are you who are poor, for yours is the reign of God.
> Blessed are you who are hungry now, for you will be filled.
> Blessed are you who weep now, for you will laugh.
> (Luke 6:20–21)

It is misleading, however, to say that the reign of God will turn things upside-down. That implies a vindictiveness foreign to Jesus' message, a vindictiveness too often characteristic of human revolutions. When the Cultural Revolution came to Communist China, former peasants ran the bureaucracy while former bureaucrats toiled in the fields without enough to eat. Subjected themselves to "ethnic cleansing," some Albanian Kosovars no sooner returned home under NATO protection than they decided to "cleanse" some Serbs.

Jesus' reversals work differently. His choice of friends and followers makes the point. He draws his closest disciples mostly from among fishermen from Galilee, people without a lot of money or education and from a part of the country known for scandalous sloppiness about Jewish law. Sure enough, he has to keep offering explanations for them. Why do they pluck the grain and eat it as they walk through wheat fields on the Sabbath? Don't they know that this is "work" unlawful on the Sabbath? (Matt. 12:1–8). "Why do your disciples break the tradition of the elders? For they do not wash their hands before they eat" (Matt. 15:2). It sounds as if Jesus is trying to change the world with a crew of teenagers wearing their baseball caps backwards.

But it's worse than that. Jesus befriended not only the oppressed but also their oppressors. One of his disciples is apparently a tax collector. In the first century, tax collectors usually paid for the right to collect taxes from a particular territory, and then tried to make a profit by collecting more than was due. Along with dice players, usurers, shepherds, and the managers of pigeon races, they were on the standard lists of disreputable people, so likely dishonest that they were not even allowed to testify in court.[8]

Yet here was Jesus, supposedly a religious teacher, going to parties with such people, acting like "a glutton and a drunkard, a friend of tax collectors and sinners" (Matt. 11:19). In a culture where women were supposed to stay home and take care of their men, he seems to have had women following him on the road from Galilee to Jerusalem. The pious must have speculated about where they slept—and with whom.

He healed the daughter of a Roman centurion—the military representative of the enemy. He touched people whose illnesses made them ritually unclean. Yet he also sat down to dinner with Pharisees—members of the party within Judaism most concerned about ritual purity. Off briefly by himself, Jesus entered into conversation with a Samaritan woman—doubly scandalous because a pious Jew would not speak to a strange woman, and Jews regarded Samaritans as heretics, who failed to keep the proper laws and were ritually unclean.[9] "Just then his disciples came. They were astonished" (John 4:27). They must have felt that this teacher of theirs was hardly fit to go out alone.

Few people match the inclusiveness of Jesus' welcome. Good liberal people in the United States find it easy to sympathize with the historically hard lot of African Americans (as indeed we should). But when a blue-collar white man with his own racial prejudices gets a raw deal, one rarely hears liberal protests. Conservatives complain (often justifiably) about the injustice imposed by liberal "political correctness," but pay less attention to continuing injustices imposed by old fashioned prejudices.

We all cheer those who have made themselves unpopular defending *our* favorite causes. However, regarding those who suffer for exposing corruption in an institution we admire, we may grudgingly admit that they're right, but they won't get much of our sympathy. Conservatives attack left-wing dictators, and liberals attack right-wing dictators, but few of us attack tyranny in all its forms with equal force.[10]

Jesus was different. In the communities he created, from his ragtag band of followers to the varied groups with whom he sat down to dinner, he would welcome *anybody*, and the stories imply that no one ever went away hungry when they came to eat with Jesus. The excluded were those who excluded themselves.

His stories often contrast the prideful and self-righteous with the humble and contrite:

> An admired man of piety thanks God in his prayers "that I am not like other people: thieves, rogues, adulterers." *He* follows the rules, fasts twice a week, and gives ten percent of his wealth to charity. But nearby in the Temple a tax collector beats his breast, confesses his sins, and ends up looking much better than this pompous example of self-righteousness (Luke 18:9–14).
>
> Leading local citizens contribute generously to their religious institutions; a widow gives two copper coins. But she gave more than all the rest, Jesus says, because those two coins were all she had (Luke 21:1–4).
>
> A woman slips into a dinner party to which Jesus has been invited, and begins "to bathe his feet with her tears and to dry them with her hair" (Luke 7:38). One can imagine the embarrassment around the table.[11] Even worse, she is locally notorious as a sinner—presumably a prostitute. This Jesus can hardly be much of a prophet, the guests start to whisper, if he can't even recognize the sort of person she is. One can almost hear the snickers around the table. But Jesus praises her action and sends her away forgiven.

In such stories we see in Jesus what Martin Luther once wrote: "God is the God of the humble, the miserable, the afflicted, the oppressed, the desperate, and of those who have been brought down to nothing at all."[12] It is not that God is out to get even with the rich and powerful, but that their self-confidence gets in the way of turning to God's mercy.

Whatever our political point of view, we usually end up firmly excluding some class of people. Jesus was different. When a rich young man tells Jesus that he has obeyed all the commandments since childhood and asks what more he should do, Jesus responds that he should sell all his possessions, give the money away to the poor, and "'then come, follow me.' When he heard this, he was shocked and went away grieving, for he had many possessions" (Mark 10:21–22). Mark says that Jesus, "looking at him loved him" (10:21)—it is the only time the Gospel describes Jesus as loving any particular individual. In this world of ours, where political conservatives would never have demanded that the young man give away his possessions and political radicals would not have loved him, Jesus represents a way of thinking about society and social change that is full of passion yet resistant to choosing sides.

To those who know they need God's mercy, Jesus proclaims that it is without limit. Again, some of the most familiar of his stories make the point. The younger of two sons asks for his share of his father's property, travels to a far country, and squanders it "in dissolute living." Reduced to the worst possible job for a Jew—tending pigs—he isn't even allowed to share in the food the pigs eat. Close to starvation, he heads home, willing now to be the lowest of the servants in his father's house. But before he even gets home, his father sees him from a distance, runs toward him, embraces and kisses him, and throws a party to celebrate his return.

It's an amazing image—the father who doesn't even wait for the confession, who gives up all his dignity to run to the errant boy (a Middle Eastern patriarch in his long robes would *never* run). Among other things, it undercuts many of our assumptions about the "father" as the symbol of stern judgment. This father symbolizes loving to the point of irresponsibility. So his older son protests:

> Listen! For all these years I have been working like a slave for you, and I have never disobeyed your command; yet you have never given me even a young goat so that I might celebrate with my friends. But when this son of yours [Note: not "my brother," but "this son of yours"] comes back, who has devoured your property with prostitutes, you killed the fatted calf for him!
>
> (Luke 15:29–30)

It's a common theme in Jesus' stories. A shepherd, he says, will rejoice more over the recovery of one lost sheep than over the ninety-nine who never went astray (Luke 15:3–7). A landowner pays workers he hired late in the afternoon, who only worked one hour, as much as those who labored the whole day (Matt. 20:1–16). God wants to rescue sinners, this God who, in Luther's words, "loves sinners, evil persons, fools and weaklings in order to make them righteous, good, wise and strong."[13]

Should we therefore, Paul imagined someone asking, "continue in sin that grace may abound?" (Rom. 6:1). Of course not! It's better to be safe in the sheepfold than wander lost on the hillside. Why would we want to be slopping the pigs and starving? It's better to feel at home knowing that God loves us than journey into a far country. Living apart from God is not the best way to live, so why not accept God's love as soon as we encounter it?

Jesus' account of God's abundant love has implications for our interaction with others. In Matthew, Jesus compares the reign of God to this story: A king forgives one of his slaves a vast debt of ten thousand talents (a wildly hyperbolic story—ten thousand talents would amount to millions of dollars).

> But that same slave, as he went out, came upon one of his fellow slaves who owed him a hundred denarii [a relatively modest sum]; and seizing him by the throat, he said, "Pay what you owe."
>
> (Matt. 18:28)

His fellow slaves complain, and "in anger his lord handed him over to be tortured" (18:34). It's not such a mysterious principle, really: if we all need justice tempered by mercy for ourselves, it only makes sense that we ought to try to be merciful to others.

In Matthew's summary of it, Jesus' message calls for repentence; it assumes that truly hearing this good news will compel radical changes in one's life. Jesus posed the highest kind of ethical ideal. The law had taught not to murder; *he* says not to be angry (Matt. 5:21–22). The law said not to commit adultery. Jesus said, "Everyone who looks at a woman with lust has already committed adultery with her in his heart" (Matt. 5:28). Ancient injunctions taught that you shouldn't escalate a fight—don't take more than an eye for an eye or a tooth for a tooth. Jesus in contrast said, "Do not resist an evil-doer. But if anyone strikes you on the right cheek, turn the other also; and if anyone wants to sue you and take your shirt, give your coat as well; and if anyone forces you to go one mile, go also the second mile" (Luke 5:39–41, translation modified).

The Reign of God's Love

To describe this ideal of overflowing mercy, the New Testament had to introduce new vocabulary. When people talked about "love" in Greek, they often used the word "*eros*," which meant "desire." *Eros* need not refer to the kind of desire we would call "erotic"; such philosophers as Plato could talk about the desire for human virtue or for justice. Still, *eros* always involves a quest for something one lacked and wanted in order to make oneself happier or better.

By this standard, God cannot love, since God lacks nothing and therefore cannot seek anything in a search for self-improvement.[14] So the New Testament authors consistently use a different word—"*agape*"—for love. *Agape* had been a colorless, rather uncommon word for "liking" someone that had already been used for God's love in the Greek translation of the Hebrew Bible. The translators redefined the word to convey the way God loves us not for anything we can give in return but simply because God is loving. The linguistic contrast is dramatic: the noun *eros* never appears in the New Testament, and the noun *agape* is absent from classical Greek literature.

The New Testament calls on us to express the *agape* with which God loves us in turn to our neighbors. When a lawyer asks Jesus, "Which commandment in the law is the greatest?" (a trick question: whatever you pick, you treat the others as less important),

> He said to him, "'You shall love the Lord your God with all your heart, and with all your soul, and with all your mind.' This is the greatest and first commandment. And a second is like it: 'You shall love your neighbor as yourself.' On these two commandments hang all the law and the prophets."
>
> (Matt. 22:37–40)

Christians sometimes contrast "Jewish legalism" with "a Christian emphasis on love." It is therefore worth noting that Jesus is here quoting two passages from the Hebrew scriptures: Deuteronomy 6:5 and Leviticus 19:18. Some rabbis would have summarized the law in just the same way.

What's important is not whether Jesus was the first to say it, but what he said. He refused to answer the question: asked for one greatest commandment, he gave two. To those who would put exclusive emphasis either on relation with God or on service to neighbors, his refusal serves as a reminder that the Christian life always includes both. Both dimensions of that life center on love, and love, as the philosopher Alfred North Whitehead once remarked, "is a little oblivious as to morals."[15]

To love God is not to try to earn God's rewards by following God's rules, but to kneel in worship before the sheer wonder of God's holiness—whether we get anything out of it or not. To love our neighbor is to free ourselves from looking over our shoulders to see how many spiritual merit badges our good behavior is winning, and simply help people because they need our help.

Perhaps the most famous of Jesus' stories comes in response to a question from a lawyer: "Who is my neighbor?" Jesus tells of a traveller wounded by robbers and left by the side of the road. Two religious officials pass him by, and it is a despised Samaritan—in most Jews' eyes, one of those appalling semi-foreigners who ignore God's laws—who stops to help. Which of the three was a "neighbor" to the victim? Clearly, the Samaritan who helped him. "Go and do likewise" (Luke 10:37). The question has been reversed. When the lawyer asked, "Who is my neighbor?" he had meant "How many people do I have to love?" But "Who *was* a neighbor?" means "How can I love—without counting on who deserves what—the way God loves?"

Love is thus the sum of Christian life. As Paul wrote to the Corinthians,

> If I have prophetic powers and understand all mysteries
> and all knowledge, and if I have all faith, so that I
> could move mountains, but do not have love, I am nothing.
> If I give away all my possessions, and if I hand over my
> body [to be burned in martyrdom], but do not love, I gain nothing.
> (1 Cor. 13:2–3, translation altered)

A life of love is not easier than following the rules. Its demands have no limits, and (as I said in chapter 3) it challenges us to imagination, to a certain gift for creative improvisation in thinking how to be most of service, in a way that rule-following never requires. But the life of love to which Christ calls us is a life of what Calvin called "Christian freedom."[16] Secure in the knowledge that God already loves us, we do the best we can, freed of "those terrors of uncertainty whether God is offended or honored by our work."[17]

I began this part with Luke's account of Jesus' sermon at Nazareth. Jesus there quotes Isaiah about being "anointed . . . to bring good news to the poor . . . release to the captives and . . . to let the oppressed go free" (Luke 4:18–19). I have tried to describe the good news of freedom we see him teaching in the Gospels. In that teaching, and in the life of his community of followers, he was introducing a way of living in which many of the values of his culture or ours get reversed and which anticipates the reign of God.

His quotation from Isaiah ended with Jesus saying he was called "to proclaim the year of the Lord's favor"—apparently a reference to the "Jubilee year" described in Leviticus 25.[18] Every fifty years, according to this part of Jewish law, "you shall proclaim liberty throughout the land to all its inhabitants. It shall be a Jubilee for you" (Lev. 25:10). Debts were to be forgiven, indentured servants released, the land itself given a rest—"you shall not sow, or reap the aftergrowth, or harvest the unpruned vines. For it is a jubilee; it shall be holy to you: you shall eat only what the field itself produces" (11–12). The Jubilee is an ethical ideal that implies we have obligations to our "neighbors" the plants as well as our human neighbors.

It is not clear that ancient Israelites ever really celebrated a Jubilee year according to all the requirements. But the law was there, and at key historical moments they at least recognized it as something they ought to be doing (Jer. 34; Neh. 10). In our own time, a movement called "Jubilee 2000," led by evangelical Christians, has advocated simply "forgiving" the international debts of third world countries. On purely political grounds, such a proposal would usually strike this constituency in particular as the worst kind of liberal leniency, but members of Congress are listening to supporters inspired by the biblical vision of Jubilee.

What could it look like to anticipate, in whatever small ways, the reign of God? Love God. Love your neighbors. Seek equality and justice. Welcome everyone to join in. Nothing we do can bring about God's reign. We live in hope that *God* will someday bring about that astonishing transformation of things, like a great mustard plant sprouted suddenly overnight. But Jesus claimed that his own ministry already manifested hints and anticipations of that reign, and he invited us to keep on anticipating it. How people reacted to *him* and his ministry was therefore integral to how they understood what he taught. The messenger was part of the message.

9

Messenger: Who Do You Say that I Am?

At the climax of each of the first three Gospels, somewhere near the middle of each story, comes a crucial moment. As Jesus teaches and acts in remarkable ways, followers and critics alike begin to ask ever more pressingly, in effect, "Who is this guy?" Finally, Jesus himself addresses the question to his disciples:

> "Who do people say that I am?" and they answered him,
> "John the Baptist"; and others, "Elijah"; and still
> others, "One of the prophets." He asked them, "But who
> do you say that I am?" Peter answered him, "You are the Messiah."
> (Mark 8:27–30)

"Messiah" is the Hebrew word translated into Greek as "Christos"—the anointed one of God. In part 1, I discussed some of the "titles" applied to Jesus in the New Testament and what they have come to mean for Christian faith. That seemed the most suitable place to consider them, since the use of those titles developed as early Christians struggled to understand the relation of human and divine in the incarnation. The place of "Messiah" and other titles in Jesus' own ministry is much harder to judge. For one thing, in the first three Gospels—especially Mark, but Matthew and Luke as well—Jesus' true identity remains generally hidden, and the way titles are used for him manifests that hiddenness.

In all three, for instance, Peter no sooner identifies Jesus as the Messiah than he is told to keep what he just said secret. In Mark, voices from heaven and the cries of angry demons identify Jesus as "the Son of God" during his ministry, but no human voice does so until after his death. Whoever speaks of such matters—even the demons!—Jesus orders to be silent.

Scholars have developed a variety of explanations for this "Messianic secret." Perhaps, one argument goes, the Gospels are preserving the memory that no one *did* understand Jesus as Messiah or Son of God until after his death. Perhaps, until he was crucified, proclamation of Jesus by such titles would in that historical context have evoked expectations of a great political or military leader who would drive the Romans out of power. Until the cross made it clear that Jesus was a different kind of savior, therefore, either in the logic of the Gospel stories or in historical fact, or both, terms so susceptible to misunderstanding needed to be avoided.

Speaking with Authority

Still, even in the first three Gospels, Jesus is not just someone who is passing on a message. What you believe about the messenger, how you respond to *him*, is a key part of your response to the message itself. Jesus spoke, people around him kept noting, "as one having authority, and not as their scribes" (Matt. 7:29). Not only did he seem to claim an authority greater than God's Law (Matt. 5:21–43), but, even though the Jerusalem Temple stood at the heart of Jewish religion, Jesus sometimes appeared to claim that it was more important to be in relation to *him* than to the Temple (Matt. 12:6). He declared himself Lord of the Sabbath (Matt. 12:8).

Above all, on no authority but his own, Jesus ordered prospective disciples to abandon their families, abandon social and religious obligations, and follow him. In the Gospel stories he does not ever justify such a preemptory demand by appealing to Scripture or tradition or citing some official status or office he held. He simply speaks the word, "Follow me," and people drop everything and come.

To be sure, the Gospels condense complex events into relatively brief narratives, and one might argue that they have simply left out intervening details—his explanations of the importance of his ministry, or some appeal to the excitement of the adventure. But the texts as we have them convey a picture of Jesus: when he commands, he evokes obedience in a way that seems more fundamental than the authority of even the most significant of religious institutions.[1]

Particularly in John's Gospel Jesus keeps proclaiming who he is: "I am the bread of life" (6:35); "I am the gate for the sheep" (10:7); "I am the good shepherd" (10:11); "I am the resurrection and the life" (11:25); "I am the way, and the truth, and the life" (14:6); "I am the true vine" (15:1).

The phrase "I am" had a particular force in a Jewish context. In Exodus, when God appeared to Moses and Moses asked God's name, "God said to Moses, 'I am who I am.' He said further, 'Thus you shall say to the Israelites, "*I am* has sent me to you"' (Exod. 3:14). Scholars have long debated the meaning of this cryptic passage. Linguists note that the Hebrew word for "I am" comes close to YHWH, the name of God so sacred that it was never spoken aloud. (Hebrew language doesn't have vowels; if the sacred name *had* been pronounced, it might have sounded something like "Yahweh.")

Biblical scholars with more philosophical interests sometimes propose that the author of Exodus meant God to be saying something like, "I am the one who causes things to be"—that it was a self-designation of God as the first cause of all things in the universe. Still other scholars read, "I am who I am," as meaning something more like, "None of your business who I am—shut up and do as you're told." However understood, "I am" was by Jesus' time something like a name of God. This explains the response in John, when Jesus says to some Jews with whom he is arguing, "Your ancestor Abraham rejoiced that he would see my day." They reply in understandable puzzlement, "You are not fifty years old, and have you seen Abraham?" He responds, "Before Abraham was, I am" (John 8:56–58). They gasp at his blasphemy and try to stone him to death. Scholars debate how such an audience would have understood that "I am" in that context, but many think it would have sounded as though Jesus were claiming to be God.

A similarly dramatic moment happens near the end of Mark—surprisingly so, for it seems out of keeping with Mark's approach. Jesus has been arrested but has refused to answer any questions.

> Again the high priest asked him, "Are you the Messiah,
> the Son of the Blessed One?" Jesus said, "I am; and
> 'you will see the Son of Man
> seated at the right hand of the Power,'
> and 'coming with the clouds of heaven.'"
> Then the high priest tore his clothes and said, "Why do
> we still need witnesses? You have heard his blasphemy!"
> (Mark 14:61–63)

A good many themes come together here: Jesus is the Messiah; the Son of God; the one who will return as Son of Man coming down from heaven to bring in the reign of God (the quotations are from the Son of Man passages in Daniel 7); and the one who can say, "I am."

Encountering God in Jesus

In the Gospel stories people encounter God in Jesus. Israel's old modes of relating to God are *not* abolished. Paul could not be more emphatic: "They are Israelites, and to them belong the adoption, the glory, the covenant, the giving of the law, the worship, and the promises" (Rom. 9:4). God made a covenant with Israel, and God does not break promises. Still, one can read much of John—and the theme is clearer there than in the other Gospels—as a list of ways in which Jesus becomes an alternative place for encountering God. For instance:

Jesus drives the money-changers and sellers of animals for sacrifice out of the Temple, though their services had become essential for ordinary Temple practice. He says that if the Temple were destroyed, he could raise it up again in three days, and the Gospel writer explains "he was speaking of the temple of his body," which would indeed be raised three days after his death (John 2:21). Jesus' own body thus will now function as a place of sacrifice to God.

People complain when Jesus performs cures on the Sabbath, but he replies, "My Father is still working and I also am working" (John 5:17). He thus proposes that his own activity is more a revelation of how God works than even the law of the Sabbath.

He tells his critics, "You search the scriptures because you think that in them you have eternal life. . . . Yet you refuse to come to me to have life" (John 5:39–40). One can come to eternal life through Jesus.

Around the time of Passover, the Jewish celebration of the Hebrews' escape from slavery in Egypt to the crossing of the Red Sea, Jesus crosses to the other side of the Sea of Galilee and feeds five thousand people who have followed him. Here is a new ritual meal and a new sea-crossing, creating a new community, in which what matters most is not Hebrew descent but community with Jesus (John 6:1–15).

Circumcision set Jews apart as the chosen people of God, and it was so important a ritual that it could even be performed on the Sabbath. Jesus says that he can heal on the Sabbath as well. By his healing (more on this in a few pages), he restores people to full membership in the community of Israel, just as circumcision initiates them into Israel in the first place.

Jews treasured the covenant between God and their ancestor Abraham as the foundation of their relation with God: "Abraham is our Father" (John 8:39). Jesus bluntly reminds them, "Abraham died, and so did the prophets" (8:52). What matters above all is not descent from Abraham, but relation to Jesus, "for I came from God, and now I am here" (8:42).

Thus, Jesus becomes Mediator between people and God. Whether it is Temple, Sabbath, Scriptures, festivals, circumcision, or descent from Abraham, none of the old ways of defining one's special relationship with God can surpass the good news offered of relationship through Jesus. John may have been written at a point where Christians had just been expelled from Jewish synagogues, so that the issue of finding an alternative way of connecting to God was particularly important to its author and his original readers.[2] For Christians today, however, the primary lesson of these texts should not be about Judaism and Christianity but about the authority of Jesus and the fact that Jesus is always the critic as well as the foundation of our own Christian rituals and institutions. He challenges them as surely as he challenged those of Israel when we try to set limits to the work of his Spirit.

Acting with Authority

So far, in thinking about what made Jesus important during his ministry, I've focused on words—on what was said by him and about him. But the Gospels convey his special authority through deeds as well. In Luke's Gospel, John the Baptist, while in prison and facing death, sends a question to Jesus: "Are you the one who is to come, or are we to wait for another?" "Go and tell John what you have seen and heard," Jesus replies. "The blind receive their sight, the lame walk, the lepers are cleansed, the deaf hear, the dead are raised, the poor have good news preached to them" (Luke 7:20–22). Jesus was God's presence, the herald of God's reign, not only because he spoke with authority but because he *acted* with authority. The Book of Acts describes Peter declaring in his first sermon that Jesus was, "A man attested to you by God with deeds of power, wonders and signs that God did through him among you" (Acts 2:22).

To be sure, the Gospels themselves take somewhat different attitudes toward "wonders and signs." In Luke and Acts, they are clearly catalysts for faith and evidences of Jesus' authority.[3] Mark takes a more negative view: as he tells the stories, not everyone finds these wonders compelling (3:22; 3:30; 6:1–6), and it is the cross and not anything that precedes it that really makes clear who Jesus is (8:14–31). In John's Gospel the picture is more complicated. Sometimes the wonders Jesus performs bring about faith (John 4:53; 10:41–42; 11:45–48; 14:11). But the text reminds us that such signs are ambiguous (10:25–26); sometimes they attract people who are only interested in being cured or fed and don't move toward true faith at all (6:26), and sometimes people reject them as not from God (9:16, 30, 34).

Many of us today find these cures and other wonders more an embarrassment than a support for our faith. We have watched television shows where a faith healer "cures" people, and we are skeptical. Surely Jesus cannot have been like this! Yet the historical evidence seems overwhelming: whatever we make of his cures, the fact that Jesus went around "curing the sick" was one of the most well-established features of his story. What took place in those cures is harder to say. Were Jesus' cures "miraculous"?

Part of the problem concerns definitions.[4] Most people today think of the world as operating—always or nearly always—according to laws of nature. We think of two options. Either, first, Aunt Mary was cured of pneumonia by the natural forces at work in the world: the disease ran its course, or the antibiotics worked, or she had a positive mental attitude. Or, second, if God actually intervened from outside that natural causal chain, then Aunt Mary was cured by a miracle, a break with how things work 99.9 percent of the time, and definitive proof that whoever did it unambiguously speaks and acts for God.

Jesus' contemporaries saw things differently. To them, the world was not such a closed system. God or the gods intervened all the time. Science had not yet produced concepts like "laws of nature." Most everyone took it for granted that people of spiritual power could work cures and do other amazing things. The book of Exodus told how Moses and Pharaoh's magicians had a kind a miracle-working contest. Moses' were more impressive, but Pharaoh's magicians did some good tricks too (Exod. 7:8–24). Pagan wonder workers could bring people back to life,[5] and Tacitus, a tough-minded ancient historian, reports how even a hardened skeptic like the Emperor Vespasian (who lived a generation or so after the time of Jesus) was reluctantly persuaded to manifest his imperial powers by spitting on the eyes of a blind man and stepping on another poor fellow's withered hand—in both cases effecting a cure.[6]

The authors of the Gospels would therefore have taken "signs" and "wonders" as what one would naturally expect from someone like Jesus.[7] *Our* questions about whether the event involved the powerful but "natural" impact of a strong personality on a psychosomatic disease, a legend developed by later exaggeration, or a genuine "violation of the laws of nature" would puzzle them.

If they had reflected on such things, they might well have agreed with Augustine that no event can "be contrary to nature when it happens by the will of God, since the will of the great Creator assuredly *is* the nature of every created thing. A portent, therefore, does not occur contrary to nature, but contrary to what is known of nature."[8] Did God cure the blind man? Well, of course—God does everything, and "nature" is a name for the sum total of what God does.

For Augustine, what distinguishes a "portent" is that, whatever its explanation, we *cannot figure out* how it worked ("contrary to what is known of nature"), and therefore it captures our attention and (perhaps) occasions faith. Was it "contrary to the laws of nature"? It is not so much that Augustine would hesitate in answering as that he would not understand the question.

Still, even if the biblical authors would not have posed such questions, it is hard for us today to repress them. Let me take a stab at an answer. First, Augustine was right: God makes everything happen. The lilies bloom on the hillside; the sparrow does not fall; the parent's love gives the child the strength to keep on living; Jesus restores a sick person to health. Was God at work? Of course—here and everywhere else.

Second, nonetheless, God normally works according to certain rules. The lilies bloom in the spring and not midwinter, for instance. I believe (and much more about this in part 4) that in at least one case in first-century Palestine—

Jesus' resurrection—God worked in a way contrary to the usual rules. Or more precisely, if we could see the pattern of creation, start to finish, we would see that at just this crucial turning point, the rules naturally operated differently.

Some of the "wonders and signs" described in the Gospels almost certainly are later legends that developed around this extraordinary man after his death. Some are probably roughly accurate accounts of ways in which a person with some sort of charismatic authority can produce the apparent cure of disease—ways modern psychologists and anthropologists studying pre-literate cultures are just beginning to understand.

In the case of the resurrection, it seems crucial to Christian faith to believe that something took place that was radically different from what usually happens to people after they die: thanks to an action of God, Jesus, who had died, yet lived. Without that, the Gospels' whole sense of Jesus' identity breaks down. Understanding the way in which the life of Jesus represents history's decisive turning point might strengthen the argument that in Jesus' healing ministry, God worked differently from the way God works in other times and places. But none of the healings seems crucial to Jesus' identity in the way that the resurrection is, so Christians can, it seems to me, in these cases be open to a variety of interpretations of what happened.[9]

The Meanings of Signs and Wonders

The meaning of these events for the Gospel narratives, however, has implications independent of how we understand the mechanism of the wonders. First, as already noted, they affirm Jesus' authority. Second, they offer an alternative to the standard religious authorities: God does not work through the Temple rituals or other official ceremonies as forcefully as through this wandering teacher, who so often works his cures on the Sabbath, when one is not supposed to work at all, and in a way that challenges the usual religious rules. Finally, the cures have a social as well as a medical function.

Take, for example, a woman who has been suffering from hemorrhages for twelve years: her menstrual bleeding never stops. In addition to her physical symptoms and discomfort, she would have been in a state of perpetual ritual uncleanness (Mark 5:25–34). Consider also a man who "was always howling and bruising himself with stones" and has been driven out of his community to live in the local graveyard, "for he had often been restrained with shackles and chains, but the chains he wrenched apart, and the shackles he broke in pieces; and no one had the strength to subdue him" (Mark 5:4). In the Gospel stories, Jesus' cures of such folk do the same thing his teaching does: they welcome outsiders into a more inclusive community. The sick are "healed" in a way that not only changes a medical condition but restores to them a social position within the culture.

Similarly, whatever else happens when Jesus feeds four or five thousand people, at the least he creates a community where everyone is welcome and there is more than enough to eat and drink. I do not know what reality lies behind these stories of the multiplication of bread and fish and wine. Maybe the invitation to share simply generated inspired people to share food they had hoarded for themselves. Maybe even crumbs sufficed if eaten in the presence of Jesus. Maybe what we can only call a "miracle" took place. Maybe the whole thing is a later story with purely symbolic meaning. I don't know. What does seem clear is that one of the things the Gospels want us to understand about Jesus is that he is a host who will always provide all that people need—and who has particular concern for those who are most needy.

Our first reaction to Jesus' spirit of generous welcome may be that no one could object to it. But anyone who has ever been a member of a club—or a church—knows that the boundaries of its inclusiveness are a common source of controversy. Such questions as well as others certainly generated controversy during Jesus' ministry.

10

Controversies

It may seem that everyone must have liked Jesus. He taught love; he welcomed sinners; he offered God's grace. Surely if you and I had been there, we would have signed up to be his disciples. But most people didn't join up. And, more significantly, Jesus evoked a good bit of hostility among some of his contemporaries. In the end, some people hated or feared him enough to have him killed. We do not understand him unless we understand why he had such enemies.

In Defense of the Pharisees

In the Gospel accounts of Jesus' ministry, we meet opponents—people out to trick him, who ask him embarrassing questions and regularly criticize him—the first-century equivalent of the Washington press corps. The text often refers to them as "scribes," "Pharisees," or "lawyers." In Christian history, the Pharisees in particular have generally gotten a bad name. Today "Pharisaic" commonly means strict, emphasizing outward form, self-righteous, or hypocritical. It's not an attractive picture.

It's also, near as we can tell, an inaccurate one. The Pharisees were a Jewish religious-political party who were committed to trying to live as pious Jews. Unlike the Sadducees, another Jewish party who focused their activities around the Temple, the Pharisees moved among the common people out in the countryside.[1] Most Jews probably admired them as trying hard to live up to the ideals of their religion. Thus, when Jesus wants to emphasize the strictness of his ethical demands, he says, "Unless your righteousness exceeds that of the scribes and Pharisees, you will never enter the kingdom of heaven" (Matt. 5:20). Being more righteous than the Pharisees, Jesus assumes, wouldn't be easy.[2]

In a culture where sharing food implied friendship, Jesus ate with Pharisees. Luke reports one occasion on which "some Pharisees" warned Jesus that Herod was out to get him, and he ought to lay low for a while (Luke 13:31), and says that after Jesus' death the Pharisee Gamaliel defended the earliest church (Acts 5:34). The Gospels thus give us hints of support for Jesus from some Pharisees, and to many of his contemporaries, Jesus might have seemed more like the Pharisees than any of the other Jewish parties of the time.

So why all the negative talk? Why would the Gospels have Jesus calling them a "brood of vipers"? (Matt. 3:7). Why would he warn against their "hypocrisy"? (Luke 12:1). Why do they appear as confronting him or, in his parables, as insufferably self-righteous? (Luke 18:9–14).

We *want* to read the story like this: "Back then the Jews in general and the Pharisees in particular were often self-righteous and hypocritical about religion; isn't it wonderful that Christianity has put an end to that!" We ought to know better. Pride, self-righteousness, and hypocrisy are characteristics of all religions—certainly of Christianity, and in all times—certainly today. The Gospels are not condemning Judaism as a bad religion, or the Pharisees as the worst of the lot.

Probably all of the New Testament—certainly the vast majority of it—was written by Jews. Even non-Jews in the Roman Empire recognized Judaism as an unusually serious and morally upright faith. Judaism attracted a good many semi-followers who stopped short of circumcision but regularly and admiringly attended Jewish worship.

The Pharisees were the most faithful Jews and probably (though the evidence is unclear) those most likely to work actively with the ordinary people and try to touch their faith and their lives.[3] Some Pharisees may have obsessively emphasized the importance of every detail of Jewish ritual, but others were more tolerant. Jesus would certainly have fallen on the more open-minded end of any continuum of Pharisees, emphasizing the spirit rather than the letter of the law—but in most matters, he would not have been off the charts. As a Christian, therefore, I read passages critical of the Pharisees to say: *Even* Jews, *even* Pharisees, fell into hypocrisy and self-righteousness. These are characteristics of every religion, and that's why Jesus wants to warn us against their manifestations in our own religiousness.

Many of my students come to college with a clear distinction in their minds between "the Old Testament God of judgment" and "the New Testament God of love," or between "Jewish legalism" (attending always to the letter rather than the spirit of the law) and "Christian forgiveness."[4] Those distinctions are simply false. As noted earlier, when Jesus summarizes the law in terms of loving God and loving neighbor, he's quoting Jewish scripture. No one has ever written more beautifully about God's love for sinful human creatures than prophets like Hosea and Isaiah. This is a point worth emphasizing because distinctions such as those I've mentioned can feed the long and tragic history of Christian anti-Semitism. Christians could profit from reflecting on one of Jesus' parables:

> Why do you see the speck in your neighbor's eye, but do not notice the log in your own eye? Or how can you say to your neighbor, "Let me take the speck out of your eye," while the log is in your own eye? You hypocrite, first take the log out of your own eye, and then you will see clearly to take the speck out of your neighbor's eye.
> (Matt. 7:3–5)

Christian self-righteousness has often been as big as a log. Just as scribes and Pharisees condemned Samaritans, so we want to identify the problem exclusively in someone else—the scribes and Pharisees—to avoid facing our own failings.

The Gospels regularly tell stories that condemn "the Pharisees" and, particularly in John, "the Jews." Quoting some of those passages has preceded the shedding of a lot of Jewish blood down the centuries. It is therefore particularly important to emphasize that Christians should read those passages as condemnations of religious hypocrisy and self-righteousness wherever it is to be found—and therefore particularly among ourselves.

Jesus' Challenge to Order and Respectability

It is hard for us to recognize Jesus' condemnations as applying to us in part because we resist admitting just how radical his challenges can be. We turn the Pharisees into fussy extremists so that we can keep an image of Jesus as more liberal than they but still, after all, a respecter of his society's basic values. If we acknowledge that the Pharisees were the respectable, pious people of the time, then we have to admit that Jesus had little patience with respectable, pious people. Consider some stories:

> To another he said, "Follow me." But he said, "Lord, first let me go and bury my father." But Jesus said to him, "Let the dead bury their own dead; but as for you, go and proclaim the kingdom of God." Another said, "I will follow you, Lord, but let me first say farewell to those at my home." Jesus said to him, "No one who puts a hand to the plow and looks back is fit for the kingdom of heaven."
> (Luke 9:59–62)

This is not a defense of traditional family values. And in the traditional Jewish culture of the first century, with its strong emphasis on honoring parents and the continuity of families, it would have been even more scandalous than it is today.

Similarly, Jesus entered the Temple and knocked down the booths in which were sold the birds and animals which enabled people to perform the proper sacrifices. As Karl Barth once ironically remarked, "'A den of thieves' is rather a harsh description for the honest, small-scale financial and commercial activities which had established themselves there."[5] If you couldn't buy the right kind of animal, then how could you sacrifice? If you couldn't sacrifice, why have a Temple? By his actions, Jesus seems to be challenging the very basis of religion.

Indeed, Jesus seems to challenge everything—family obligations, religious rites, economic order. Surely every culture has its honored, valued, most respectable people. But to those elites in Israel, Jesus can only say, "Woe to you Pharisees! For you love to have the seat of honor in the synagogues and to be greeted with respect in the marketplaces. Woe to you!" (Luke 11:43–44). The sheer force of the love of God just rolls over all such human distinctions between more and less respected; those who try to hold on to them risk getting rolled over too.

In an adult Sunday School class in my church we were reading a widely used book on effective ministry. The author told about a young pastor who dropped by local bars (always, it was emphasized, just drinking a Coke) and talked to people there about their problems. A number of them started coming to church and growing into good members. Our author acknowledged the value of all this in a condescending way but then said that of course the young pastor had had to give it up—there was too much occasion for potential scandal. I was proud that everyone in our class disagreed with the book, insisting that of course following Jesus will involve scandal.

Yet Christians down the centuries have wanted to preserve order and respectability. The beginnings of New England provide Americans with a good example. John Cotton, the first preacher in Boston, concluded that the observably "holy" are "apt to live . . . in the strength of their gifts and not in the strength of Christ."[6] Their confidence in their own virtue will render them less inclined to understand how much they need God's grace. "Hence observe: God doth sometimes pour out the Spirit of grace upon the most bloody, and most heinous, and most desperate, and most prophane [sic], and most abominable of sinners."[7]

His fellow clergy could not agree. If Cotton were right, the town drunk might be more filled with the Spirit of God than the most respectable of church elders or local professionals. How would one keep order in a society like that, they wondered. How would one keep people in line? Cotton backed off, and his most passionate disciple, Anne Hutchinson, was as a result driven out of the colony. In the centuries since then, most churches in America have tried to become and stay respectable (and if the first generation of a new religious movement revels in its radicality, the second or third usually seeks respectability).

Still, no matter how hard Christians try to hide it, the challenge of Jesus' ministry keeps presenting itself to us through the pages of the New Testament. Jesus' vision of a community of love rather than fear, equality rather than hierarchy, where only those who cling to their privileges risk exclusion has perhaps spread no more among Christians down the centuries than it did among the Pharisees, but it remains the message of the Gospel.

11

Homosexuality

As I noted earlier, here and in the two parts that follow I will discuss an ethical issue of contemporary significance, by way of reflecting on how the things we say about Jesus affect how we think about ethical issues in our own lives. I use three issues—homosexuality, prisons, and war—simply as examples without claiming that they are the most important or most central moral questions facing Christians today. Since we have just been considering Jesus' controversial openness to the outsiders of his society, the topic of homosexuality seems appropriate to this chapter: it generates great controversy in our society, and it concerns people often relegated to outsider status.

Even so, it is at one level odd to treat homosexuality as such an important issue in Christian ethics. We have no evidence that Jesus himself ever expressed an opinion on this matter, one way or the other. In the whole of the Bible, sexual intercourse between people of the same sex is mentioned only about half a dozen times, and never at any length. It is hard to imagine how anyone, reading the Bible through, could come up with homosexuality as one of the central topics it lays out for ethical reflection.

Yet this is an issue that may yet split (and already divides) several major Protestant denominations in the United States. At national gatherings, it often consumes more time, energy, and passion than any other ethical topic. The reasons for that emphasis fall, I think, under the expertise of a sociologist, not a theologian. They grow out of events and attitudes in contemporary American society, not out of the emphases of Scripture. Still, the very prominence of the issue in the church today makes it worth attention.

Right at the start, however, we encounter a problem about terminology. While I use the word "homosexuality" in reference to biblical times as well as today, some scholars argue that "homosexuality" should properly refer to a certain style of life that is only about a hundred years old. Before that time, various people, for various reasons, did have sex with others of their own sex, but they weren't "homosexuals" in our modern sense. Same-sex intercourse is in some cultures part of religious rituals. In other cultures, people engage in it during one particular stage of their lives but not other stages. The relation between the partners may be socially defined in particular ways. One cannot simply describe people living in very different cultural contexts as "homosexuals" with the same meaning that word has in our society. Still, "homosexuality" seems the most neutral term available, so I will fall back fairly often on it, with enough ponderous references to "sexual intercourse between people of the same sex" to remind myself and my readers of the linguistic problem.

Sexuality and the Bible

Homosexuality is a sexual orientation, and questions about sexuality are important in Christian ethics. Sex matters to Christian life, first, because the body matters. As I noted in part 1, Jesus' bodiliness reminds us that having a body is a part of being human, not an evil to be escaped or an extraneous factor to be ignored, but a good feature of the way God made us. Therefore, what we do with our bodies matters—whether we use them to satisfy momentary pleasures, indifferent to longer term consequences, or act through them to express authentic love to our neighbors, find rich joy God intended for us, and glorify the God who made us, bodies and all.

Sex also matters because Christians understand (again as discussed in part 1) that human beings exist in relation. Jesus modeled the compassion and care that we ought to show to others. God's relation with Israel particularly manifests what it means to be faithful to a relationship, even when one's covenant partner is faithless. Even when the people of Israel worshipped other gods, the Lord did not abandon them, and that faithfulness challenges us with a standard of behavior to aim for when we enter into a covenant relationship like marriage. If our sexuality is an important part of who we are, then we ought to express it with care and compassion and in faithful relationships. None of these conclusions need imply anything about whether those relationships have to be heterosexual.[1] On that issue, the Bible has surprisingly little to say. Two passages in Leviticus condemn male homosexual intercourse (Lev. 18:22; 20:13). Some scholars take these passages as ethical injunctions against homosexual activity—period.

Others argue that ritual homosexual prostitution was associated with the worship of some of the pagan gods, and it was that context that led to denunication of homosexual intercourse in Hebrew law. Since today we lack Baal temple prostitution, the argument continues, the condemnation no longer applies.[2]

Still others propose that such intercourse, like certain types of heterosexual intercourse (between a man and a menstruating woman, for instance) made one impure according to the laws of ancient Israel, and so the issue actually has to do with ritual purity rather than ethical responsibility. In fact, according to Leviticus, if an adult male raped a boy or had intercourse with an animal, the boy or the animal would be killed as well as the perpetrator (Lev. 20:13, 15), and that does suggest that it is ritually purifying the community rather than punishing a misdeed that is at issue.[3] Therefore, one might conclude, this prohibition no longer applies to contemporary Christians, any more than do all the other Old Testament commandments concerning ritual purity or kosher food.

There simply isn't a consensus of scholarly interpretation on these passages. By contrast, most contemporary scholars agree that the most famous Old Testament text "about homosexuality" does not in fact address the subject. In the story of Sodom and Gomorrah (Genesis 19), when two angels visit Lot, the "men of Sodom" try to break into his house to gang-rape his visitors, whom they do not recognize as angels. Lot carries a host's obligations to extremes by offering the Sodomites his daughters for their sexual advances if only they will leave his guests alone. Offering *daughters* for sexual intercourse makes no sense at all, if we think of the "Sodomites" as homosexuals. These Sodomites are violent bullies who carry their excesses to the point of attempted rape. Such behavior still occurs in the aftermath of battle, in prisons, or among violent gangs. Those who perform such forced sexual intercourse consistently insist that they are not homosexual, and their actions seem indeed to be intended to assert power rather than to express sexual attraction.[4] So the sin of Sodom is not homosexuality.

Paul and Homosexuality

New Testament passages raise, I think, harder questions on this issue. 1 Corinthians lists types of sinners who will not inherit the reign of God: "Fornicators, idolaters, adulterers, male prostitutes [*malakoi*], men who have sex with other men [*arsenokoitai*], thieves, the greedy, drunkards, revilers, robbers" (1 Cor. 6:9–10). 1 Timothy offers a similar list: "murderers, fornicators, men who have sex with other men [*arsenokoitai*], slave traders, liars, perjurors, and whatever else is contrary to the sound teaching that conforms to the glorious gospel of the blessed God" (1 Tim. 1:9–11).[5]

Neither of these passages contains a word that exactly means "homosexual" in our usual modern sense; there is no such word in ancient Greek. Near as we can tell, as in our culture, most people around the eastern Mediterranean in the first century were erotically attracted to the opposite sex, but some were attracted to members of their own sex. Quite independently of those general preferences, however, in some parts of Greek society, an adolescent boy would spend a few years as the passive sexual partner of a young adult man who would help initiate him into adulthood. Then he would switch roles, and then he would marry a woman and have children.

Several of Plato's dialogues take all this for granted and praise the virtues of courage and honor that could result from such relationships;[6] even in the time of Paul, centuries later, similar practices continued. There were specific words for all of these activities and for the people who participated in them, but none corresponds to our word for "homosexual." There were insulting words (some of them used in low comedy)—for instance, for men who liked boys who were too young, or for males who continued to play the passive role in a sexual relationship even when they were too old—but they referred to specific kinds of behavior. The words used for other forms of homosexual behavior didn't imply insult at all.[7]

What about these two New Testament words? "*Malakoi*" is slang for boys who played the passive role in sexual intercourse. "*Arsenokoitai*" is an unusual word—these New Testament passages are its first recorded use in Greek—but it seems to have been formed from a phrase that meant "lying with a male."[8] Both terms refer to men engaged in some sort of homosexual activity, but whether they refer to all homosexual activity or just some, we don't know enough about first-century Greek usage to be sure.[9] One scholar proposes that these passages refer only to "youthful callboys and their customers,"[10] but I think that's an implausibly narrow reading.

In the most extensive biblical passage on the topic, Paul discusses the moral consequences for those who, down the centuries, have failed to worship the true God. Because of their worship of false idols, Paul says,

> God gave them up to degrading passions. Their women exchanged natural intercourse for unnatural, and in the same way also the men, giving up natural intercourse with women, were consumed with passion for one another. Men committed shameless acts with men and received in their own persons the due penalty for their error.
>
> (Rom. 1:26–27)

This is the only biblical passage to refer to same-sex relationships between women, and the most explicit concerning men.

Though some scholars argue the point, I think it is fairly clear that Paul considered the intercourse he saw around him between people of the same sex sinful. Some Christians conclude that that settles the matter—speaking with the authority of Scripture, Paul condemns homosexual intercourse (like all the biblical passages, this one concerns *behavior* and not "homosexuality" as a sexual orientation), and therefore so should we.[11] Others feel that Paul simply reflected the prejudices of a Jew who had come in contact with Hellenistic culture, and therefore there is no reason to adopt his point of view as our own.[12]

I find my own views lying in the admittedly muddier ground between those two extremes. In the Hellenistic world Paul witnessed (how closely and how often we have no idea) particular culturally shaped forms of homosexual activity. The behavior may well have been mostly homosexual *activities* in one social context, by people who also engaged in heterosexual activities and who were not culturally defined as "homosexuals." At least among men these relationships were about power as well as (or sometimes instead of) love: the active male partner's superiority to the passive partner in the sexual act was crucial to how people understood the activity. Much of it involved boys young enough that we would classify them as children.[13]

Paul condemned what he saw, and we encounter that condemnation in the pages of the Bible. I take that seriously. If we trust the Bible enough to think that it can tell us who Jesus was, and thereby who God is, then we cannot dismiss what the Bible says on other issues because we find it inconvenient or uncongenial.

On the other hand, we are not sure *why* Paul condemned what he saw. Would he have felt differently if everyone involved had been an adult? If the relation had been understood as between equals? If "homosexuality" had defined some people throughout their lives, rather being part of the lives of lots of people who also had other forms of sex? For him, in a culture where men and women had hierarchically defined roles, was the issue that homosexual activity disrupted social order? Would the issue therefore be different in a society like ours whose ideal is to treat men and women as equals?[14] Such questions have no obvious answer. We can state the question: Would very different forms of homosexual activity have seemed wrong in the same way to Paul? But we cannot summon him up from the dead, introduce him to contemporary forms of homosexuality, and find out what he would have thought of them.

Some Tentative Conclusions

Does Paul teach that homosexual intercourse is always sinful? For the reasons I have been indicating, I think that's a question on which honest Christians can disagree. Is homosexuality one of the sins Christians should worry most about? That's by contrast an easy question, and the answer is "no." Scripture discusses same-sex intercourse only briefly, and in complicated contexts. However we interpret those passages, there is something very wrong in current attitudes in many churches, where condemning homosexuality appears to be the most important of all ethical topics. Moreover (and this is how, I believe, this topic fits into a general discussion of Jesus' ministry), Jesus clearly did *not* deliver his most forceful condemnations about the sins that generated the most social antagonism in his culture, as homosexuality often does in ours, but rather reserved them for the flaws in those his society viewed as most respectable.

A number of years ago I served on a committee that wrote a new statement of faith for the Presbyterian church. Representatives of a very powerful "conservative" congregation came calling, and expressed their hope that we would reaffirm the church's "traditional beliefs." That sounded like a good idea to me, and I hoped they had the Trinity or the doctrine of grace in mind. Which of those beliefs were particularly important to them, I asked. A strong doctrine of the authority of Scripture, they replied. And why is that so important? Because it gives us the basis for the condemnation of homosexuality. It seemed to me that their priorities were misplaced, and their reasoning had not begun with Scripture.

Any honest reading of the Bible will make clear that it takes sins like greed, hatred, and lack of compassion much more seriously than it takes any sins having to do with our genitals.[15] It says things about marriage and the place of women that most "mainline" denominations ignore. For that matter, Jesus' prohibition of remarriage after divorce (Mark 10:11–12) is much clearer than any biblical comment on homosexuality but is not taken very seriously even in very conservative churches.[16]

If a denomination singles out homosexuals for judgment and doesn't speak and act forcefully on other matters where the Bible is far more forceful, therefore, it looks as though its motive is not faithfulness to Scripture, but accepting the prejudices of contemporary society. In such cases, while Christians may claim to stand up against the values of our culture, in fact they are yielding to them.

Friends I respect who struggle with this issue sometimes say, "But the church needs to take a stand somewhere. We have given up on any number of points, but at some point we need to draw a line and say that this behavior may be increasingly acceptable in our society, but it is not acceptable to the Christian community." I understand that concern. But, if we learn anything about moral judgment from the Gospels, it is surely that Christians should focus on the sins that our society rarely criticizes, especially when they are committed by the rich and powerful, not those already condemned and despised, as homosexuality so often is.

Even if one concedes that homosexual intercourse is a sin—and, for reasons already noted, the biblical evidence does not persuade me of that—it is also a form of behavior that gets people fired from their jobs, beaten up, called rude names, generally treated with contempt in many parts of our society, and sometimes even murdered. As I write this, the top selling album in the country, by a young white "rapper," Eminem, includes songs that talk vividly about beating up and killing homosexuals. A version of the album for sale in chain stores in more conservative parts of the country has the worst of its profanity eliminated, but leaves these references to violence unchanged.

Those who grow up gay generally have a hard time of it in contemporary America. Thus, the pattern of Jesus' ministry would clearly imply that, even if homosexual behavior were a sin, here is precisely *not* the place to "draw the line." Far better to draw it in the face of a sin like greed, which our culture generally treats with something like admiration, especially when it is masked as "success."[17]

Jesus, after all, singled out for particular condemnation the sins that his society accepted as compatible with respectability. Those who were condemned by society anyway he tended to treat rather generously. Here as elsewhere, Jesus stood with the outsiders, the disreputable, and the fearful, rather than the self-confident and self-righteous.

12

Preaching

Jesus' ministry of questioning the self-righteous and welcoming outcasts fulfilled theologian Reinhold Niebuhr's definition of good preaching: it comforted the afflicted and afflicted the comfortable. Preaching is the "mark of the church" that most obviously continues what Jesus did in his ministry, just as, to note Calvin's two other "marks of the church," communion relates more to the cross and baptism to the resurrection. Jesus' ministry stands in a succession that not only reaches back to the prophets but forward to Christian preachers. Not only did he preach himself, he commissioned his disciples to preach, sending them out even during his ministry to the towns and villages of Galilee (Mark 6:6–13; Luke 9:1–6; Luke 10:1–12).

Most contemporary Christian preachers play things safer than Jesus did. I do not mean to single preachers out for criticism: their pattern of caution may have more to do with what congregations are willing to listen to than with what preachers are willing to say. Sometimes, for that matter, congregations' impatience is justified. While some preaching tackles hard questions and properly challenges the comfortable assumptions of the people in the pews, sometimes the preacher is just riding his or her own hobbyhorse and calling the exercise "prophetic preaching."

How can one preach "with authority"? How can one deliver a message that a congregation does not want to hear in a way that leads them to admit that maybe they ought to listen? Perhaps we should go back and look again at Jesus' preaching. "Preaching," to be sure, can have broader and narrower meanings. In one sense Christians can and should "preach" the transformative power of the Gospel through the examples of our lives. Teaching children, informally explaining our faith to nonbelievers, and any number of other activities could also count as preaching in a broad sense.

More precisely, though, "preaching" means what Jesus did in the synagogue at Nazareth—interpreting Scripture in the context of worship. Protestants have always known that Calvin and other Reformers thought it crucial to the health of the church that preaching be done, and done right, but new research into the history of preaching indicates how consistently good preaching has also been important in the Catholic and Orthodox traditions.[1]

Preaching in the New Testament

The New Testament gives us a good many examples of preaching: Jesus preaches in the Gospels, and Acts recounts a number of the sermons of the early disciples.[2] One feature stands out: these sermons are always grounded in interpreting Scripture. (For the very first Christians, of course, "Scripture" meant the Hebrew Scriptures we call the Old Testament.) When Jesus or Peter preached, often just after they had worked miracles, we might expect that they would hardly have needed to appeal to the authority of some book. After all, didn't they speak with their own authority? And as we have seen in other contexts, Jesus felt comfortable challenging the Law. But with some consistency, when Jesus or the disciples preach, they first quote a passage of Scripture and then explain its application for their hearers.

For Christians, the Bible sets the framework for a description of the whole world, from creation to end, and we each understand our life aright when we put it into the context of that framework. Therefore, whether Christian preaching is talking about the good news of Jesus or its implications for our lives, it needs constantly to subject itself to the guidance and judgment of the Bible.

This part of this book, on Jesus' ministry, began with Jesus' "sermon" on Isaiah in the synagogue at Nazareth. It's one of several such more or less formal sermons the Gospels describe. In the Gospel of Matthew, near the end of his ministry, Jesus speaks in the Temple at Jerusalem, offering expositions of a series of texts (Isa. 54; Ps. 118; Deut. 6:5; Lev. 19:18; and Ps. 110) in explanation of his teaching and his vigorous debate with various opponents. Luke offers another model of a kind of preaching in the story of the walk to Emmaus. When Jesus "preached" to Cleopas and his friend on the road to Emmaus, "beginning with Moses and all the prophets, he interpreted to them the things about himself in all the scriptures"[3] (Luke 24:27).

At Pentecost, when the Holy Spirit descends like tongues of fire on the apostles, Peter preaches on a passage from the prophet Joel and then some Psalms (Acts 2:14–36). Under arrest and facing death, Stephen reviews virtually the whole history of Israel, quoting a wide range of scriptural passages (Acts 7:1–53). Someone about to be killed obviously does not quote texts out of antiquarian interest. Stephen—like Peter, and like Jesus—was speaking out of the conviction that these biblical stories provide the best guide for understanding the events of the moment.

Take Peter's speech at Pentecost as an example. Peter in effect says to his audience, "You've just seen this strange phenomenon of people receiving the Holy Spirit and speaking in all sorts of different languages. You must wonder what to make of it. Well, let me set it in a context that makes sense of it; to start with, let me quote the prophet Joel. . . . " And then he lays out a framework for understanding history into which the extraordinary events that just happened fit. Similarly, Jesus on the road to Emmaus sets his own death and now his empty tomb in a context "beginning with Moses and all the prophets."

Why should preaching start with Scripture? The word the New Testament uses for "preaching" or "proclamation" often referred to the news a herald would bring of some major event. The preacher, thus, has *news* to offer—not just entertainment or even good advice. Preachers begin with the Bible because that's where they got the news. Preaching, Karl Barth has written, "must not be boring." And yet, "To a large extent the pastor and boredom are synonymous." The problem, Barth believed, is that too many pastors rely on their own resources of ideas and anecdotes, and rather quickly run out of interesting things to say. Therefore,

> Against boredom the only defense is . . . being biblical. If a sermon is biblical it will not be boring. Holy scripture is in fact so interesting and has so much that is new and exciting to tell us that listeners cannot even think about dropping off to sleep.[4]

The purpose of the sermon is not to convey the preacher's interesting or uninteresting ideas but to report like a herald the news the Bible has to tell us. "The text protects us," Jean Jacques von Allmen, a contemporary Swiss theologian, once remarked. "It protects us from our imagination by setting its limits and from lack of imagination by stimulating what we have."[5] Not a bad thing, Barth noted, given all the preachers who want to pursue their own personal agendas, if "on the pulpit, as a final warning to those who ascend it, there is a big Bible."[6]

Good preaching therefore does not depend on a charismatic preacher. The famous nineteenth-century preacher Phillips Brooks (among other things, he wrote "O Little Town of Bethlehem") described preaching as "truth through personality." That's one model of preaching: we're supposed to go home thinking what a great, charismatic preacher we heard. But that is not what the New Testament calls for, "for what we preach is not ourselves, but Jesus Christ as Lord" (2 Cor. 4:5). Preachers should therefore read a passage from Scripture. Having in advance studied it, prayed, and thought about it, they should then explain as best they can what it means to the lives of the people in their congregation. And then they should sit down. To the extent that they are honestly interpreting the passage at hand, their words become God's word to the people. What is essential to Christian worship is the *reading* of Scripture. At least as an exercise, preachers might begin by asking whether the text and its applications for the congregation are clear enough without a sermon; such reflection would recall us to preaching's real purpose.

"This does not mean," Barth admitted, "that congregations must say Yea and Amen to all the words of their reverend pastors. Pastors are sinners."[7] They can be prejudiced or stupid and get the text wrong. But when they are faithful interpreters, as Calvin said, it is "the best and most useful exercise in humility" that God leads us to hear, recognize, and obey

> his Word, even though it be preached through people like us and sometimes even by those of lesser worth than we. . . . When a puny man risen from the dust speaks in God's name, at this point we best evidence our piety and obedience toward God if we show ourselves teachable toward his minister although he excels us in nothing.[8]

What matters, after all, is not the greatness of the preacher but the truth of the word being preached.

The Christian conviction about the truth of the Bible, however, means not just that it reports truthfully about long ago and far away, but that what it says makes sense of the very world in which we live. Faithfully *interpreting* Scripture therefore also means applying it to people's lives here and now. Preachers should "speak to other people for their upbringing and encouragement and consolation" (1 Cor. 14:3). They should connect what they have to say to the lives of their listeners. "What advantage would there be," Calvin once asked his congregation, "if we were to stay here half a day and I were to expound half a book without considering you or your profit and edification?"[9]

Even here, though, connecting with the congregation does not have to mean telling funny stories or making references to contemporary culture. If the Bible is what Christians believe it to be, then nothing connects to our lives better than what it has to say. The preacher's job is simply to show how that works.

Preachers ought to care about the people to whom they are speaking; they ought to speak in love. As Paul put it, "If I speak in the tongues of men and of angels, but do not have love, I am a noisy gong or a clanging cymbal" (1 Cor. 13:1). Preaching of the Gospel is by definition preaching "good news." If it feels like anger or hatred, something has gone wrong.

Still, however much compassion preachers have for those to whom they preach, they should not try to shoulder the burden of ultimate responsibility for the success or failure of their preaching. They are not "pedlars of God's word," Paul once observed (2 Cor. 2:17). In Luke Jesus commissions seventy preachers to try spreading the word in each town to which they come, but if they get no positive reaction, they are to move on to the next place (Luke 10:1–12).

Preachers are called to do their duty as best they can; what comes of it rests finally in God's hands. The Holy Spirit who inspired the authors of Scripture inspires preachers and hearers. "The Word itself," Calvin insisted, "is not quite certain for us unless it be confirmed by the testimony of the Spirit."[10] That Spirit, like the wind, "blows where it chooses" (John 3:8), according to plans known to God but utterly mysterious to us. Mediocre preaching can transform lives; on the wrong day, the best of preaching can produce no discernible result. Failure and success are not to be measured by empirical criteria. One preaches what Scripture seems to call for, and trusts in the Lord. When preachers do that, they continue the ministry of Christ and his disciples. To say that is not to guarantee that they will always have an easy time of it. The disciples' careers were not easy, and Jesus' ministry, after all, led him to the cross.

PART 3

The Cross

The Cross

The cross is the most pervasive Christian symbol. Whether on the window of a ghetto storefront, at the top of a great cathedral, or in an archeological site in the deserts of central Asia, the cross signals the presence of Christians. Everything else in the Gospels seems to lead to the accounts of the last few days before Jesus' execution. These "passion narratives," as they are called, take up a fourth or more of each Gospel.[1] In John the risen Jesus proves his identity to doubting Thomas by inviting him to touch the nail marks in his hands, as if to say, the marks of crucifixion are the sign that this is really *me*. "I have resolved," Paul says, "to know nothing among you except Jesus Christ, and him crucified" (1 Cor. 2:2).

Yet how odd a place for faith to begin. The beauty of golden crosses and Renaissance paintings tempts us to forget that this most basic of Christian symbols was first of all a particularly brutal means of execution. Crucifixion was a terrible way to die—excruciating pain, slow suffocation, the shame of dying, naked or nearly so, with nature's processes running their course, out by a garbage dump near one of the lesser gates of the city.[2] Imagine some new religious cult in the United States claiming that its founder was unjustly put to death, and placing a working model of an electric chair at the front of each of their places of worship.

If we face it honestly, the cross makes us uncomfortable for more personal reasons. "The cross places suffering at the heart of God's character and at the heart of meaningful, faithful human life," the Old Testament scholar Walter Brueggemann has written, and therefore, "our North American dominant cultural values are massively resistant to a theology of the cross."[3]

The whole course of Christ's obedience led him to crucifixion. What does it mean, then, to be one of his followers in a sinful world? If we stand up for the implications of our faith when they happen to be unpopular in our neighborhood, nothing may come of it—or we may get a few nasty anonymous phone calls, or a rock through the window, or some crazed fanatic may kill us. The cross should remind us of the possibility of such consequences. Too often, however, we do not think about its meaning because we want to call ourselves Christians while avoiding the thought that the implications of our faith might threaten our comfort.

Critics of the Cross

It might seem that those who are committed to social action and want their fellow Christians to become similarly involved in taking risks or making sacrifices to help the oppressed would particularly emphasize the cross in their theologies. Yet today some of the Christian theologians who are most concerned about suffering and injustice in the world also want to move the cross out of its central place in Christian faith. They fear that the idea that Jesus died on the cross "for our sins" pictures a vindictive Father God, angry at humankind and unappeased until his only son is murdered for the sake of the Father's satisfaction—which places child abuse at the heart of Christian faith.[4]

They also fear that the image of the cross encourages oppressed people simply to accept their suffering as a way of following Christ. Feminist theologians Joanne Carlson Brown and Rebecca Parker express this concern with respect to women:

> Christianity has been a primary—in many women's lives *the* primary—force in shaping our acceptance of abuse. The central image of Christ on the cross as the savior of the world communicates the message that suffering is redemptive. If the best person who ever lived gave his life for others, then, to be of value we should likewise sacrifice ourselves. Any sense that we have a right to care for our own need is in conflict with being a faithful follower of Jesus.[5]

And so, they argue, the abused wife goes back to her husband for another beating—following the crucified Jesus.

Do we have only a hard choice between two alternatives: either accepting the importance of the cross, thereby inadvertently fostering child abuse and wife beating, or getting rid of the cross, and its power to disrupt our comfortable lives?

I think there's another way of understanding the meaning of the cross for Christian faith. God did not stand by and watch someone else die on the cross—such an interpretation denies the divinity of Christ. In Jesus Christ, God was there, dying. We thus see how much God loves us, even as God acts, accomplishing what the Christian tradition has called our "reconciliation" and "redemption" (topics to be discussed in later chapters). Thus the cross is not a model for passively accepting one's suffering, but for acting boldly to make the world a better place. As such, it continues to challenge those who would call themselves Jesus' followers. As Martin Luther King Jr. wrote from a jail cell in Birmingham,

> There was a time when the church was very powerful. It was during that period when the early Christians rejoiced when they were deemed worthy to suffer for what they believed. In those days the church was

> not merely a thermometer that recorded the ideas and principles of popular opinion; it was a thermostat that transformed the mores of society. . . . Things are different now. . . . If the church of today does not recapture the sacrificial spirit of the early church, it will lose its authentic ring, forfeit the loyalty of millions, and be dismissed as an irrelevant social club with no meaning for the twentieth century.[6]

If the cross means that God pays a price for rescuing sinners, then it properly speaks of God's reckless love. If the cross means that we have to take risks for our faith, then it properly indicates what it means to follow Jesus.

Interpreting the Cross

In the Bible, Jesus' crucifixion takes place in the context of the passion narratives. These narratives also include Jesus' last meal, the foundation of the sacrament of the Lord's Supper. Earlier parts of the Gospels sometimes may seem to be just collections of sayings and events, but here we read connected stories—narratives where the four Gospels have more consistency among them than anywhere else. Thus in the following chapters I will look at the passion narratives and then at the Lord's Supper, one of the "marks of the church."

After looking at the stories, I will turn to theological reflection on their meaning, and here we will discover something remarkable: the Christian tradition has never taken an "official" position on *how* Christ's death helps save us. Christian theologians down the centuries have distinguished orthodoxy from heresy on a large number of issues, some of them apparently quite trivial. By contrast, the claim that Christ's death played the crucial role in accomplishing our salvation seems as central as anything in Christian faith. Nevertheless, the church has tolerated a wide range of explanations of its meaning.

No one ever accused John Calvin of being a wishy-washy relativist, for instance; yet listen to him acknowledge a plurality of possibilities: "If the death of Christ be our redemption, then we were captives; if it be satisfaction, we were debtors; if it be atonement, we were guilty; if it be cleansing, we were unclean."[7] None of these images is wrong, he is saying; none is uniquely correct. The Presbyterian Church's Confession of 1967 states the diversity frankly:

> God's reconciling act in Jesus Christ is a mystery which the Scriptures describe in various ways. It is called the sacrifice of a lamb, a shepherd's life given for his sheep, atonement by a priest; again it is ransom of a slave, payment of a debt, vicarious satisfaction of a legal penalty, and victory over the powers of evil. These are expressions of a truth which remains beyond the reach of all theory in the depths of God's love.[8]

After dicussing the passion narratives and the Lord's Supper, then, I will look at three interpretations of what Christ did by dying on the cross—I've labeled those interpretations (1) solidarity, (2) reconciliation, and (3) redemption. Each of these ideas addresses a part of our problem as sinners. To oversimplify our threefold problem: (1) We feel alone and afraid. (2) Our relation with God is broken or frayed. (3) We have fallen under the sway of the power of evil. Christ thus responds in a threefold way, by (1) showing solidarity with us, thanks to which we no longer feel so radically alone; (2) reconciling us with God; and (3) redeeming us from the power of evil. Solidarity (again oversimplifying) speaks to a condition within ourselves; reconciliation to a two-part relation between ourselves and God; and redemption to a three-part problem involving ourselves, God, and evil.

Particularly in addressing reconciliation and redemption, the Bible draws heavily on the imagery of sacrifice. Partly because that imagery is so foreign to most people today, I want to pause part way through the chapter to discuss the meaning of sacrifice; that discussion will also provide the occasion to review the Old Testament context of Christ's "office" as priest. If Jesus was a high priest, he was also a condemned prisoner, and so, in applying the lessons of this chapter to a particular contemporary ethical issue, it seems appropriate to think about prisons and criminal justice.

13

The Way to the Cross in the Passion Narratives

The passion narratives operate on two levels. On one, they tell the story of a brave, frightened, lonely young man who is killed by powerful people and institutions in his society. On the other, they recount how the Son of God saves humankind. Here above all the Gospels do what I described in chapter 5: they show Christ doing divine things in a human way and human things in a divine way, so that the two sides of the story remain always the story of one person.

Since we cannot separate the two stories and be faithful to these texts, we cannot think about the story of our salvation without also reflecting on the human story of the particular way in which Jesus died. As the Mennonite theologian John Howard Yoder once wrote, "The cross of Calvary was not a difficult family situation, not a frustration of visions of personal fulfillment, a crushing debt, or a nagging in-law; it was the political logically-to-be-expected result of a moral clash with the powers ruling his society."[1] The brutal politics of power and Jesus' resistance to them are unavoidably part of the story of our salvation.

Mark's Story

Characteristically, Mark begins this part of his story abruptly and moves it forward quickly:

> They were on the road, going up to Jerusalem, and Jesus was walking ahead of them; they were amazed, and those who followed were afraid.
>
> (Mark 10:32)

In what follows, even this first sentence warns us, there will be cause for amazement but also for fear. Jesus is walking ahead—this is a story about following him. Like that ascending road, everything in the Gospel is coming to a climax, human conflict and divine victory: "See, we are going up to Jerusalem," Jesus says, "and the Son of Man will be handed over to the chief priests and the scribes, and they will condemn him to death; then they will hand him over to the Gentiles; they will mock him and spit upon him, and flog him, and kill him; and after three days he will rise again" (Mark 10:33–34).

> When Jesus arrives in Jerusalem, riding on a donkey, crowds waving branches welcome him like a triumphant hero, crying,
> Hosanna!
> Blessed is the one who comes in the name of the Lord!
> Blessed is the coming kingdom of our ancestor David!
> (Mark 11:9–10)

At this, Mark's Jewish readers would have recalled a passage from the book of Zechariah. In one of the darkest periods in Israel's history, the fourth or fifth century B.C., an anonymous prophet whose words are included in Zechariah lived among Jews who had been allowed to return from exile but remained disorganized and spiritless: "The dreamers tell false dreams, and give empty consolation. . . . the people wander like sheep; they suffer for lack of a shepherd" (Zech. 10:2). Nevertheless, this unknown prophet envisioned hope:

> Shout aloud, O daughter Jerusalem!
> Lo, your king comes to you;
> Triumphant and victorious is he,
> humble and riding on a donkey,
> on a colt, the foal of a donkey.
> (Zech. 9:9)

The image from the prophet offers a way of saying yes, Jesus is a monarch, but not the kind of monarch who will lead us into violence. Rather, he is a monarch unlike any other, who arrives not on a war stallion but on the foal of a donkey, no doubt looking a little ridiculous in the midst of a triumphant procession. He has nothing to do with violence, but in his own way he is going to war.

Within a few days, as Mark tells the story, Jesus challenged the most fundamental features of first-century Jewish society: He knocked down the tables of the money changers in the Temple (Mark 11:15). He seemed to feel free to rewrite the Law of God itself, and he refused to explain his authority (Mark 11:33). He predicted the destruction of the Temple (Mark 13:2). He denounced the pious scribes as those who "devour widows' houses and for the sake of appearance say long prayers" (Mark 12:40). In the end, when the high priest demanded, "Are you the Messiah, the Son of the Blessed One," he replied, "I am; and 'you will see the Son of Man seated at the right hand of the Power,' and 'coming with the clouds of heaven' " (Mark 14:62).

Jesus was challenging the status quo, but his challenge reached beyond the Temple practices of Judaism or Roman provincial governance. He was concerned with addressing universal forms of human sin that exist in every political and religious institution, and the revolution he was proposing was therefore more radical than any that would merely replace one power structure with another.

Not surprisingly, every social group and political party abandoned him. Religious and political leaders condemned him; the disciples fell asleep just when he needed their companionship; Judas betrayed him; Peter denied him; a crowd (some of the same folk, perhaps, who had shouted hosannas a few days earlier) called for his death. Yet somehow Jesus was doing his work of salvation. At one level, he had fallen victim to social and political establishments, but at another he was working out the plan of God.

In Mark 13 a dramatic interruption occurs in the story; this chapter suddenly introduces prophecies of wars and earthquakes, the darkening of the sun, stars falling from heaven, and "the Son of Man coming in clouds with great power and glory" (Mark 13:26). This apocalyptic language seems so uncharacteristic of Mark that some scholars imagine he must have made the chapter out of a fragment of an earlier text, reworking it for his own purposes.[2]

However one explains Mark 13, though, it's worth recalling (as I noted in chapters 2 and 8) the way in which apocalyptic language both was and was not political. These dramatic symbols can serve as a code for saying in secret what cannot be expressed openly: the end of Roman rule is portrayed as the end of the world. But it's never *merely* a secret code, for apocalyptic visionaries were hoping for far more than the replacement of one government with a slightly better one. They dreamed of the kind of radical change in the underlying order of things-as-they-are that only God can bring—a change whose character they literally could not imagine. Apocalyptic, with its wild efforts to stretch beyond the limits of our imaginations, thus provides the right kind of language for the tension Mark wants to keep alive between the two sides of his one story: human struggle with the powers-that-be and divine action for the salvation of the world.

With good reason, we are suspicious of apocalyptic predictions, at least as they have often been used in our culture. The wild bearded man with the signboard proclaiming, "The end is at hand," has become a figure we see mostly in cartoons. But Mark does not really offer predictions (other than that times will be hard and we will be tested, which is surely safe enough for those who follow Christ). Jesus' call is simply to live life in readiness: If anyone says, "Here is the Messiah!" or "There he is!" we are not to believe, for "about that day or hour no one knows." Therefore, only this: "keep alert; for you do not know when the time will come" (Mark 13:21, 32–33).

After sharing a Passover meal with his friends (more about that in the next section), Jesus went off to the Garden of Gethsemane to pray. He "shudders in distress" and "anguishes"—many translations do not convey the forcefulness of the verbs.[3] "Abba, Father," he cried—the most intimate appeal to God (Mark 14:36). He asked God if he must really drink the cup of suffering that awaited him, "yet," he prayed, "not what I want but what you want" (Mark 14:36).

Fully God yet fully human: Mark stretches that tension as close to the breaking point as imaginable. Jesus was most fully obedient, most at one with God, in taking a path which led him most radically away from God into fear and doubt, until at the end he cried out from the cross, "My God, my God, why have you forsaken me?" The cry quotes the beginning of Psalm 22, whose author saw himself "scorned by others, and despised by the people. All who see me mock at me" (Ps. 22:6–7). This is the first time in Mark that Jesus does not call God "Father," and the question—that desperate "Why?"—apparently receives no answer. Yet it is this bruised body of a despairing man abandoned by everyone and sensing himself forsaken even by God upon which a Roman centurion looks and says, "Truly this man was God's Son!" (Mark 15:39).

Theme and Variations

Mark's story is all sharp edges. Matthew and Luke follow its outline (Matthew more closely) but occasionally temper its bleakness. In the Gospel of Matthew, Jesus prophesies all that will happen; he thus seems more confident and feels less sense of abandonment by God. In Luke, Jesus is healing and forgiving even during the darkest moments of the story: he restores the severed ear of one of the high priest's servants; he forgives those who have killed him; and he promises the penitent thief dying beside him, "Today you will be with me in Paradise" (Luke 23:43). His final words are a cry not of forsakenness but of acceptance: "Father, into your hands I commend my spirit" (Luke 23:46).

Still, the story remains one of condemnation, scourging, and humiliating death. In Luke's Gospel too, Jesus is ridiculed even as he is dying. The one positive voice comes from a convicted criminal, one of those hanging beside him on another cross, who says, "This man has done nothing wrong," and addresses him simply as, "Jesus" (the only time in the Gospel someone uses the name without any title), one dying man to another (Luke 23:41–42).

The Gospel of John presents greater differences. The events differ in a good many details, and the time-frame is changed. In the first three Gospels, Jesus shares a Passover meal with his disciples as their last supper together. But John moves everything back a day, so that Pilate condemns Jesus at noon before Passover, just at the moment Temple officials would have begun to kill the lambs for the Passover meal. Even more significantly, though, as Raymond Brown has written,

> Whereas the Jesus of Mark/Matt[hew] is mocked on the cross, and the Jesus of Luke is forgiving, the Jesus of John is triumphant. . . . until the moment he dies, the Marcan Jesus is victor only in the eyes of God, the Lucan Jesus is a victor in the eyes of his believing followers; but the Johannine Jesus is a victor for all to see.[4]

In the Gospel of John, Pilate writes an inscription, "Jesus of Nazareth, King of the Jews," to display on the cross. At one level, a sophisticated Roman procurator was showing his cultured irony and taking the opportunity to annoy the Jewish leaders, who of course pleaded that this convicted criminal not be identified as their king (John 19:19–21). And yet, of course, from the Gospel writer's point of view, Pilate got it right.[5]

No one mocks this Jesus on the cross. He is not abandoned; his mother, her sister, and that mysterious figure, "the disciple Jesus loved," remain by him near the cross, and he commends his mother to this disciple's care. Even in death, he is still in charge of things. Saying, "It is finished," he "bowed his head and gave up his spirit," as if even his death was something he chose rather than merely suffered (John 19:30).

So—four Gospels and their stories. Many historians properly remind us that we cannot trust the historical accuracy of their details; some even think that there was no historical memory of Jesus' last days, and the whole story is a legend.[6] Even the less skeptical have to admit that we cannot know on historical evidence what Jesus felt or thought as he faced his death. It's worth noting, therefore, that while the four Gospels can tell the story with very different details and very different pictures of Jesus' frame of mind, it remains recognizably the same story, with its two levels—at once the young man facing the power structure, and the Son of God saving the world. The story retains its identity in spite of the variations in its four versions, suggesting that the details that differ from one Gospel to another—and might vary further if we knew more historical facts—are oddly inessential to the meaning of the story.

A Historical Question: The Role of the Jewish Leaders

One point, though, particularly given the tragic place of the Holocaust in our century's history, does deserve some attention concerning its historical accuracy. Christian anti-Semites have often appealed to aspects of these stories—John's repeated references to "the Jews," or the moment in Matthew where Pilate refuses to take responsibility for Jesus' death and "the people as a whole answered, 'His blood be on us and on our children!' " (Matt. 27:25). Are the narratives as we have them necessarily anti-Semitic? Is it therefore crucial to probe behind the narratives and ask if any Jews were really involved in Jesus' death?

In considering such questions, it helps to think about how the Gospels came to be written. They emerged from small Christian communities that had been expelled from Jewish synagogues and were under threat of Roman persecution, communities that never thought of themselves as likely to have the power to persecute others. These Christians therefore didn't consider the potential damage their language could cause were they ever to achieve power. They could write about "the Jews," meaning only the Jewish leaders in Jerusalem at a particular time, and not think about the impact such references would have in different circumstances. Thus reading the Gospels should remind us of the dangers of simply identifying God's cause with the oppressed: today's oppressed may be the next century's oppressors.

Moreover, the authors of the Gospels had good reason to downplay the Roman role in Jesus' death and shift blame elsewhere. The idea that Jesus himself had been a rebel against a Roman governor would have further compromised his followers, already regarded with suspicion by the Roman government. The scenes in which the Roman procurator Pontius Pilate plays a relatively sympathetic role thus must fall under particular suspicion. But the Gospels never deny the basic reality: crucifixion was a *Roman* penalty, not for violation of religious orthodoxy but for something like treason or sedition. Whatever else he was doing, Jesus was at least perceived to be challenging Caesar.

Some scholars have wanted to push the argument one step further and try to show historically that Jews were not involved in Jesus' death at all. If it was *purely* a Roman act, their argument goes, wouldn't that be a wonderful way of clearing away Christian anti-Jewish prejudice?

I don't think so. Suppose some first-century Jewish leaders did encourage Jesus' crucifixion. That would have nothing to do with how Christians today ought to feel about our Jewish brothers and sisters. After all, since crucifixion was a Roman penalty, the Roman authorities *must* have had something to do with Jesus' death. But Christians do not have prejudices against Italians. We do not mistrust all New Englanders today because of the Salem witch trials. It is dangerous to try to show that anti-Semitism is wrong by showing that no Jewish leaders had any involvement in Jesus' death, since such arguments risk implying the bizarre view that, if they *were* involved, then anti-Semitism would be acceptable.

Moreover, we religious folk would like to say, "Well, it was the evil political and military leaders who killed Jesus." We need to remember how often in history *religious* leaders have been complicit in the worst kinds of persecution and violence. The presence of some of the religious leaders of Jesus' time in the story of his death reminds us of the evil that religion, in any form, can do.

Of course, politics and religion were hard to distinguish in first-century Palestine. Still, though we cannot claim to know as historians what Jesus was thinking or feeling at the end of his life, unless the Gospels got him completely wrong, he did not have a political or military plot in mind. In the circumstances, however, anyone of intelligence would have recognized that he was following a course toward confrontation in a brutal world. Whether he expected some miraculous intervention even before his death we cannot know, but the Gospels present him as at once in despair as to his fate and utterly obedient to God's will.

His followers very soon grew convinced that his obedience had accomplished their salvation. Some early Christian, possibly a follower of the apostle Peter, writing to a church suffering under persecution, put it this way:

> For to this you have been called, because Christ also
> suffered for you, leaving you an example, so that you
> should follow in his steps.
> "He committed no sin,
> and no deceit was found in his mouth."
> When he was abused, he did not return abuse; when he
> suffered, he did not threaten; but he entrusted himself
> to the one who judges justly. He himself bore our sins
> in his body on the cross, so that, free from sins, we
> might live for righteousness; by his wounds you have been
> healed. For you were going astray like sheep, but now
> you have returned to the shepherd and guardian of your souls.
> (1 Pet. 2:21–25)

By his wounds, we have been healed. But how? Before thinking about that question, we need to return to a part of the story this account skipped—Jesus' last meal—and its ongoing meaning in the life of the church.

14

The Lord's Supper

The first three Gospels all tell how, in the last meal he ate with his disciples before his crucifixion,

> [Jesus] took a loaf of bread, and after blessing it he broke it, gave it to them, and said, "Take, this is my body." Then he took a cup, and after giving thanks he gave it to them, and all of them drank from it. He said to them, "This is my blood of the covenant, which is poured out for many. Truly I tell you, I will never again drink of the fruit of the vine until that day when I drink it new in the reign of God."
>
> (Mark 14:22–25, translation modified)

In chapter 12 I showed how preaching keeps Jesus' teaching present in the life of the church. The Lord's Supper serves a similar function for his passion (just as, as chapter 24 explains, baptism does with the new life given in Jesus' resurrection). Different Christian traditions use different terms for this shared bread and wine: Communion, Lord's Supper, Eucharist (which means "thanksgiving"). I've chosen "Lord's Supper" for no better reason than that it is the term I learned as a child. Whatever this meal is called, it has been a feature of Christian worship from its very earliest days.

For the first Christians, sharing the bread and wine came at the end of a regular meal. After dinner, someone would repeat Jesus' words, and the people would share in the bread and wine. The meal functioned as a form of charity: the community gathered for the ritual, but those who didn't have enough to eat would come and be fed by the generosity of the more advantaged. Paul is angry when he hears that sometimes among the Corinthian Christians "each of you goes ahead with your own supper," so that some eat or drink too much and others go away hungry (1 Cor. 11:21).

Hope, Memory, Presence

Jesus' supper is not to be like that. To someone reading the Gospels straight through, the "last supper" evokes memories of earlier meals Jesus shared—how he ate with despised tax collectors and sinners, how he miraculously fed thousands. When Jesus sat down to dinner, it seems, everyone was welcome, and there was always plenty to go around.[1]

Such stories of meals would have raised other memories among Jews of Jesus' time. In the Book of Exodus, Moses and the elders climbed the mountain of the Lord at the reception of the ten commandments

> and they saw the God of Israel. Under his feet there was something like a pavement of sapphire stone, like the very heaven for clearness. God did not lay his hand on the chief men of the people of Israel; also they beheld God, and they ate and drank.
>
> (Exod. 24:9–11)

In ancient Israel, people believed that no one could see God without dying, and this image of sitting down to eat with him is thus an amazing one. (Note the surprise that "God did not lay his hand" on them—in other words, did not kill them on the spot.) Such a meal isn't the sort of thing that happens in human history; it anticipates the reign of God, which lies beyond all current experience. The idea of a banquet with God at the end of time became one of the symbols of Israel's hope. Listen to the prophet Isaiah:

> On this mountain the Lord of hosts will make for all peoples
> a feast of rich food, a feast of well-aged wines, of rich
> food filled with marrow, of well-aged wines strained clear. . . .
> It will be said on that day,
> Lo, this is our God; we have waited for him, so that he might save us.
> This is the Lord for whom we have waited;
> let us be glad and rejoice in his salvation.
>
> (Isaiah 25:6, 9)

Thus when Christians eat and drink the bread and wine, we joyously anticipate the future in which we shall be with God.[2] In repeating these acts, Paul says, we "proclaim the Lord's death *until he comes*" (1 Cor. 11:26)—thereby keeping the memory alive until the future feast.

Jesus' Supper offers hope for the future, however, only because it is connected to specific memories of the past. We remember Jesus and his meal with his disciples. That means our joy is tempered, for we remember that this was a meal "on the evening before he suffered," "on the night when he was betrayed." We proclaim *the Lord's death* until he comes. Yet what we remember is not just his death. "Do this in remembrance *of me*," he says in the Gospel accounts—not just in memory of his death, but of the whole course of his obedience.[3]

Moreover, we do not "just remember." The Great Jewish rabbi Gamaliel wrote of how Jews, reenacting the Passover meal, were not just remembering what had happened in the time of Moses but were somehow present with the Hebrew slaves that night in Egypt: "Every man in every generation must regard himself as having been personally delivered from Egypt. Every Israelite must know that he personally has been freed from slavery."[4] In reenacting the event, Jews relive its reality.

And so it is also with Christians and the Lord's Supper. As the New Testament scholar C. H. Dodd once wrote,

> At each Eucharist we are *there*—we are in the night in which he was betrayed, at Golgotha, before the empty tomb on Easter Day, and in the upper room where he appeared; *and* we are at the moment of his coming with angels and archangels and all the company of heaven, in the twinkling of an eye at the last trump.[5]

The Lord's Supper, then, looks forward to the great feast and backward to Jesus' last night, but more than that it experiences Christ as *present* in the shared bread and cup. The Supper is thus, as Aquinas said, a foretelling of future glory, a reminder of Christ's passion, and an indication of the grace effected in us.[6] The traditional liturgy for the feast of the body of Christ (*corpus Christi*) in the Catholic tradition includes those words: "The memorial of his passion is renewed, the mind is filled with grace, and a pledge of future glory is given to us."[7]

The Nature of Christ's Presence

Just how Christ is "present," however, has long been a matter of theological dispute. Even in the early second century, Christian theologians affirmed that the bread and wine *were* Christ's body and blood.[8] Debates in the early Middle Ages led to a rejection of the idea that reference to Christ's body and blood was "just a symbol" or a remembrance. Rather, some insisted the body and blood were really present. Indeed, in the Middle Ages, legends grew of bread that started bleeding, or of a human being somehow visible in the consecrated bread.

Thomas Aquinas and other Catholic theologians have used Aristotle's philosophy to find a middle ground between that kind of physical literalism and theories of merely symbolic remembrance. Aristotle had distinguished between a *substance* and its *properties*. An onion, for instance, he observed, is a substance which has the properties of white color, strong smell, circular layers, and so forth. In the Eucharist, Aquinas said, the *properties* of the elements remain the same—the bread still looks and smells like bread; it doesn't bleed. But the *substance* is "transubstantiated," so that it becomes the body and blood of Christ. Transubstantiation became Catholic doctrine at the Lateran Council in 1215.

Nearly all Protestants rejected transubstantiation, although they did not agree on a theory to replace it. Luther wanted to emphasize that the bread and wine remained bread and wine even while becoming Christ's body and blood. Lutheran theology thus talks about "consubstantiation"—both substances present together rather than one transformed to the other. Calvin wanted to resist offering any particular philosophical explanation of what happens. "If anyone should ask me how this takes place," he wrote, "I shall not be ashamed to confess that it is a secret too lofty for either my mind to comprehend or my words to declare."[9] He proposed simply affirming that Christ is "really present." In contrast, more radical Reformed Protestants like the Swiss reformer Ulrich Zwingli took the Lord's Supper to be nothing more than a way of remembering what Christ had done in dying for our sins.

Today some Protestant and Catholic theologians are finding common ground on these issues. Aristotle thought the world was fundamentally made up of observable substances—people, loaves of bread, rocks, and so on—and Aquinas generally borrowed that conceptual framework. Some Catholic theologians today admit that this philosophy seems in some ways out of date, as we acknowledge that the physical world is made up of electrons and protons or quarks, and much contemporary philosophy urges us to think of persons with different categories than we use for purely physical objects.

It's not that Aquinas was wrong, this argument goes—*if* you use Aristotle's categories, then transubstantiation would be the right thing to say. But in today's context it might make better sense to use, with respect to Christ's presence in this sacrament, the categories for affirming the presence of a person.[10] As one Catholic writer puts it,

> This change is not a change in molecular structure. Christ is not "under" or "behind" or "inside" the physical realities involved. He gives Himself in His own way, in sovereign freedom from all the conditions of material existence. He gives Himself, in short, in mystery.[11]

Calvin could have agreed.

Just as some Catholics are moving closer to Protestant views, so Protestants like the contemporary German Lutheran Wolfhart Pannenberg move nearer to traditional Catholic terminology. Pannenberg argues that Aristotle's most basic definition of "substance" is simply "what is." The distinctions between substance and properties, he says, are less important to Aristotle's thought. And, if "transubstantiation" means only that, in the most important sense for Christians, the bread and the wine of the Lord's Supper *are* the body and blood of Christ, then followers of Luther and Calvin need not deny it.[12]

Sharing the Bread and Wine

It is important that, on this and other issues, many Christian groups are coming closer to agreements that may make it possible for their members all to share someday in the same Eucharist. The fact that Christians from different denominations cannot eat the bread and wine together is a great Christian scandal, for this meal should be a symbol of the church's unity. "Because there is one bread," Paul wrote the Corinthians, "we who are many are one body, for we all partake of the one bread" (1 Cor. 10:17).

One of the earliest Christians texts from outside the New Testament, the *Didache*, a manual of church advice from second-century Syria, makes the symbolism clear in a prayer to Christ: "As this piece [of bread] was scattered over the hills and then was brought together and made one, so let your church be brought together from the ends of the earth into your Reign."[13] Augustine preached the same theme to his congregation several centuries later. Many grains of wheat, he said, made one loaf of bread only after being crushed, moistened, and baked. Likewise, many Christians became one church through discipline, baptism, and the fire of the Holy Spirit.[14]

For Christians, "the body of Christ" refers both to the bread of the Lord's Supper and to the church itself. The unity of the one symbolizes what ought to be the unity of the other. Ancient liturgical tradition required that the Supper be celebrated only once in a given day on a given altar. Churches that have circumvented this by having different services for different sorts of people—the service for those who like to dress informally, the service for those who want traditional music, and so forth—may have had practical reasons for their actions, but they miss the point: there should not be separate communions for the rich or the young or any other subgroup of the one Christian community.

The inclusiveness of the Supper means not only that all should share together but that all are welcome. If only the "pure" or those "purged from sin" could come to the table, Calvin once wrote, this "would debar" all "who ever were or are on earth from the use of this sacrament."[15] Jesus scandalously sat down to dinner with tax collectors and sinners; he rejected no one. The table of the Lord's Supper is his, not ours; it is not our place to institute selectivity that he never imposed. This is a table for sinners who share, one with another, in the heavenly feast by sharing in the presence of the one who died for their sins—in communion with Jesus only to the extent that we share the meal with everyone else who comes.[16] Then we take bread and wine from the shared meal to the bedfast or those in prison in sign that they remain members of the community.

That sharing, now as in the earliest church, needs to extend beyond this bread and wine. Writing in fourth-century North Africa, Cyprian demanded of wealthy Christians, "You are wealthy and rich, and do you think that you celebrate the Lord's Supper? . . . For your eyes, overcast with the gloom of blackness and shadowed in night, do not see the needy and poor."[17] Those who ignore the poor do not truly celebrate the Supper of the Lord who fed the poor. In the early church, the "offertory" involved bringing all sorts of food and money and other goods forward for sharing with members of the community in need as well as the bread and wine to be used for the Supper, to make as clear as possible the relationship between our sharing of the bread and wine and our sharing in whatever else the poor among us may need.

Many congregations today have so rearranged their services that a connection between communion and "collecting the offering" never occurs to anyone. Such services lose track of part of the meaning of both these elements of worship. In the early second century, Ignatius of Antioch identified those who abstain from the Supper with those who "care nothing about love: they have no concern for widows or orphans, for the oppressed, for those in prison or released, for the hungry or the thirsty."[18]

If we come authentically to *this* meal, we commit ourselves to sharing with those in need just as Jesus shared his very life with sinners. In the words of a recent document jointly signed by representatives of nearly all Christian groups, Protestant and Catholic:

> As Jesus went out to publicans and sinners and had table fellowship with them during his earthly ministry, so Christians are called in the Eucharist to be in solidarity with the outcast and to become signs of the love of Christ who lived and sacrificed himself for all and now gives himself in the Eucharist.[19]

This meal, which anticipates God's reign, remembers Jesus' passion, and makes Jesus present to his church, ought to be a meal that unites the church and leads it to service of the poor whom Jesus fed. It makes present among us what Christ did for our salvation. But that leads back to the issue—in his death on the cross in particular, what did he do, and how did he do it?

15

Solidarity

First of all, Christ saves us simply by being God with us. I'm calling that theme "solidarity" to point to the way he stands in solidarity with us even in the worst of our suffering and sins. To read about Christ's scourging, mocking, and crucifixion is to realize how fully he endured the worst that can come of being human. The cross represents the culmination of the incarnation: divinity fully united with humanity. Christ did not take on a "higher" human nature while avoiding the tough side of it. "We do not have a high priest who is unable to sympathize with our weaknesses, but we have one who in every respect has been tested as we are" (Heb. 4:15). "Jesus' death," Elizabeth Johnson has written, "included all that makes death terrifying: state torture, physical anguish, brutal injustice, hatred by enemies, the mockery of their victorious voices, collapse of his life's work in ruins, betrayal by some close friends, the experience of abandonment by God."[1]

The last point deserves particular attention. We are apt to think, "Jesus was God, so of course he knew it would turn out all right, and it was just a matter of getting through the pain." But as I discussed in chapter 4, such assumptions run against what the Gospels say, for they emphasize Jesus' terror and his sense of abandonment by the one he had always called "Father." By contrast, they don't much dwell on the purely physical side of his suffering. He was "distressed and agitated" (Mark 14:33). He "offered up prayers and supplications, with loud cries and tears, to the one who was able to save him from death" (Heb. 5:7). "My God, my God, why have you forsaken me?" Mark says he cried at the end (Mark 15:34). "To say he was pretending," Calvin once wrote, "is a foul evasion."[2]

Therefore, nothing that can happen to us—no pain, no humiliation, no journey into a far country or even into the valley of the shadow of death—can "separate us from the love of God in Christ Jesus our Lord" (Rom. 8:39). The

Incarnation shows that in Christ God is with us. The cross shows that in Christ God is with us, no matter what. Even when we doubt or disbelieve or think ourselves completely cut off from God, Christ has been there before us. Christ is, as the philosopher Alfred North Whitehead said of God, "the great companion—the fellow sufferer who understands."[3]

Christians from a variety of perspectives have understood Christ's solidarity with those who feel most abandoned and rejected. Aquinas quoted St. Jerome on how Christ was crucified in the company of thieves, "a guilty one among the guilty."[4] African Americans have understood Jesus as, in Jacquelyn Grant's phrase, "a divine co-sufferer who empowered them in situations of oppression."[5]

To find that comfort in Christ's identification with us, however, we have to be willing to share a sense of identification with the thieves and outsiders with whom Christ identifies. In the words of the contemporary theologian Rowan Williams, "Christ as criminal, Christ as madman, Christ as alcoholic vagrant: all this and more is implied in the unconditional identification of God with the victim."[6] If, like the Pharisee who thanked God "that I am not like other people; thieves, rogues, adulterers" (Luke 18:11), we contrast our own relative rectitude with the moral corruption of others, then we distance ourselves from those with whom Christ identifies, and thus from Christ.

Descent into Hell

Reflecting on the line in the Apostles' Creed which speaks of Christ's "descent into Hell" can help make clear the full extent of Christ's solidarity with those who are separated from God. In the First Letter of Peter, a brief passage declares that Christ "was put to death in the flesh, but made alive in the spirit, in which also he went and made a proclamation to the spirits in prison" (1 Pet. 3:18–19). The most honest interpretation would be, I think, that no one really knows what this phrase means.

But as early as the third century, Christian writers were interpreting it to mean that, between his death and his resurrection, Christ had gone to Hell to rescue the best people of ancient Israel and take them up to Heaven with him.[7] This interpretation offered one way of dealing with a worrisome question: if salvation depended on Christ, then what about all the people who died before his lifetime? Indeed, some scholars argue that the idea of Christ's descent into Hell originally developed out of reflection on these issues and independently of the passage in 1 Peter.

In any event, the phrase "he descended into Hell" came to be part of the Apostles' Creed, one of the most widely used Christian creedal statements. Until the Reformation, the standard interpretation of the phrase was that it described a rescue mission among souls already dead.[8] Luther emphasized Christ's defeat of the devil, so that the descent became a military expedition more than a rescue operation, but it was still a trip to Hell *after* Jesus' death.

Calvin, however, thought the phrase referred to the doubt and fear that Christ underwent *before* death. "Hell" was the agony of facing death without the presence of God, for, "No more terrible abyss can be conceived than to feel yourself forsaken and estranged from God; and when you call upon him, not to be heard."[9] In order fully to occupy the place of sinners, Christ "must also grapple hand to hand with the armies of hell and the dread of everlasting death . . . suffering in his soul the terrible torments of a condemned and forsaken man."[10] It was in those torments before death that he experienced Hell.

Calvin's interpretation powerfully captures Christ's sense of abandonment on the cross, but it seems a forced way of reading the passage in the creed. If we say that Christ "was crucified, dead, and buried; he descended into Hell; the third day he rose again from the dead," the most natural reading is surely that this "descent" took place after his death rather than before.

The twentieth-century Roman Catholic theologian Hans Urs von Balthasar understood the descent into Hell in a way that combined elements of Calvin's reading and earlier ones. Yes, von Balthasar said, this "descent" happened after Christ's death, but it was no triumphant victory march. Instead, on Holy Saturday (the day between Good Friday and Easter) Jesus descended into "solidarity . . . with those who have lost their way from God." Some sinners really have "chosen to put their I [their egotism] in place of God's selfless love" and therefore would be eternally apart from God, except that,

> Into this finality (of death) the Dead Son descends, no longer acting in any way, but stripped by the cross of every power and initiative of his own, as one purely to be used, debased to mere matter. . . . He is (out of an ultimate love, however) dead together with them. And exactly in that way he disturbs the absolute loneliness striven for by the sinner: the sinner, who wants to be "damned" apart from God, finds God again in his loneliness, but God in the absolute weakness of love who unfathomably . . . enters into solidarity with those damning themselves.[11]

Von Balthasar's idea here is powerful but difficult. One reason for the difficulty is that it's hard to know how to think about Hell. I do not believe that it is a physical place; I think all those "flames" are metaphors. I trust that those enveloped by God's grace enter into God's presence after death, and I believe that non-Christians will be included among them.

Still, I recognize that some people, even to the moment they die, have turned away from God and rejected grace and hope alike. It just seems dishonest to pretend that everyone comes around right at the last minute. And it trivializes human freedom and the meaning of human lives to say that how people end their lives in relation to God doesn't matter. Nevertheless, even if their last impulse rejects God, von Balthasar is saying, however dark and lonely the mysterious reality in which they would then exist, Christ is there, and so the love of God also is there.

The Assurance of God's Love

Christ's death on the cross and his descent into Hell thus reassure us that we can never wander so far astray as to be outside the humanity with which Christ has identified. In so fully manifesting God's love, Christ ought to evoke our loving response. Writing in the twelfth century, Peter Abelard affirmed that in Christ's passion God "has more fully bound us to himself by love, with the result that our hearts should be enkindled by such a gift of divine grace, and true charity should not now shrink from enduring anything for him."[12] Part of the way Christ's passion changes our lives is that it so fills us with wonder at how much God loves us that we want to be more loving in return—to God and to the rest of the creation God loves. As Abelard concluded, "Everyone is made more righteous, that is, more loving towards God after the passion of Christ than he had been before, because a realized gift invites greater love than that which is only hoped for."[13]

Abelard has been one of the most criticized of Christian theologians. His critics point out that an account of how Christ's death inspires us to greater love cannot be the whole story. Christ provides something more than a moral example. Fair enough. But it *can* be *part* of the story. Seeing what God was willing to do for us should fill us with love, just as it should comfort us to know that nothing we do can carry us outside of the humanity which Christ brought into unity with God.

But we are sinners, and our problems are deeper than such measures, or anything that offers only a good example, can cure. We have broken our relation with God and fallen under the power of evil. If the cross is to accomplish our salvation, it must address those problems too. The language the Bible uses to explain how that happens draws on the practice of performing sacrifices to God, so first I need to say something about sacrifice and Christ's "office" as priest.

16

Priest and Sacrifice

Imagine walking through the Jerusalem Temple at the time of Jesus. We would be astonished, even horrified—by the animals being herded to their deaths, by the cries of dying birds and beasts, by the stench of blood.[1] From Mexico to Greece to India to Israel, however, sacrifice was part of the central stuff of religion. We modern Christians tend to use the language of "sacrifice" too casually, forgetting its context in sharpened knives, outstretched necks, and bloody dying. Yet listen to John Calvin on Christ's "priestly office":

> As a pure and stainless Mediator he is by his holiness to reconcile us to God. But God's righteous curse bars our access to him, and God in his capacity as judge is angry toward us. Hence, an expiation must intervene in order that Christ as priest may obtain God's favor for us and appease his wrath. Thus Christ to perform this office had to come forward with a sacrifice. . . . The priestly office belongs to Christ alone because by the sacrifice of his death he blotted out our own guilt and made satisfaction for our sins.[2]

For those of us who live in a democracy, monarchs seem a foreign idea, and most modern people have trouble understanding the inspiration of prophets. "Priest" may at first seem the most accessible of Christ's three "offices"—after all, we all know priests—until we realize how tied up with sacrificial rituals the biblical ideas of priesthood were.

Calvin was trying to take those biblical ideas seriously. Because of God's holiness, he proposed, we need a Mediator to bridge the gap between this holy God and human beings who have wandered astray. In ancient Israel, the high priest served this role; for Christians it is Christ. But because of our sin, that's not enough—we also need "expiation," we need some clearing away of the stain of our sins before mediation can take place. And, as we see in the letter to the Hebrews, "under the law almost everything is purified with blood, and without the shedding of blood there is no forgiveness of sins" (Heb. 9:22). So we come back to the idea of sacrifice.

Sacrifice in Israel

From their beginnings, the people of Israel brought burnt offerings and grain offerings to the Lord as symbols of their loyalty to the covenant and their gratitude for God's blessings.[3] Leviticus 1 and 2, for instance, give instructions on how to kill animals, splash their blood around the altar, and then burn the meat as "an offering by fire of pleasing odor to the Lord," and how to take flour, mix it with oil and frankincense, and turn it "into smoke on the altar, an offering by fire of pleasing odor to the Lord."

At least one level of symbolism seems clear enough. The Lord has given us everything we have. We are grateful, and so we take a portion (an especially good one—an animal without blemish, or choice flour) and give it back. God does not *need* our sacrifices ("for the world is mine, and all that it contains" Ps. 50:12), but the pleasant odor of their smoke symbolically affirms the mutuality of the covenant relationship. Not only is God faithful, but the people, in part and in some degree, remain faithful too.

So King Saul, preparing to face the Philistines in battle, finding his troops are slipping away from him, and remembering that he has failed to "entreat" the Lord, offers a burnt offering (1 Sam. 13:12). The sacrifice "entreats," and that "covers a wide range of motives: homage, thanksgiving, appeasement, expiation."[4] But all reaffirm the covenantal relationship: yes, you are our God, and we are your people.

"Sin offerings" had a more specific function. Beginning in chapter 4, Leviticus lays out a variety of specific rules: "If it is the anointed priest who sins, thus bringing guilt on the people . . . "; "If the whole congregation of Israel errs unintentionally . . . "; "When a ruler sins . . . "; "When any of you sin and commit a trespass against the Lord by deceiving a neighbor . . . . " In every case there follows the appropriate ritual for a sacrifice. Some scholars argue that "sin offering" is not the right term here.[5] The faults to be corrected have to do primarily with ritual impurities and unintentional violations of the law, they propose, and not with the deliberate and morally offensive kind of act that we would call a "sin." Ancient cultures, however, often drew no sharp line between ethical lapse and ritual impurity.[6] In either case, something about people made them unworthy to come before God, and so something needed to be done to repair that state of affairs.

In Israel's most dramatic ritual, on the Day of Atonement, the high priest entered the Holy of Holies in the center of the Temple for the only time during the year. There sat the Ark, which was believed to have originally held the tablets of the Law Moses received on Sinai, and above it was the "mercy seat," a cover above the Ark that was the throne of God. Here was a place so holy that it needed to be approached with caution. "Tell your brother Aaron," God tells Moses in Leviticus, "not to come just at any time into the sanctuary inside the curtain before the mercy seat that is upon the ark, or he will die; for I appear in the cloud upon the mercy seat" (Lev. 16:1).

The Day of Atonement ritual is full of paradoxes. One of God's greatest gifts to Israel is that there is this place—the Temple, and particularly the mercy seat on the Ark—where God reliably is. And yet, the space where God sits is empty; it represents, in Rowan Williams' lovely phrase, the "space where God would be if God were anywhere."[7] This is the place where God reaches out to the people in mercy, and yet such is the holiness of God that without the appropriate ritual no one can come to this space without dying. It is not that God would lash out against sin, but that in the presence of God's holiness a sinful person would just combust, self-destruct, were it not for God's mercy. The situation symbolizes the mysterious and terrifying yet loving God both Christians and Jews worship.

The central purpose of the sacrifice is not to "change God's mind" but to purify a space in the human world so that God can be present there. The Jewish scholar Baruch Levine explains,

> Human beings have always sought the nearness and presence of God (or of the gods, in polytheistic environments). We are filled with anxiety at the prospect of God's withdrawal, or absence, or distance from the human scene. . . . Emotionally, we expect that God, as the power who sustains the universe and grants the petitions of his worshippers, responds to our needs more readily if he is near and present and that he is less likely to do so from heaven. . . . But to retain the nearness of God, it was necessary to provide a sacred environment acceptable to him.[8]

God loves. But God is holy. And it is the nature of holiness to be incompatible with sin or impurity. We have to enact the drama that purifies the space in which we sinners can then be in God's presence. For Israel it was the Ark in the Temple, the place where God is and is not, that guaranteed the possibility of that approach, and so the rituals centered there. For Christians, it is Jesus on the cross, who is and is not God—God with us, but also the God-forsaken one—who is the place where we can encounter God. In sacrificial rituals, people enacted a drama that often involved slaying a victim, and then God would expiate their sins. In Christ, it is God who enacts the drama of expiation and becomes the victim.

Jesus' contemporaries understood such dramas. Shortly before the time of Jesus, tyrannical Greek rulers of a state based in Damascus ruled Israel. One of them, Antiochus Epiphanes, even demanded that sacrifices to Zeus be performed in the Jerusalem Temple. The Maccabee family led a revolt within Israel, and seven heroic Maccabee brothers were captured and executed, setting an inspiring example that eventually led to a Jewish victory. As a Jewish historian wrote,

> These then, having consecrated themselves for the sake of God, are now honored not only with this distinction but also by the fact that through them our enemies did not prevail against our nation, and the tyrant was punished and our land purified, since they became, as it were, a ransom for the sin of our nation. Through the blood of these righteous ones and through the propitiation of their death the divine providence rescued Israel.[9]

The people had betrayed the covenant through their impurities, and so they could no longer approach the Lord, but the sacrifice of these brave martyrs purified the land and made such an approach possible once again.

Christian Interpretations of Sacrifice

Such ideas would have been in circulation in the time of Jesus. They imply that a heroic sacrifice can call a covenant community back to its higher ideals. Such a view, however, attributes the sacrifice's significance only to a psychological change; it works in us. As with Abelard's theory, nothing objective happens in God or our relation with God.

On the other hand, to think of God as finding pleasure in the death of a brave human being is an even worse interpretation. It is also unbiblical, for in the Bible it is never an angry God that is reconciled to us, but always *we* who are reconciled.

Sometimes, though, human suffering, like a grain or animal sacrifice, can enact a purification that closes the gap between us and God. If we have been somehow purified, then the holy God can come among sinners without destroying us. The Maccabean martyrs served such a role for the Jewish people. Could anyone do it for the whole of humanity? Only God could do that. But only a human being could do it. Only Jesus Christ could do it.

The most famous argument along these lines in the history of Christian theology was developed by Anselm, the Archbishop of Canterbury around 1100. Anselm argued that by sinning human beings dishonor God, and "he who violates another's honor does not enough by merely rendering honor again, but must, according to the extent of the injury done, make restoration in some way satisfactory to the person whom he has dishonored."[10] In the feudal system of Anselm's time, honor mattered a lot. If you dishonored a feudal lord, you owed a good bit more than your normal payment in recompense.

Since God is our lord, we owe God much in repayment for sin, Anselm argued. But we already owed God *everything*. So how can we render satisfaction for our sin? "If in justice I owe God myself and all my powers, even when I do not sin, I have nothing left to render to him for my sin."[11] Indeed, only God can make the requisite payment. But if it is a payment for human sin, it has to be made by a human being—and therefore it could only be made by one who was both God and human.

Anselm's argument has generated vast scholarly debate. Both his critics and his defenders often distort Anselm's idea. For instance, when one shifts the argument from Anselm's feudal language of honor to the commercial language of repaying debts, the whole affair sounds too much like a business transaction, and that changes the character of Anselm's argument. Again, when one emphasizes the distinctive roles of "Son" and "Father" in the story, the "Father" starts to seem selfish and oppressive. But Anselm begins and ends by saying that it is "God" who seeks and accomplishes human salvation.

Anselm is better than many of his interpreters. Debating what flaws, if any, remain in his argument once misinterpretations have been cleared away would lead too far astray from the concerns of this book. I have followed some of the general form of his argument while preferring the biblical language of God's holiness and the imagery of sacrifice to his references to God's honor. Thinking in terms of God's "holiness" seems to me the best way (better than honor, and certainly better than debts and credits) to convey the fact that sin simply *cannot endure* to be in the presence of God, and therefore something has to be done before sinners can enter God's presence.

Whatever language one uses, what remains is the idea that sinners are unworthy of relationship with God, and that that state of affairs has to be changed if we are to find our way home to God's love. As I've already discussed, the Hebrew people often thought about how to make that change in terms of sacrifices, and Christians too have used sacrificial language.

Christ Our Sacrifice

References to the sacrificial rituals of Israel appear again and again when the New Testament talks about what Jesus does for our salvation. John the Baptist sees Jesus approaching him, and calls out, "Here is the Lamb of God who takes away the sin of the world" (John 1:29). Jesus sits down to a meal with his disciples, passes around a cup of wine, and says, "This is my blood of the covenant, which is poured out for many" (Mark 14:24). The author of

Hebrews writes, "For if the blood of goats and bulls, with the sprinkling of the ashes of a heifer, sanctifies those who have been defiled so that their flesh is purified, how much more will the blood of Christ, who through the eternal Spirit offered himself without blemish to God, purify our conscience from dead works to worship the living God" (Heb. 9:13–14). And in the great vision of Revelation, the inhabitants of heaven sing their song to the Lamb that was slain:

> For you were slaughtered and by your blood you ransomed for
> God
> saints from every tribe and language and people and nation. . . .
> Worthy is the Lamb that was slaughtered
> to receive power and wealth and wisdom and might
> and honor and glory and blessing.
>
> (Rev. 5:9,12)

Christ is our sacrifice. His blood transforms us into people who can once again come into the presence of the holy God. Christ is the new holy place where God's presence is manifest—now not just to Israel but to the world. And Christ's sacrifice is what makes it possible for sinful humanity to enter into that holy place and live our lives in Christ, reconciled to God. To understand what that means, we need to explore further the idea of reconciliation.

17

Reconciliation

Think of what happens when one friend lies to another, or betrays a friendship, or a spouse is unfaithful to the marriage vow. The relationship is broken, or at least badly injured. If the betrayed one says, "Oh, never mind; it didn't really amount to anything," then the relationship was of little value from the start. When we love someone, betrayal *does* hurt. It matters that we are not sure we can still trust someone we used to think was our friend. The relationship is just no longer the same.

Human sin creates that kind of damaged relationship between us and God. The God who loves us knows we have turned away. How can God not feel something equivalent (however mysteriously) to the sorrow we would feel in such a situation? But such a broken relationship comes hard to the betrayer as well. Once I have broken our trust, how can I say, "Oh, you can trust me again now," without sounding absurd? If you offer to forgive me, what does it mean for me to accept that forgiveness? Can I really believe that our relationship is mended?

Christians have believed that in Christ God healed the relationship that human sin had betrayed. As Paul wrote to the Corinthians,

> So if anyone is in Christ, there is a new creation: everything old has passed away; see, everything has become new! All this is from God, who reconciled us to himself through Christ, and has given us the ministry of reconciliation; that is, in Christ God was reconciling the world to himself, not counting their trespasses against them, and entrusting the message of reconciliation to us.
>
> (2 Cor. 5:17–19)

The Angry Father?

It might seem obvious that this is good news. Still, as I noted at the beginning of this part, the way the story has been told by some Christian theologians (or at least the way it has been heard) made it sound horrible. God the Father, so this account goes, was angry with humankind, and could not be appeased until Christ offered himself, dying on the cross to pay the penalty accrued by human sin.

"How cruel and wicked it seems," Peter Abelard wrote in the twelfth century, "that anyone should demand the blood of an innocent person as the price for anything . . . still less that God should consider the death of his Son so agreeable that by it he should be reconciled to the whole world!"[1] The contemporary feminist theologian Rita Nakashima Brock insists that the problem is built into any discussion of reconciliation or atonement ("atonement" means making us one with God, and thus the same thing as "reconciliation"): "The shadow of the punitive father must always lurk behind the atonement. He haunts images of forgiving grace."[2]

Indeed, as I've argued earlier, something has gone wrong with the story if it tells how the sacrifice of the Son appeased the angry Father. In fact, several things have gone wrong.

First, as John Calvin put it, "It was not after we were reconciled to him through the blood of his Son that he began to love us. Rather, he has loved us before the world was created."[3] After all, one of the most famous of all Bible verses says, "For God so loved the world that he gave his only Son . . . " (John 3:16). The First Person of the Trinity is not sulking until the Word wins back the divine mercy, and does not look on with indifference as Christ goes off to death. There is pain in heaven in contemplation of the death on Golgotha.[4]

Second, to think of the "Son" appeasing the "Father" would misunderstand the Trinity, whose Persons do not work in opposition, or have to win one another over, but operate in perfect unity. Therefore, any sense of conflict, of one Person paying a price to appease another Person, has the story wrong. The Triune God works together to achieve our salvation.

Third, in that corporate work, Christ is not a victim but a volunteer. In Aquinas's words, "It is indeed a wicked and cruel act to hand over an innocent man to torment and to death against his will. Yet God the Father did not so deliver up Christ, but inspired him with the will to suffer for us."[5] Just as the one who sends Christ to suffer is not exempt from the suffering, so Christ is not exempt from the process of deciding that the task must be undertaken. It is the Triune God that reconciles, and the Triune God that determines to act for our reconciliation.

But what is the problem to which reconciliation responds? Just as with Old Testament patterns of sacrificial ritual, the New Testament never speaks of *God* needing to be reconciled to *us*. God always loves; it is our sin that has broken down the relationship between us, and therefore *we* who need to be reconciled to *God*. The image of the angry God who needs to be won over is therefore wrong from the start.

And yet the language of divine anger is not entirely wrong. The second-century theologian Origen proposed that "anger" is just a kind of rhetorical device on God's part:

> It is a matter of verbal usage for the sake of a child. We put on threatening looks, not because we are angry, but for the child's good; if we always show our love and never correct the child, it is the worse for him. It is in this way that God is said to be angry, so as to change and better us.[6]

Calvin made a similar point. Scripture, he said, portrays the cross as "an astonishing display of the wrath of God that he did not spare even his only begotten Son, and was not appeased in any other way than by that price of expiation."[7]

How to reconcile such language with the assurance that God "loved us before the world was created"?[8] Calvin thinks of it as an instance of divine "accommodation": "It is the part of a wise teacher to accommodate himself to the capacity of those whom he has undertaken to instruct, so that in dealing with the weak and ignorant, he drops in his instructions little by little, lest it should run over, if poured in more abundantly."[9] *If* we were simply told that God has loved us all along, in spite of our sins, we would "experience and feel *something*" of what we owe to God's mercy. *But*, when we hear that God was angry with us or hated us until "Christ interceded," Calvin says, then we will be even more struck by the greatness of the calamity from which we have been saved and therefore all the more grateful to Christ for having saved us.[10]

Such cautionary notes offer valuable warnings against taking the language of the "wrath" of God too literally. We humans cannot understand what it would mean for God to be angry. Yet this language conveys something important. The anger that sin arouses in the Lord is a common theme of the prophets. Is God unjust "to inflict wrath on us?" Paul asks. "By no means! For then how could God judge the world?" (Rom. 3:5–6). In human terms, we know that a passionate reaction to betrayal is part of what it means to love. If betrayal left me unaffected, I would not have loved. We know that God loves us, and that our sins betray God.

When we sin, we find ourselves unable to face God, like Adam and Eve in the story of the Garden, who hide when they hear the sound of the Lord God walking in the evening. We sense that there is something about the holiness of God that would burn sinners. And we're not imagining this. It's not just our shame and guilt. Our human experience of anger does not resemble any reality within God, but there is something real in the betrayed love of God when confronted with sin that appropriately engenders our sense that the relation has been shattered and we should turn away and hide.[11]

Christ Stands in the Place of Sin

But in Christ God was reconciling the world to God's own self. Christ stands with us in our place of sin, and therefore it is no longer a place separated from God. Christ made our sin his own, Karl Barth explained. "He bore it and suffered it with all its most bitter consequences. . . . He elected it as his own suffering."[12] "He was not a sinful person. But inwardly and outwardly His situation was that of a sinful person."[13] It is an old idea in the Christian tradition. "Christ also is called disobedient on my account," Gregory of Nazianzus wrote in the fourth century, "He makes his own our folly and our transgressions."[14] Or Calvin: "This is our acquittal: that guilt that held us liable for punishment has been transferred to the head of the Son of God."[15]

We were running away from God, looking for a place to hide, and we found that God was running beside us, sharing our fear and shame. The sense that we had irreparably damaged our relation with God disappears, and we can stop running away. *We* have been reconciled—God loved us all along, and what needed fixing was the way we had turned away from God. Yet God's love really did take the form of wrath as long as we were alone in the place of sin—"wrath" here not referring to an emotional reaction on the part of God, but functioning as the only way to describe the broken relation from God's side.

The place of sin, however, is not a physical place. It is a spiritual, psychological space of pain and anguish and sense of separation from God. Thus if Christ is to share that space with us, Christ must experience all the anguish of sin. To quote Calvin again, "The death which he underwent must therefore have been full of horror, because he could not render satisfaction for us without feeling, in his own experience, the dreadful judgment of God."[16] This is the Christ who prays that the cup might pass from him, who cries out from the cross, "My God, my God, why have you forsaken me?" "And through him, God was pleased to reconcile to himself to all things, whether on earth or in heaven, by making peace through the blood of his cross" (Col. 1:20).

Reconciliation, then, is not about how Christ's suffering appeases an angry Father. Our suffering has cut us off from God, and we can experience God's love only as anger. God comes to be with us in the place of sin, as the way to bridge the abyss that lay between us, so that we can be in loving relation with God again. But coming into the place of sin is a painful business that costs a heavy price. It is a price that God, in love, is willing to pay.

18

Redemption

We have seen how Christ's *solidarity* with us relieves our own doubts and fears, and Christ's work of *reconciliation* restores our good relationship with God. But we are also captives of forces of evil, and Christ frees us from them by working our *redemption*. Just as Christ's solidarity with our doubts and sufferings on the cross is the culmination of the incarnation, so Christ's work of redemption on the cross anticipates the victory of the resurrection. Seeing the relations among these themes shows how the cross is the center of Christ's work of salvation. So, having discussed solidarity and reconciliation, we turn now to redemption.

Meanings of "Redemption" in the Ancient World

"Redeem" and "ransom" both derive from the same Latin word, which means "buy back." In the most literal kind of example, needing money in an emergency, you pawn something at a pawn shop. Some time later, in better financial circumstances, you go back and "redeem" your property—you buy it back.

In much of the ancient world, one could redeem not only the family silver but human beings as well. People who fell into slavery as a result of debt or capture in wartime could be redeemed if someone paid their new master an appropriate sum of money. In ancient Israel, the responsibility for doing this fell to the male next of kin, who was one's "redeemer" (see, for instance, Ruth 2:20). In a culture in which family relations had great importance, there was considerable comfort in knowing that, if you really got into trouble, you had a redeemer, someone who would "bail you out" (see, for instance, Job 19:25). For those on the outside of society, who had no relatives to redeem them, the hope was that the Lord would be their redeemer, so that redemption by the Lord was particularly the hope of the abandoned and isolated.

Not everyone in need of redemption was the victim of bad luck. Some people were responsible for their own enslavement. If you had had to sell yourself into slavery in order to pay gambling debts or because of wild extravagance, for instance, then your redeemer was rescuing you not only from your new owner but also from the consequences of your own wrongdoing.

A second kind of "redemption" was even more clearly related to the consequences of wrongdoing. If you faced a penalty for harm you had done someone, you could redeem *yourself* by paying an appropriate penalty to your victim or your victim's next of kin:

> the person shall make full restitution for the wrong, adding one fifth to it, and giving it to the one who was wronged. If the injured party has no next of kin to whom restitution may be made for the wrong, the restitution for wrong shall go to the Lord for the priest, in addition to the ram of atonement with which atonement is made for the guilty party.
>
> (Num. 5:7–8)

Some crimes were judged too awful to permit redemption; murderers, for instance, could neither redeem themselves nor be redeemed by their kinfolk (Num. 35:31).

When the Israelites were led into exile in Babylonia and hoped that they might someday be free and return home, they used this language of redemption. There was no one but God to whom they could turn, so they clung to the hope that the Lord would "ransom" or "redeem" them (Jer. 31:11).

Since prophets like Jeremiah insisted that exile had come as punishment for Israel's sins, it followed that the Lord was ransoming the people not only from the power of the Babylonians but also from the consequences of their own unfaithfulness. If the people repent, the Lord will redeem them:

> Our transgressions indeed are with us,
> and we know our iniquities:
> transgressing, and denying the Lord,
> and turning away from following our God. . . .
> The Lord saw . . . that there was no one to intervene;
> so his own arm brought him victory,
> and his righteousness upheld him. . . .
> And he will come to Zion as Redeemer,
> to those in Jacob who turn from transgression,
> says the Lord.
>
> (Isa. 59:12–13, 15–16, 20)

Christian Interpretations of Redemption

The first Christians, searching for ways to talk about how Jesus had changed their lives and the world, further developed this category of redemption. In a new context, however, the idea of redemption took on different connotations. Three of them are particularly worth noting.

1. Christians combined the idea of God as redeemer with the idea that someone's next of kin or friend could get them out of slavery or punishment by volunteering to take their place, at whatever cost in suffering. "You know," the author of First Peter wrote to a Christian community facing persecution, "that you were ransomed from the futile ways inherited from your ancestors not with perishable things like silver or gold, but with the precious blood of Christ, like that of a lamb without defect or blemish" (1 Pet. 1:18–19).

In Christ God did redeem people, but God did it by taking on suffering in a way that had previously been considered imaginable only with respect to human redeemers. Christ, who "came not to be served but to serve . . . gave his life a ransom for many" (Mark 10:45). "Christ Jesus, himself human . . . gave himself a ransom for all" (1 Tim. 2:6).[1] Like the redeemer who had to become a slave so that someone else might go free, Christ suffered in order to redeem.

2. Christians expanded the scope of redemption to include the consequences of all human sin. The Hebrew prophets had usually talked about the ransom of one nation, Israel, from the consequences of their unfaithfulness to the covenant. Christ, in contrast, ransomed "saints from every tribe and language and people and nation" (Rev. 5:10) from the consequences of the sin into which all humankind had fallen from its very beginnings.

Writing in the second century, Irenaeus contrasted Adam's disobedience with Christ's obedience.[2] "Adam" here represents the universal condition of sinful humanity, though no doubt Irenaeus also thought of him as an actual historical figure. Whether symbolically or historically, Adam sinned, and all of humankind inherits the consequences of that sin. Through Christ's obedience, which culminated in the sacrifice on the cross, we were redeemed from the powers of evil under whose sway we had fallen as a result of Adam's sin. As Paul had written, "for as all die in Adam, so all will be made alive in Christ" (1 Cor. 15:22). We can still make a mess of our lives, and all of us in one degree or another do, but the door of the prison of sin has been opened, and we have at least the possibility of living as redeemed people.

3. Christians pictured Christ as actively redeeming people from cosmic forces of evil. The Lord had redeemed Israel from the Babylonians, but, Paul wrote to the Galatians, "Christ redeemed us from the curse of the law by becoming a curse for us—for it is written, 'Cursed is everyone who hangs on a tree' " (Gal. 3:13). He is quoting Deuteronomy 21:23, which declares that

anyone who has been hanged from the bough of a tree must be buried at once, lest their continued visible presence "defile the land." Paul thinks of Christ, who died on the wood of the cross and thus on a kind of "tree," as therefore also cursed and defiled by this shameful death.

Paul's interpretation of Deuteronomy may stretch a point, but his meaning is clear enough. Human beings are trapped by the consequences of sin. It is easy to think of addicts, so caught up in the power of the heroin that they cannot seem to break free of it. But remember also the rich young man who wants to enter the kingdom of heaven but is so captured by the power of his wealth that when Jesus tells him to give up all that he has, he goes away grieving (Mark 10:17–22). One way or another, we are all caught up by what Paul calls "the curse of the law."

But Christ has taken on the curse that imprisoned us. Paul brings us back to the idea of a redeemer who takes the place of the one who needs redemption. As Martin Luther explained this passage in Galatians, Christ was counted a sinner

> as a magistrate takes him for a thief and punishes him whom he finds among thieves, though he never committed any deed worthy of death. So Christ . . . would also be a companion of sinners, taking upon him the flesh and blood of those who were sinners, and plunged into all kinds of sin. When the law therefore found him among thieves it condemned and killed him as a thief.[3]

Luther sees Christ's victory as the outcome of a kind of combat:

> Sin also is a most mighty and cruel tyrant ruling and reigning over the whole world, subduing and bringing all men into bondage. . . . this tyrant, I say, flies upon Christ, and would swallow him up as he does all others. But he sees not that he is a person of invincible and everlasting righteousness. Therefore, in this combat, sin must be vanquished and killed and righteousness must overcome, live, and reign.[4]

Notice that the image of the redeemer has changed. The ancient Hebrew redeemer who took someone's place simply went into jail or slavery and sat there. In contrast, Luther imagines a redeemer who enters the place of sin and defeats the forces that had imprisoned us so that "there is now no sin, no curse, no death, no devil to hurt us anymore, for Christ has vanquished and abolished all these things."[262]

Christ the Victor

Long before Luther wrote those words, Christian theologians had been exploring these images of combat, often combat with Satan. Who is this Satan?

"Satan" means "the adversary." We first hear of him in the book of Job and the prophet Zechariah, where he is a reasonably respectable character, one of the officials of heaven whose particular job it is to test people—a sort of prosecuting attorney in the divine court (Job 1:6–12; Zech. 3:1–2). He may be tough, but he is in no sense operating in opposition to God.

By the time of Jesus, however, Jews had come to think of "Satan" or "the devil" as a real opponent to God—though always one of God's creatures and never anywhere near God's equal.[6] He was identified with the tricky serpent in Genesis. He is still testing people, but no longer as part of God's own procedures. In the New Testament he tries to tempt even Jesus; he corrupts Judas into his act of betrayal. Since Satan "has been sinning from the beginning" (1 John 3:8), God is fully justified in acting to "crush" him "under your feet" (Rom. 16:20).

Early Christian theologians therefore came to think that our sin had trapped us under the power of Satan ("the devil," "the evil one"), so that it was from the devil that Christ had to ransom us. As Origen put it around the end of the second century,

> To whom did he give his life as "a ransom for many"? Certainly not to God! Was it not then to the evil one? For he had power over us until the ransom, even the soul of Jesus, was paid to him, since he was deceived into thinking that he could be its lord, and not seeing that he could not bear the torment of holding it.[7]

Not only battle but trickery is at work—and how fitting that the oldest of tricksters should himself be tricked.

In the fourth century, Gregory of Nyssa explained the issue like this: because of sin, all human beings lay under the power of Satan. We have gone to the devil voluntarily, and thus we are in no position to dispute the justice of his Lordship. To Satan Christ was one more sinful human being, and so he tried to snatch him up. But in reaching for a sinless one who was also God, he overreached, and any claim he might have made to legitimate authority came to an end. "That was the reason why the Godhead was veiled in flesh, that Satan should observe what was familiar and congenial and thus have no fear in approaching the transcendent power."[8] In an image repeated from Augustine to Luther and beyond, Gregory even described Christ's humanity as a bait which hid "the hook of divinity" until the devil had swallowed it.[9]

It makes for a good story: the rapacious devil finally overreaches himself, the trickster is tricked, and God finds a way to rescue us without simply overriding Satan's legitimate rights. But there's also something a bit unnerving in this version of things. Even Gregory of Nyssa's friend Gregory of Nazianzus protested the inappropriateness of God paying a ransom to the devil: "How shameful that that robber should receive not only a ransom, but a ransom consisting of God Himself."[10] A long tradition of Christian thought has rebelled against the idea of redemption as divine trickery and the incarnation as the baiting of a fishhook.[11]

Yet such imagery conveys something important about Christ's work in our salvation. Let's start with the devil. Forget about pictures of horns and goat hooves. Simply face a reality to which Scripture and our own experience both testify: evil has its own kind of power. Whether it's the logic of warfare that seems to require murdering innocent people, or the sexual affair that gathers its own momentum, or the economic situation that forces a factory closure, or the history of abuse that goes down the generations in a family, there are countless situations in which the evil that surrounds us seems greater than the sum of the bad deeds of the human agents involved.

We make free choices, but then we find ourselves entrapped. We can blame the military-industrial complex, or the media, or the corrupt politicians, and all that often contains a measure of truth, but beyond it lies a power that evil itself seems to exercise on all those who have fallen under its sway. Evil seems to have its own kind of cunning, as if it were plotting to entrap sinners yet further into the consequences of our sin. Whether or not there is someone named "Satan," we can certainly experience evil as a malevolent force beyond any of the human persons we confront.

Therefore, if God is to rescue us from the mess we are in, it is not enough that we be comforted by the thought of God's solidarity with us, or even that we be reconciled to God. Something needs to be done about the power that evil has over us. Evil needs to be defeated. It is hard to know how to describe "victories" in the realm of spiritual warfare. Those who have held the hand of a sinner struggling through a long night—or those who have been such a sinner—know that something like a battle has taken place, but we lack the categories for describing the fields on which such battles occur or the weapons with which we are called to fight them. The images of "demonic possession" in popular films often trivialize evil, as if Satan went around making little girls vomit, while Hitler was acting on his own. Still, the idea of struggling with the devil points to realities hidden by the cool winds of Enlightenment rationality.

Victories of Love

What we learn most about such conflicts from Scripture is the proper way to "fight" them. Trying to defeat evil with its own weapons of force and violence, in this kind of warfare as in any other, ensures that evil simply triumphs, whoever wins. One aggrieved party avenges its grievance, creating a grievance for its opponent, and the blood flows through history.[12]

Take, for example, segregation and racial injustice in the American South—here was evil aplenty, from casual degradation to terrible violence, and an evil that somehow trapped its perpetrators as much as its victims. One strategy against this evil would have been to match hatred for hatred, violence for violence. Burn down the segregated restaurants; shoot the bigoted sheriff. Could anyone justifiably have complained that this was monstrously unjust? And yet, its effect would only have been to perpetuate a cycle of violence.

Those who battled for civil rights generally followed a different strategy. They sat peaceably at lunch counters, waiting for service that would not come, as a crowd around them yelled insults and sometimes beat them. They claimed their rights with a commitment against violence that led them to be willing to suffer. They loved those who hated them, and thus they interrupted the spiral of violence.

Christians are called to return hatred with love, violence with forgiveness, lies with truth. When we think of how Christ is our redeemer, we recognize two things: (1) God will not abandon us to the power of evil, but also (2) God will not turn to violence to defeat that power. The way God redeems us thus offers the model for our own struggles with opponents of any sort. Irenaeus spoke of how God worked for our redemption

> by means of persuasion, as became a God of counsel, who does not use violent means to obtain what he desires; so that neither should justice be infringed upon, nor the ancient handiwork of God go to destruction.[13]

For God, as for us, turning away from all violence involves risk. As Augustine wrote,

> Since the devil, by the fault of his own perversity, was made a lover of power, and a forsaker and assailant of righteousness . . . it pleased God, that . . . the devil should be conquered, not by power, but by righteousness; and that so also men, imitating Christ, should seek to conquer the devil by righteousness, not by power.[14]

Commenting on this passage from Augustine, Aquinas explained, "Christ came to destroy the works of the devil, not by powerful deeds, but rather by suffering from him and his members, so as to conquer the devil by righteousness, and not by power."[15]

The Book of Revelation provides the extraordinary image of the conquering slaughtered Lamb. At one of the climaxes of the story it seems that no one in heaven is worthy to open the scroll that contains the secret plan of history. Then one of the elders of heaven points out "the Lion of the tribe of Judah," who "has conquered, so that he can open the scroll and its seven seals." But then, with no transition, the author sees "a Lamb standing as if it had been slaughtered," and the elders fall down in worship before the Lamb, singing,

> You are worthy to take the scroll and to open its seals,
> for you were slaughtered and by your blood you ransomed for
> God
> saints from every tribe and language and people and nation.
> (Rev. 5:5–10)

To the puzzlement of a long tradition of scholarly commentators, the conquering Lion seems to turn into a slaughtered Lamb, but the Lamb is still the symbol of triumph.

Christ confronts evil with no weapons but sinlessness and love, and triumphs not through violence but through willingness to suffer. But sometimes, even in struggle against the worst of evil, that can suffice. And so we are liberated, ransomed, from the evil that had enslaved us, even as the bloody body of Christ reminds us of the price that was paid for our freedom.

Christ says to us, "Turn away from violence; love your enemies." I reply, "But that's risky and painful." And Christ answers, "I know. I took the risk; I know the pain." Human wisdom teaches us, all too often, that the only alternatives are accepting evil or turning its own weapons against it. Christ's triumph shows another path, for without violence he has been our redeemer.[16]

19

Visiting Prisoners

Of the three ethical issues I discuss in this book to show some ethical implications of following Jesus, two receive wide discussion: homosexuality (part 2) is deeply dividing many denominations; violence (part 4) is a prominent and perennial topic for Christian ethics. One can read a good many books about the moral and political implications of Christian faith, however, without finding much discussion of prisons. Even when Americans worry (as we should) about capital punishment, those worries rarely spread to concern about the penal system in general.

American Prisons

Jails and prisons become an ever more important topic in American society; we live in a country gone mad on sending people to prison. Consider some statistics. From the early twentieth century until the mid-1970s, the United States imprisoned about 110 people for every 100,000 of population. The figure doubled in the late 1970s and 1980s and doubled again in the 1990s, so that today 445 out of every 100,000 Americans are in prison.[1] Other countries come nowhere close in such figures: compared to that 445, there are 36 per 100,000 in Japan, from 50 to 120 in the countries of Western Europe, 229 in the famous "police state" of Singapore, and 368 in South Africa before the change to majority rule.[2]

California alone has "more inmates in its jails and prisons than do France, Great Britain, Germany, Japan, Singapore, and the Netherlands combined."[3] The Gulag or the Nazi concentration camps, with their political prisoners or whole races imprisoned, incarcerated larger percentages of their total populations, but, counting only criminals in the usual sense of the word, the United States has a larger portion of its population in prison or jail now than any society in history.

Consideration of most social issues in the United States, if we are honest, leads us sooner rather than later to prisons. Take race for example: one in every three young African American men in the United States is either in a jail or prison, on probation or parole, or under pretrial release—in many cities the figure is more than half. Nationwide, more black men are in jail or prison than in college—in California, four times as many.[4] Black males in the United States are incarcerated at four times the rate of black males in South Africa.[5]

Prison conditions are often dreadful. In my own state of Indiana, young men under twenty-one, some guilty of violent crimes, some not, can be assigned to a facility where most of them sleep in large dormitory areas which are essentially unpatrolled at night. Some inmates, unable to defend themselves against sexual predators, quickly become flamboyantly effeminate, concluding that having forced sex is better than being beaten. The administrators of the facility can hardly claim to be unaware of what is happening. Indeed, the threat of rape has unofficially become part of the deterrent policy of American prisons. In a widely publicized program called "Scared Straight," teenage boys identified as potential troublemakers are taken to prisons where inmates harangue them about how eagerly they will welcome such good-looking boys as sexual victims.

Some states have reinstituted chain gangs. New laws keep lowering the age at which capital punishment is permitted. Yet conservative American rhetoric continually talks about how "soft" we are on our prisoners and denounces the supposed "luxury" of the prison system. Running for President in 1996, Bob Dole called the American criminal justice system a "liberal-leaning laboratory of leniency."

When groups concerned about criminal justice have carefully investigated some of the cases of prisoners on Illinois' death row, over half of those reviewed have been proven innocent of the crimes of which they had been convicted. Even a cynic might expect that death penalty cases would have been reviewed in the first place more carefully than those that merely involved prison sentences, so one suspects many prisoners not on death row are innocent too.

Social programs to keep young people out of trouble, even if they have only mixed success, come far cheaper than paying for prisons, but prisons are far more politically popular. Opening high school gyms for "midnight basketball," for instance, demonstrably lowers crime in the surrounding neighborhoods, but has often been dismissed with ridicule in political debates, even as we keep building more prisons.

Even the American political left has been scared off the prison issue. Appearing to be "soft on crime" seems such a horrible risk that no one wants to chance it. Candidates remember the fate of Michael Dukakis who, running for president, faced ads about Willie Horton, an African American who had committed a murder while in a Massachusetts furlough program when Dukakis was governor. No other politician wants to be identified as on the side of criminals—perhaps, if truth were told, least of all on the side of African American criminals. So Bill Clinton paused in his first presidential campaign to approve the execution of a man so severely retarded that he did not understand that he was going to die (he asked that the pie from his last meal be saved so he could eat it later). And the number of people whose killing he had approved sometimes seemed George W. Bush's principal qualification for high office.

The Politics of Prisons

The United States certainly has a serious problem with violent crime, but it is not clear that putting more people in prison reduces crime rates. From 1985 to 1995, American rates of imprisonment and crime rates *both* dramatically increased. Since 1995, crime rates have substantially declined in some states, but there is no particular correlation between severity of sentencing and decline of crime.[6] Admittedly, different sets of statistics sometimes seem to point toward different implications, but a consensus of studies supports the following conclusions:

A high probability of arrest, followed fairly promptly by time in jail or prison, has a serious deterrent effect.

Particularly when the probability of arrest is relatively low, increases in the length of sentence soon cease to have much effect. Someone who thinks it unlikely he or she will be caught will not be more deterred by the threat of thirty years in prison than twenty. To a teenager, two years seems a lifetime; the threat of five years will not much increase deterrence.

Rehabilitation programs have very mixed success, but a prison system that cuts inmates off from family and society, does not offer substance abuse treatment or any educational opportunities, and provides no support services after release makes it very likely that released inmates will soon commit further crimes. People who come out of prison with untreated drug habits and no marketable skills, unsurprisingly, tend to go back to crime rather quickly.

Prison brutality that forces prisoners to be constantly ready to defend themselves and challenges male prisoners' masculinity makes additional crime even more likely after they are released.

Nevertheless, while recent years have seen some improvement in police work (with a greater chance that criminals will be arrested), American public policy generally involves dramatic cutbacks in services available to prisoners, coupled with increased expenditures on new prisons to accommodate those sentenced to longer terms.[7] The American criminal justice system has simply become irrational. What most political figures say about "luxurious" prisons bears little relation to their actual brutality. Our prisons—and by extension we as a society—are responsible for great human suffering without for the most part accomplishing any useful social goals (like lowering crime). With the exception of some evangelical groups, ministry to prisons and prisoners is not a part of the life of most congregations, and poll data indicate that self-identified Christians are more inclined than the national average to favor capital punishment and more severe sentencing.

The Bible on Prisoners

Talk about prisoners—and fairly radical talk at that—however, has a significant place in the New Testament. In the Synoptic Gospels, Jesus' programmatic declaration of the purpose of his ministry quotes Isaiah:

> The Spirit of the Lord is upon me,
> because he has anointed me to bring good news to the poor.
> He has sent me to proclaim release to the captives
> and recovery of sight to the blind,
> to let the oppressed go free,
> to proclaim the year of the Lord's favor.
> (Luke 4:18–19 and parallels)

"Release to the captives" and "letting the oppressed go free" are prominent here. The reference to "the year of the Lord's favor" evokes the Jubilee year, which was supposed to occur every fifty years in ancient Israel and in which prisoners and slaves would simply be freed (Lev. 25:10, 41). As I noted in part 2, it is not clear whether Israelites ever put this idea into practice, but even its presence in theory testifies to a conviction that mercy can displace retribution.[8]

In Matthew, Jesus imagines the returning Son of Man distinguishing the righteous from the accursed in that the righteous had fed the hungry, welcomed the stranger, clothed the naked, cared for the sick, and visited prisoners (Matt. 25:35–36). Until quite recently, visiting prisoners was an important part of Christian life. Many of the dramatic scenes of early Christian faith take place in prison cells, and the accounts of their time with condemned prisoners from John and Charles Wesley, the founders of Methodism, are among the most moving passages in their writings.[9] Some prison visits by pious Christians were no doubt condescending or manipulative, but at least people who regularly visited prisoners knew what the inside of a prison looked like. They would not in general denounce its luxury, and they might (and sometimes did) work to improve prison conditions.

Practices like visiting prisoners grew out of the core of Christian faith. After all, Jesus was a crucified criminal. He was not merely punished, one important strand of Christian theology has maintained—he was guilty, for he had taken on our guilt. "For our sake," Paul wrote, God made Christ "to be sin who knew no sin, so that in him we might become the righteousness of God" (2 Cor. 5:21).

Luther insisted that this passage means what it says. Christ "says to me," he wrote, "'You are no longer a sinner, but I am. I am your substitute. You have not sinned, but I have. . . . All your sins are to rest on Me and not on you.' "[10] The law thus looks at Christ and declares, "'I find him a sinner, who takes upon Himself the sins of all men. I do not see any other sins than those in Him. Therefore let Him die on the cross.' And so it attacks Him and kills Him. By this deed the whole world is purged."[11]

Christ takes on our sin, and frees us from it. Some of us may have a more immediate need of rehabiliation, or more need to be prevented from doing harm to others in the short run, but according to Christian faith it makes no sense to think of "distinguishing the innocent from the guilty." Apart from Christ, we are all guilty. In Christ, we can all be found innocent.[12] We may need to be helped, both by being protected from doing further wrong, and by being helped to be better, but there is no reason to *punish* anyone. As the contemporary theologian John Milbank has written,

> The trial and punishment of Jesus itself condemns, in some measure, all other trials and punishment, and all forms of alien discipline. . . . The only finally tolerable, and non-sinful punishment, for Christians, must be the self-punishment inherent in sin. When a person commits an evil act, he cuts himself off from social peace, and this nearly always means that he is visited with social anger. But the aim should be to reduce this anger to a calm fury against the sin, and to offer the sinner nothing but goodwill, so bringing him to the point of realizing that his isolation is self-imposed. . . . The Church, while recognizing the tragic necessity of "alien," external punishment, should also seek to be an asylum, a house of refuge from its operations, a social space where a different, forgiving and restitutionary practice is pursued. This practice should also be "atoning," in that we acknowledge that an individual's sin is never his alone, that its endurance harms us all, and therefore its cancellation is also the responsibility of all.[13]

In short, we face pragmatic questions of how to protect potential victims and rehabilitate criminals to lead better lives, but Christians can think about such questions free of the need to distinguish innocent and guilty, and free of the need for punishment.

Christians and Prisoners

What would that mean in practice? Charles Colson, a conservative Republican who first got interested in prisons when he was sentenced to one for his part in the Watergate scandal, has founded the Prison Fellowship and the Justice Fellowship to try to help American prisoners. His work offers a particularly useful example, since Colson is such a tough-minded conservative that his views cannot be dismissed as typical liberal softness on crime. In the Prison Fellowship, Christians work with prisoners in seminars and Bible studies and just in general visit prisoners and serve as their pen pals. They arrange for community service for furloughed prisoners, and they pair released prisoners with members of Christian congregations who will help them in their efforts to readjust to life "outside." Prisoners are not treated as outsiders, but as potential and then actual members of Christian communities. Welcoming prisoners into such communities even while they are imprisoned and the promise of a greater degree of fellowship after their release are crucial to the program's success. So here is a place for individuals or congregations to begin: visit prisoners; establish human contact; offer to help them get settled when they are released; invite them to join a Christian congregation.

The influential contemporary Christian ethicist Stanley Hauerwas, though he has not talked much about prisons, argues in general for such a model of Christian action: act through local congregations, one on one; don't get involved as Christians in politics to try to change governmental policies.[14] Political involvement, he says, compromises Christian witness, since in politics we inevitably make regrettable compromises.

In Colson's programs, however, the work of the Justice Fellowship supplements that of the Prison Fellowship, campaigning for alternative forms of punishment for nonviolent offenders, for an end to the worst abuses within the prison system, and so on.[15] How, Colson asks, can one visit prisoners, connecting with them as Christian brothers and sisters, and hear their stories of brutality or sexual abuse within their prisons without doing something by way of publicity or political lobbying to improve their condition? How could prisoners accept as sincere invitations to join Christian communities whose members were not trying, through political activity, to reduce brutality and injustice?[16] It is hard to believe someone who says, "I really care about you, but I'm not going to vote against the sheriff who lines his pocket by cutting back on your food. I don't want to corrupt myself by political participation."

If Christians were to start working with prisoners in significant numbers, it might be the beginning of radical changes in our criminal justice system. Or it might lead to rather modest decreases in brutality and improvements in rehabilitation. I see no need to try to predict the end before we begin. As Will Campbell and James Holloway have written,

> We constantly discover men and women who have been in various types of prisons for decades without *one single visitor* having signed

> their record card. We have suggested on other occasions that each institutional church adopt three prisoners purely and simply for purposes of visitation—so that at least once each week every man and woman and child behind bars could have one human being with whom he could have community, to whom the prisoner could tell his story. And the visitor his. We have advocated that because we are convinced that this elementary act of charity alone would provide all the prison reform that society could tolerate.[17]

To be sure, Christians cannot expect that our non-Christian neighbors will share our view that we are all sinners just like the inmates of the local jail, and that their sin, like ours, has been taken on by Christ. Christians have theological reasons for welcoming prisoners into our congregations and families which others in our society do not share, and non-Christians may not want to emulate our practices. But we ought to be able to persuade non-Christians too that the present prison system is not working and that, even on purely pragmatic grounds, its brutality and lack of counselling and support programs do more harm than good. We should at least remind our neighbors of what prisons are like—something we will know if we have been visiting prisoners. If we do not engage in such "political" activity, prisoners will regard our overtures with justified suspicion. Moreover, if we are visiting prisons, our hearts will compel us to try to change them. How radically? We can only find out if we begin.[18]

PART 4

Resurrection

Resurrection

The first three stages of the story of Jesus Christ have already provided a great deal of "gospel"—that is, of good news. From the incarnation we learn about God's reckless love and how humanity has been transformed by being united with divinity. In Jesus' life and ministry we find a model of the life of obedience and love that God invites us to live. In the cross we encounter God's reconciling and redeeming forgiveness.

If that were the end of the story, though, all that good news would collapse. For Jesus died condemned as a blasphemer and general troublemaker by the religious authorities established by God. He had made big claims: that he spoke for God with unique authority, that people's relation with God and the future that God was planning depended on their response to him. Now he was dead, and in a particularly shameful and scandalous fashion. On the face of it, his big claims had been false.

Certainly, if death had put an end to him, then he could not offer hope beyond death for anyone else. For some people, on some days, that might be all right. The goodness of this life suffices. As we will see, through much of the history of Israel people held only vague hopes about the individual's survival after death. The focus was on this life: You lead a rich and interesting life, perhaps you have children and grandchildren who will remember you with love. If, after eighty years or so, it all comes to an end—a dead end—would one have any grounds for complaint?

But not everyone was or is so lucky. Children born with devastating handicaps or in the midst of famine or war die young, their brief lives full of pain. Some heroes fight their battles with torturers in secret prison cells, and no one who would admire them ever knows about it. Some people just seemed dogged by bad luck, partially but not entirely of their own making. In the face of such sorrows, we ask: Is God really in charge of the world?

If so, does God treat some people like garbage, casting them aside into nothingness without anything good ever happening to them? Can I live with myself if I am content to say, "Well, I've been lucky in my life; I won't worry about how God treats the world's unfortunate victims"?

On the other hand, what if God is not in charge of the world? Then the dictator who can wipe out an ethnic population, or the lunatic who kills us on a streetcorner, or the disease that strikes us down truly can have the last word in our lives. If that is so, then it makes little sense to follow this Jesus who claimed that love can overcome violence and that the true master must be a servant. The God we know in him would not be truly Lord of the world.

Jesus' resurrection, however, offers hope that transcends death. It offers hope for the world's victims and challenges the lordship of all the forces in the world that can kill us. To the powers and principalities that threaten us, even with death, we can reply that Jesus survived the worst they can do, and so can we. In the words of contemporary poet Kurt Marti,

> it might suit many lords fine
> if everything were settled in death
> the dominion of the lords
> the servitude of the slaves
> would be confirmed forever
>
> it might suit many lords fine
> if in eternity they stayed lords
> in expensive private tombs
> and their slaves stayed slaves
> in rows of common graves
>
> but a resurrection's coming
> quite different from what we thought
> a resurrection's coming which is
> god's rising against the lords
> and against the lord of all lords—death[1]

Jesus' resurrection is therefore not an extra burden to Christian faith—something we believe reluctantly and only because it's there in the Bible. If his story really ended on the cross, then it's hard to explain why we should follow him, or what hope we can draw from him for ourselves or our world. As Paul wrote to the Christians at Corinth, "If Christ has not been raised, then our proclamation has been in vain and your faith has been in vain. . . . If for this life only we have hoped in Christ, we are of all people most to be pitied" (1 Cor. 15:14, 19). But if he was raised from the dead, then neither death nor those who think they have absolute power because they can kill have the last word.

20

Hopes of Resurrection

When Jesus' early followers claimed that he had been "raised from the dead," what did they mean? How would his contemporaries have understood the proclamation of his resurrection? Though it is a Greek word in the New Testament that we translate as "resurrection," the idea was a Hebrew one. According to Acts, when Paul preached in Athens, his Greek audience was intrigued by his message until he got to the idea of resurrection, at which point they scoffed (Acts 17:32). Although many Greeks believed that the soul was immortal, the idea of bodies being raised from the dead seemed ridiculous to them.

Ideas of Resurrection in Ancient Israel

For that matter, during most of the history of Israel, there hadn't been much talk of life after death. In Genesis the Lord promises Abram that he will be famous and the ancestor of a great nation (12:2) and that his descendants will be as numerous as the stars (15:5). No reassurances about life after death. There was, to be sure, a dark and static "Sheol" where the dead existed in shadowy form, but nothing happened to them there: "There is no work or thought or knowledge or wisdom in Sheol" (Eccl. 9:10).

A few Old Testament passages talk about odd events. "Enoch walked with God; then he was no more, because God took him." Took him where? The text doesn't say (Gen. 5:24). In 1 Samuel King Saul, wanting to know about the future, has a witch call the prophet Samuel up from the dead, and, to make things even more mysterious, the text calls Samuel a "divine being" or "god" (1 Sam. 28). Such cryptic passages, however, had little influence on the religion of Israel as the Hebrew Scriptures present it. In general, a person hoped for a good life, lots of descendants, and a reputation worthy of memory. But when you died, you'd be dead.

This picture changed a few centuries before Jesus' birth (and has continued to change in a variety of ways in the subsequent history of Judaism). One exile or conquest had followed another, and that hope or comfort of being the ancestor of a great nation, or even having settled descendants who would remember you, was stretching thin. Instead, people couldn't be confident that after death they would survive in family or memory or any other earthly way. Jews began to hope that God could restore their individual lives somehow after they died.

"Resurrection," in Hebrew as in Greek, derives from words that have to do with being lifted. Someone could raise you up if you fell down, or raise you up if you had "fallen" asleep. By extension, a dead person could be "raised" back to life—and that was resurrection.[1] Some prophets broached the idea tentatively: Ezekiel imagined a valley of dry bones brought back to life (Ezek. 37:1–14), and an anonymous prophecy included in Isaiah promised,

> Your dead shall live, their corpses shall rise.
> O dwellers in the dust, awake and sing for joy.
> (Isa. 26:19)

But these are isolated examples, and we can only guess at their meaning or their influence.

The only clear Old Testament passage about resurrection comes from the Book of Daniel. Daniel was brought together in its current form when a Greek ruler based in Syria, Antiochus Epiphanes, desecrated the holy Temple in Jerusalem and erected a pagan altar on its grounds. Jews reacted with horror and despair. The author of Daniel, writing in the apocalyptic tradition I first discussed in chapter 2, reassures his readers that God will eventually triumph, however bad things look in the meantime. But that was no longer enough. People's lives were so dreadful that they couldn't be satisfied with the promise that life would be better (for future generations) in some distant future. What good would that do *them*? Daniel answers: you will be brought back to enjoy the triumph.

> At that time . . . many of those who sleep in the dust of the earth shall awake, some to everlasting life, and some to shame and everlasting contempt. Those who are wise shall shine like the brightness of the sky, and those who lead many to righteousness, like the stars forever and ever.
> (Dan. 12:2–3)

Notice that not everyone comes back—apparently only those who ended their lives particularly deserving of reward or punishment.

Antiochus did not long remain in control of Jerusalem. A priest named Mattathias and his sons (the "Maccabees") led a successful Jewish revolt, and in only a few years the Temple was purified and rededicated. But Antiochus's son took up the fight, defeated the Jewish forces, and proceeded to exact vengeance. Second Maccabees, a Jewish text of the period which is part of the "Apocrypha" (Jewish works written in Greek and found in some Christian Bibles), reports in horrifying detail the torture of a mother and her seven sons who had fought in the Jewish resistance: hair ripped from heads, limbs pulled off one by one, bodies fried in huge pans.

In chapter 16 we saw how some Jews thought that these heroic sacrifices had purified all of Israel so that it could be reconciled to God. But the young heroes and their mother were sustained, according to 2 Maccabees, not only by their courage and the conviction that they were serving their people, but also by hope of resurrection. One of the young men declares to the ruler who has ordered his execution:

> You accursed wretch, you dismiss us from this present life, but the King of the universe will raise us up to an everlasting renewal of life, because we have died for his laws. . . . One cannot but choose to die at the hands of mortals and to cherish the hope God gives of being raised again by him. But for you there will be no resurrection of life.
>
> (2 Macc. 7:9, 14)

Resurrection would give these brave rebels their ultimate vindication, and prove the ultimate triumph of God's justice. If their oppressors came back after death at all, it would be only for punishment.

People today often assume that the point of resurrection is that human beings shouldn't die—or at least shouldn't stay dead. The dominant argument for resurrection in the Jewish tradition, however, was primarily about *justice*—the idea that some people so obviously don't get a fair shake in this life that they are due further reward or punishment—and about the conviction that God is ultimately in charge of things. As 1 Enoch, a Jewish text written a bit later than Daniel, summarizes:

> Therefore, you righteous ones, do not be afraid when you see the wicked grow strong and prosper. Do not join in their ways, but keep far from their violence, for you will become companions of the hosts of heaven.
>
> (1 Enoch 104:5)

Beliefs about Resurrection in the Time of Jesus

Even in Jesus' time, however, not all Jews accepted the idea of resurrection. The Pharisees believed in it; the Sadducees (the party that centered around the Jerusalem Temple) did not. At one point in Acts, in fact, Paul extricates himself from a difficult situation by announcing that he is really on trial for believing in the resurrection of the dead, thereby setting these two parties against one another (Acts 23:6–9.)[2] Moreover, some Jews expected the resurrection only of the righteous, some of the conspicuously righteous and wicked, some of everyone.[3] Although most Jews thought of the body as essential to being human, so that people could live after death only if their bodies were resurrected, a few had begun to adopt the Greek idea that human beings have an immortal soul which death cannot destroy.[4] Even in those texts from around Jesus' time that affirm resurrection, it remains a minor theme, with immortality even less important.[5]

Furthermore, "resurrection" meant different things in different texts. In the Daniel and Isaiah passages, the bodies of the dead are restored out of dust to dwell in an everlasting kingdom on earth—presumably like the bodies we have now, but built to last forever. Others described the righteous dead as raised to shine like stars in heaven.[6] In the Syriac Apocalypse of Baruch, a Jewish text written about the same time as the Gospels, bodies are first raised in the same form in which they lived previously (so that they can recognize each other!), but then the wicked undergo a transformation for the worse, while the good change "from beauty into loveliness, and from light into the splendor of glory."[7]

A number of texts refer to a "spiritual body," though what they mean is far from clear. In 2 Enoch, the Archangel Michael takes Enoch out of his "earthly garments" and puts him into the garments of God's glory—a spiritual body like those of the angels (22:9–10). The spiritual body needs no food, and its face has to be "frozen" so that people can recognize him; even so, when he returns to earth, they can kiss him.[8]

When Jesus' contemporaries first heard the news, "He is raised from the dead," then, their culture did not provide them with a clear or consistent account of what that meant. Still, they would quickly have drawn some conclusions. First, because it was God who raised the dead, belief in Jesus' resurrection would have implied that Jesus, who had seemed to be abandoned and rejected by God, must have been speaking the truth after all. Resurrection vindicated him. If God had raised him, Jesus must have been who he said he was.

Second, because nearly all talk of resurrection referred to a general resurrection in the last days, this individual resurrection in the midst of history would have come as a surprise. It suggested a relation between Jesus' life and death and the end of history and God's final judgment.

Finally, to those who had trusted in Jesus and believed in his message, his resurrection would have confirmed God's justice and power. In the face of the powers that had put this innocent man to death, God had brought him to victory. Earthly powers can kill us, kill our children, wipe out our memory—Jews had come to know that only too well—but God has the last word. Belief in Jesus' resurrection implied that Jesus *was* God's last word. But what did it mean when early Christians said that Jesus had been raised from the dead, and why did they believe it?

21

What Happened When Jesus Was Raised?

At the end of the eighteenth century, the cynical German historian Hermann Samuel Reimarus came up with his own theory about Jesus' resurrection. The disciples, he said, had discovered that there was a better living to be made in preaching than in fishing. Therefore, when Jesus died, they invented the story of his resurrection to keep themselves in their new, more lucrative line of business.[1]

Reimarus did not originate suspicion about Jesus' resurrection. Both the New Testament itself and early Jewish critiques of Christianity imply that some people around Jerusalem shortly after Jesus' death claimed that his disciples had stolen his body (Matt. 27:62–64). Something like Reimarus' theory is reproclaimed, sometimes with great fanfare, every few years, as a new discovery.[2] So let me reiterate what I said earlier: if Jesus' resurrection is just a made-up story, then there's no reason to be a Christian.[3] Christians have to *deny* some sorts of skepticism concerning the resurrection, or we lose the core of our reason to follow Jesus and our ultimate confidence in the face of this world's powers of death.

It is much less clear, however, what Christians need to *affirm* about Jesus' resurrection. Different theologians give different answers. My own answer tries to preserve a place for mystery between two extremes that seem to me to try to explain too much.

At one end of a spectrum of opinions, the great German scholar Rudolf Bultmann argued that, when Christians started preaching how faith in Jesus could transform your life, Jesus "was raised" *in that preaching*, not in some miraculous event that preceded it.[4] Some Christians today, following roughly the same line of thought, talk about Jesus' presence in the lives of his disciples, and say that that's what "resurrection" really means.[5] At the other end of the spectrum, a sophisticated Christian philosopher insists, "A camera could have taken a snapshot of the risen Jesus."[6]

I prefer a view that is in between the risen Jesus as risen-in-the-faith-of-the-apostles and the risen Jesus as an-object-that-could-have-been-photographed, and considerably more cautious than either of those views. Calvin once wrote that he would try to give "some suggestion of the manner of resurrection. I use this language because Paul, calling it 'a mystery,' urges us to sobriety and restrains us from philosophizing too freely and subtly."[7] Sobriety and restraint indeed seem like a good idea when talking about this topic. A resurrection from the dead, a transformation of the meaning of things, an inbreaking of the ultimate triumph of God into the midst of history—we might expect that such an event would be a little hard to describe.

Moreover, the biblical texts themselves invite caution. The stories of Jesus' ministry and death raise all sorts of historical puzzles, but at least the stories as stories for the most part present coherent and clear narratives. The resurrection accounts are another matter altogether. Each Gospel presents a different set of events. Mark has an empty tomb but no appearances of the resurrected Jesus. Paul talks about appearances but never mentions the empty tomb. In Acts, Luke says that Paul saw something like a light in the sky, but Luke's Gospel describes a period of forty days during which Jesus appeared, talked, ate, and could be touched before he "ascended."

Matthew and John do not define a forty-day period, but they describe appearances of the resurrected Jesus as involving a person who could walk around and indeed was so much a "normal-looking" human being that he could be mistaken for someone else.[8] Luke has Jesus appear to the disciples near Jerusalem; in Matthew's version it happens in Galilee. John has a different set of stories altogether. People who knew Jesus well sometimes do not recognize him. Many react with fear. Some doubt (Matt. 28:17). Everything seems fragmentary, contradictory, incoherent.[9]

The authors of the New Testament are certainly able to tell a straightforward story when they want. If they so obviously fail to do so about the resurrection, it is perhaps because what had happened to them was not very straightforward either. "The stories themselves," the English theologian Rowan Williams writes, "are about difficulty, unexpected outcomes, silences, errors, about what is not readily accessible or readily understood."[10] Still, even given all the need for caution, Christians can and should say some things about what we believe of Jesus' resurrection.

Since the New Testament references to Jesus' resurrection discuss both appearances of the risen Jesus and the discovery of the empty tomb, let me review some conclusions I believe we can draw first about very general issues, then about the appearances, and then about the empty tomb.

Some Basics

Within a rather short time after Jesus' death, some of his followers were proclaiming his "resurrection" and urging others to join them in following him.

The New Testament never describes Jesus' resurrection, which remains—in the lovely phrase Ignatius of Antioch used early in the second century—"in the silence of God."[11]

In contrast, say, with the stories of Jesus' birth, the resurrection narratives rarely explicitly cite the fulfillment of Old Testament prophecies. The accounts are mysterious and inconsistent, but they are not obviously rearranged to fulfill the words of earlier prophets.[12]

Believing in Jesus' resurrection means wanting to follow him. Those who believed they had encountered the risen Jesus had their lives transformed.

Resurrection Appearances

The New Testament authors seem to assume that "resurrection appearances" were events that happened to a few people over a limited period of time; they aren't just another name for what happens when you become a Christian, or even for any sort of apparently "miraculous" conversion. Paul talks about "visions and revelations of the Lord" in the church at Corinth (2 Cor. 12:1); Stephen sees Jesus in heaven (Acts 7:55); at Pentecost the people assembled experience the rushing wind of the Holy Spirit. But none of those is a "resurrection appearance."

Paul is the only New Testament author who claims that Jesus appeared to him, our only eyewitness. His account is also the most reticent of the New Testament reports of such an event. Jesus "appeared," "was revealed," he says, and that's all—whether Paul is describing what happened to him or to others.[13] Luke's accounts in Acts of Paul's experience describe a voice and a light that shone from heaven, but these stories do not come from Paul himself.[14] Still, although Paul had many enemies in the early church, we have no hint of anyone denying the authenticity of his experience of the resurrected Jesus.

The Empty Tomb

References in both Christian and Jewish sources to accusations that Jesus' disciples had stolen his body may suggest that even opponents of his early followers conceded that there was an empty tomb, which needed some sort of explanation—though such an argument can only be very tentative.[15]

In a culture where women were not considered trustworthy to testify in court, it is hard to imagine why women would be cited as those who found the tomb empty unless this recalled some historical reality. This provides a rather stronger argument for the empty tomb tradition.[16]

The Christian practice of worship on the first day of the week, rather than on the Jewish Sabbath, began early and was associated with the resurrection. That the church preserved a memory of something "on the first day of the week" is at least a plausible explanation for this.[17]

Everyone seems to admit that the whole business of the resurrection was mysterious, hard to describe, unsettling, and even frightening. As Calvin said, we need to proceed with caution. We cannot imagine what it was like to encounter the resurrected Jesus. (And we certainly cannot imagine what it was like for Jesus to be resurrected!) Most modern historians would say that it makes no sense to try to evaluate the evidence for an event such as someone being raised from the dead. After all, historical arguments seek the most probable explanation of the data. How could we argue for the probability of an actual resurrection, as opposed to some other explanation, when the Bible itself would insist that the whole thing was utterly improbable?[18]

But even if we were to take resurrection from the dead as one possible explanation of the available evidence, the stories as we have them would leave us deeply puzzled about what led people to conclude that Jesus had been raised.

Some of Jesus' followers, it seems, encountered him shortly after his death and joyously concluded that the one who had been killed was raised and lived. I'm not sure we need to say (or can with any confidence say) much more than that about the nature of these "appearances." The choices are not easy. Just for a start, one would have to take as the paradigm either Paul-as-described-in-Acts (a voice and a light in the sky) or Matthew-Luke-John (a figure that could be mistaken for a living human being), or else allow for two quite different sorts of events, both described as resurrection appearances.

For a good many years, I thought the whole empty tomb tradition was just a story that had grown up later among Christians. The fact that Paul never mentions the empty tomb seemed to count decisively against its truth. If someone had invented the story, however, I can think of no reason why women would have been cited as the witnesses. As a result I've come to think that there probably was an empty tomb. Others may not find that argument persuasive, and historical argument cannot rule out the possibility that the empty tomb might have been the result of confusion or theft.

John Dominic Crossan has recently declared rather melodramatically that Jesus' body was eaten by dogs. He is convinced that the body of a convicted criminal would have been denied burial—that was part of the humiliating punishment—and likely consumed by scavenger dogs. Thus, Jesus was never buried in the first place.

But we lack detailed historical information about the context of the end of Jesus' life from sources other than the Gospels. If we treat the Gospel narratives skeptically, therefore, we cannot know much about the historical details. What were the internal politics of Jerusalem around 30 A.D.? Did Jesus have influential friends? Faced with questions like these, crucial to a historical account of Jesus' death and its aftermath, we have to say that we just don't know.

Indeed, looking at the "evidence" gets us only so far in speculations about Jesus' resurrection. I believe it is important that Christians not simply yield the field to the skeptics. If we cannot describe what happened, we can certainly identify those accounts that we believe to be false. Confident "historical" accounts (like Crossan's) of "what really happened" that expose the traditional Christian view as illusion turn out consistently to rest on their own sets of assumptions and guesses, and their flaws are worth pointing out. We do not have enough evidence for a confident answer of *any* kind based purely on historical evidence. It is equally the case that most Christians who start arguing for a historical basis for faith quickly start claiming more than they can know, or more certainty than historical research can ever provide.

What's the solution? Looking at these matters in terms of historical evidence generates only agnosticism. It is only when our minds and hearts have been captured by the Jesus we meet—whether we meet him in the stories that describe "the whole course of his obedience," in the life of the church that worships him, or in some other way—that we will be persuaded that the resurrection narratives point, however inadequately, to the reality that after his death he yet lived. And we will in turn find the stories of Jesus persuasive only as they illuminate our understanding of the world and how we should live our lives.

For Christians, therefore, Jesus' resurrection can never be *just* a historical question. We cannot separate asking "What happened?" from asking "What does it mean?" What does it mean for the way we understand the world and for the way we live our lives?

22

Bodily Resurrection and Eternal Life

If Jesus was raised to new life after his death, Christians believe, his resurrection offers a radically new perspective on how we live, because it offers hope for what will happen to us after our deaths. "Christ has been raised from the dead," Paul wrote to the Corinthians, "the first fruits of those who have died" (1 Cor. 15:20). We hope to be included in the general harvest that will follow those first fruits.

Such a hope assumes some kind of analogy between what happened to Jesus and what will happen to us; if they are totally different, then his ressurrection wouldn't imply anything about ours. Christians cannot separate our understanding of Jesus' resurrection from our own hopes for something beyond death. But that makes things complicated. I used to walk past a cemetery in New Haven, Connecticut, where the dead were buried facing toward Jerusalem so that they would see Jesus (presumably in heaven directly over Jerusalem) when their bodies were raised. I smiled at such naïveté. But if we don't believe in that kind of resurrection for ourselves, what do we believe?

Bodily Resurrection

As already mentioned, in the Greco-Roman culture into which Christianity began to spread, many people lessened the fear of death by hoping for the immortality of the soul. They believed that the soul has a natural immortality, and death only frees the soul from the body, which is an evil thing to be escaped. The Greek philosopher Plato said that the philosopher will welcome death as a liberation from the body and its distractions, freeing the soul for the pure quest of truth.[1] The Roman philosopher Seneca spoke of "this clogging burden of a body, to which nature has fettered me."[2]

As I noted earlier, the dominant Jewish view (with exceptions) was that the spirit and the body *together* are what makes one human. When the body dies, far from being freed, we stop existing (unless in a very shadowy way in Sheol). To live in a way that has any value after death, therefore, one's body will need to be resurrected. That resurrection isn't something natural to human bodies, but a gift of God. In the story in John's Gospel, when Lazarus died, Jesus did not congratulate Lazarus' sisters on the liberation of his soul—he wept, and then he brought Lazarus' *body* back to life (John 11:1–44). Jesus lived after *his* death only because God had resurrected his body, in however different a way from what the New Testament reports happened to Lazarus.

In part 1, I pointed out, in discussing the incarnation, that many Christians have failed to understand the positive value the Bible assigns to the human body. They have come to think of the body and its functions and pleasures as something we should be ashamed of.

But that's not what early Christian writers taught, and the contrast becomes clear in what those writers said about the resurrection. In the third century Tertullian asked,

> Shall that very flesh which the Divine Creator formed with His own hands in the image of God . . . not rise again? God forbid, God forbid (I repeat), that he should abandon to everlasting destruction the labor of his own hands, the care of his own thoughts.[3]

God made human bodies too, and cares about them. Tertullian's contemporary and fellow Christian, Athenagoras, accepted the Greek model that "the whole nature of human beings in general is composed of an immortal soul and a body which was fitted to it in the creation." But the body is no dispensible shell:

> that which has received both understanding and reason is the human being, not the soul by itself. The human being, therefore, who consists of the two parts, must continue forever.

But this is impossible unless our *bodies* are raised.

> For if no resurrection were to take place, the nature of human beings as human beings would not continue.[4]

God made our bodies, and they are therefore good—not prisons to be escaped, but essential to who we are. To deny their goodness not only damages people psychologically but betrays the teaching of Bible and early church.

The New Testament talks about Jesus' *bodily* resurrection, but it never much clarifies what it means to say that the risen Christ had a body. Remember Paul's reticence in describing his encounter with the risen Jesus. He has a good bit more to say about resurrection in 1 Corinthians, but his comments there raise more questions than they answer. What is resurrected, Paul says, is a body, but a *spiritual* body rather than a *physical* body.

> Flesh and blood cannot inherit the kingdom of God, nor does the perishable inherit the imperishable. Listen, I will tell you a mystery! We will not all die, but we will all be changed, in a moment, in the twinkling of an eye, at the last trumpet. For the trumpet will sound, and the dead will be raised imperishable, and we will be changed. For this perishable body must put on imperishability, and this mortal body must put on immortality.
> (1 Cor. 15:50–53)

This new body will be as different from the old as a stalk of wheat is from a wheat seed:

> What is sown is perishable, what is raised is imperishable. It is sown in dishonor, it is raised in glory. It is sown in weakness, it is raised in power. It is sown a physical body, it is raised a spiritual body.
> (1 Cor. 15:42–44)

But what will it be like? Paul has an abrupt answer for those who ask that question: "Fool!" (15:36). He himself encountered the risen Jesus, and he tells us we cannot even imagine the reality of a spiritual body.

With respect to the meaning of "spiritual body," Augustine admitted, "I confess that I have not yet read anywhere anything which I would esteem sufficiently established to deserve to be either learned or taught."[5] We hope, after we die, that we will be raised in communion with Christ above the vicissitudes of time and trouble. As Paul wrote in another letter, Christ "will transform the body of our humiliation that it may be conformed to the body of our glory" (Phil. 3:21). But a body just seems the sort of thing that by its nature is involved in process and decay. Yet, if we shift away from bodies to the immortality of the soul, we move away from the important biblical affirmation of our bodies as good parts of our identities.

Eternal Life

One reason we find it so hard to think about life after death is that, whether we think of a resurrected body or an immortal soul, we tend to think of it as still existing in time. We die, but then we go on living. To Gregory of Nyssa that sounded like a bad idea. "If human bodies return to life in the same condition in which they left it," he wrote, "then we are looking forward to endless misfortune in the resurrection."[6] Imagining the anxieties of this life going on forever is a depressing thought. More of the same, stretching on literally forever, sounds more like punishment than reward.

Christian theology therefore usually distinguishes between "time" and "eternity." "Eternity" does not mean just endless time. Rather, it means a different kind of time, something different altogether from time as we know it. The Bible, to be honest, does not help much here. Neither Greek nor Hebrew makes a sharp distinction between very distant or extended time and what subsequent philosophers would call "eternity."[7] The sources of such distinctions lie rather in Greek philosophy. Plotinus, for example, defined "eternity" as "a life never varying, not becoming what previously it was not, the thing immutably itself, broken by no interval."[8]

Thomas Aquinas used the analogy of a circle. The center of the circle is equally related to every point on the circumference but is not *at* any point on the circumference; so, similarly, eternity is not at any point *in* time but is equally related to every point of time.[9] Another analogy compares a spectator high on a mountain above a road with travellers on the road. The travellers can see only the bit of the road around them, but the distant spectator sees all points on the road simultaneously.

Ever since Einstein, physicists have insisted that we should not take our commonsense ideas about time for granted. To note one of many paradoxes, if you travel at a speed approaching the speed of light while I stand still, then, when you return from your trip, less time will have passed for you than for me. If we were the same age when we started, you will be younger. Puzzles like this remind us that we cannot simply trust our instincts about time. We cannot point to the clock on the wall and say, "There, that's what time it is." Time turns out to be far more complicated, and we need the help of philosophers as well as physicists in understanding it.

As we rethink our understanding of time, I find most helpful those philosophers who reflect on how we experience it, who start with questions about what time feels like to us.[10] Mostly, many of them say, we experience time anxiously. The past can be a burden, or we worry that it is slipping from memory. The future fills us with a mix of worry and hope. The present constantly disappears, like the landscape seen from the window of a fast-moving train. An infinite span of this kind of time, any number of theologians tell us, would not be worth having. Christian hope is for something different—for an experience of eternity in which past, present, and future come together without tension. Listen to Karl Barth:

> What distinguishes eternity from time is the fact that there is . . . not opposition or competition or conflict, but peace between origin, movement and goal, between present and future, between "not yet," "now" and "no more," . . . a totality without gap or rift, free from the threat of death under which time, our time, stands.[11]

Many philosophical accounts work by negation: eternity is *not* time. Barth says that it's a *different kind* of time, one rich and full but without the tensions that inevitably afflict our current temporal experience. Living in eternity would involve experiencing temporal things, but experiencing them whole.

God experiences things that way—that is, God lives in eternity. In this life, we catch glimpses of it. In the mystic's vision, the focus of the artist or athlete, or the passion of love, we fleetingly experience a different kind of temporality than our normal sense of things—but only fleetingly. As T. S. Eliot put it,

> . . . to apprehend
> The point of intersection of the timeless
> With time, is an occupation for the saint—
> No occupation either, but something given
> And taken, in a lifetime's death in love,
> Ardour and selflessness and self-surrender.
> For most of us, there is only the unattended
> Moment, the moment in and out of time,
> The distraction fit, lost in a shaft of sunlight,
> The wild thyme unseen, or the winter lightning
> Or the waterfall, or music heard so deeply
> That it is not heard at all, but you are the music
> While the music lasts. These are only hints and guesses,
> Hints followed by guesses; and the rest
> Is prayer, observance, discipline, thought and action.[12]

Only beyond death can we really hope for eternity.

Bodies in Eternity

The language of eternity, however, has often been associated with the idea of the soul that escapes the body—and understandably so. The body seems so obviously the sort of thing that exists in time. In the fourth century, Gregory of Nyssa struggled with just this problem. After the death of his brother Basil, he fell into a kind of despair. The thought of death and decay terrified him, yet they seemed inseparable from the reality of having a body. Gregory visited his saintly sister Macrina, who was herself dying, and his dialogue, *On the Soul and the Resurrection*, recounts what she taught him.

Human nature, she said, gives up "dishonor, corruption, weakness," and aging at death, "but it does not give up being itself." Its change is as radical as that from a seed to a stalk of wheat,[13] but having a body is part of what it means to be human. In eternal life, Macrina continued, we will therefore be bodily creatures, but with different kinds of bodies than we have now.

One of Jesus' parables tells how poor Lazarus looks down from the bosom of Abraham at the rich man who ignored him in this life, now suffering in Hades. "Father Abraham," the rich man begs, "have mercy on me, and send Lazarus to dip the tip of his finger in water and cool my tongue; for I am in agony in these flames" (Luke 16:24). But words like "finger" and "tongue," Macrina explained, here mean something altogether different from their meanings in this life. In eternity, our bodies will be unimaginably different.

After the resurrection, "a kind of all-inclusive human being will come into being so that nothing of the resurrected person will be missing in the risen person, the newly-born, the infant, the child, the adolescent, the adult, the parent, the old person, and all the stages in between"[14]—bodily but eternal. Our hope, as Augustine wrote, is "not the escape from any kind of body but the possession of an imperishable body,"[15] and an imperishable body is not one that goes through time as we do without ever stopping, but a body living in the kind of time called eternity.

It is probably best not even to attempt to imagine what this will be like, but simply trust that in God nothing is lost—as Barth puts it, "No suffering or joy . . . no ray of sunlight; no note which has ever sounded . . . no wing-beat of the day-fly in the far flung epochs of geological time."[16] God lives in eternity, and God welcomes us into that eternity, so that, in the words of Gerard Manley Hopkins,

> In a flash, at a trumpet crash,
> I am all at once what Christ is, since he was what I am, and
> This Jack, joke, poor potsherd, patch, matchwood, immortal diamond,
> Is immortal diamond.[17]

On the road to Damascus, when Paul encountered Christ, Christ already lived in that eternity. Paul didn't try to describe what Eliot called "the point of intersection of the timeless with time," but he did leave the assurance that, "neither death, nor life, nor angels, nor rulers, nor things present, nor things to come, nor powers, nor height, nor depth, nor anything else in all creation, will be able to separate us from the love of God in Christ Jesus our Lord" (Rom. 8:38–39).

23

The Resurrection Narratives in the Gospels

One of my assumptions in this book has been that, while trying to understand the Bible sometimes appropriately raises the historical question, "What really happened?" it is best to begin by reading biblical stories simply as stories, and see what they intend to convey about the identity of God or of Jesus. Having earlier considered the resurrection narratives as a kind of historical evidence, I will now look at some of the stories themselves.

The Road to Emmaus

In the introduction I discussed Jesus' appearance to Cleopas and his friend on the road to Emmaus. These two followers of Jesus describe the despair that they feel in the aftermath of Jesus' crucifixion to a man they do not recognize who has joined them on the road. "Oh, how foolish you are," their unknown companion exclaims, and proceeds to explain how Jesus' suffering and death were not the sign of his failure but rather the fulfillment of what the prophets had proclaimed about the Messiah. Cleopas and his companion are fascinated by the stranger's comments and invite him to join them for dinner.

> So he went to stay with them. When he was at the table with them, he took bread, blessed and broke it, and gave it to them. Then their eyes were opened, and they said to each other, "Were not our hearts burning within us while he was talking to us on the road, and while he was opening the scriptures to us?"
>
> (Luke 24:29–32)

They get up at once and return to Jerusalem, only to be met with the news that Jesus has appeared to Peter too.

Considering the resurrection narratives for the moment simply as stories, without worrying about their historical reliability, the road to Emmaus is a good place to begin. I have no idea whether or not this encounter really happened. Maybe the author is recounting an actual event; maybe it's a legend that was exaggerated as it passed from one person to another. Or maybe, faced with the literally indescribable experience of encountering the risen Jesus Christ, the author of Luke did what Jesus did when he told about the good Samaritan or the prodigal son—try to convey something locked in mystery by telling a story.

What can we learn from the story? For one thing, we learn that in reading Scripture and sharing in the meal in which we remember him, we encounter Jesus. Like a number of other resurrection narratives, this story shifts from a particular event in the days immediately after Jesus' death to actions and responses that belong to the life of the church. Cleopas and his companion recognize Jesus only in his teaching and his sharing of the bread—both contexts though which readers of the story can themselves encounter Jesus in the church community.

By the Sea of Galilee

Consider too the strange story at the end of the gospel of John. The book seems to end in chapter 20 with what sound like final words:

> Now Jesus did many other signs in the presence of his disciples, which are not written in this book. But these are written so that you may come to believe that Jesus is the Messiah, the Son of God, and that through believing you may have life in his name.
>
> (John 20:30–31)

But then the story starts up again in chapter 21 (some scholars propose that this may be a later addition). The disciples are back home in Galilee, fishing in the Sea of Tiberias, when they see a stranger on the beach. They have had so little luck fishing that they even follow his odd instruction to try casting the net on the other side of the boat, "and now they were not able to haul it in because there were so many fish." Only then does the always unnamed "disciple whom Jesus loved" say to Peter, "It is the Lord." Peter jumps into the sea to swim to Jesus in a kind of baptism. "Come and have breakfast," Jesus says, so they sit down, and he takes bread and gives it to them, but "none of the disciples dared to ask him, 'Who are you?' because they knew it was the Lord" (John 21:12).

Here too, is mystery, an initially unknown stranger, teaching, and the sharing of a meal. The emphasis falls not on the qualities of this event that were uniquely available to the first disciples, but on those features of it that any Christian can experience in word and sacraments.

Three times Jesus asks Peter, "Do you love me?" Three times Peter says yes, and three times Jesus responds, "Then feed my sheep."[1] "After this he said to him, 'Follow me.' " As the narrative moves from description to call to discipleship, yet again we move from the particularity of Peter's experience to an experience of discipleship we readers can share.

Then the Gospel distinguishes two sorts of leadership within the church that follows Jesus. Peter receives his authority and responsibility, even as "the disciple Jesus loved" remains present in the background. Peter sees that disciple "following them" and asks, "Lord, what about him?"

What do these two disciples symbolize? Peter stands for the hierarchical organization and rules about who is included and excluded, which Jesus' followers will need to develop if the church is to survive through history. The other disciple reminds readers of this story that human rules can never encompass God's grace. There is always that anonymous disciple who seems to have secrets unknown even to Peter. Jesus' final words in the last Gospel respond to Peter's question, "Lord, what about him?" "What is that to you?" Jesus replies.[2] The text reminds us that no structures or institutions, however necessary (and they *are* necessary), can encompass the mystery and the startling love of Jesus still at work in the world.

Such an interpretation of what the end of John is about assumes that these stories of Jesus' resurrection appearances are also stories about the life of the church. The text itself invites that assumption. Even in the form of the narrative, something odd happens at the end of John. The storyteller keeps moving outside the story. For instance, when Jesus speaks to Peter, the narrator explains that his remark predicts how Peter will meet his death (John 21:19). Similarly, an enigmatic comment about the beloved disciple is conjoined with a rumor later "spread in the community" that the disciple would not die (21:23).

Finally, we jump out of the frame of the story altogether: the next-to-last verse reveals that this beloved disciple "is the disciple who is testifying to these things and has written them, and we know that his testimony is true"—not only an identification of the source of the story, but also a "we" who testify to his reliability (21:24). The story of Jesus' resurrection appearances almost merges with the story of the life of the church.

Raymond Brown, perhaps the greatest New Testament scholar of our time, put it this way in his great commentary on John:

> Throughout the Gospel, and more particularly in the Last Discourse, in what the evangelist has been describing on the stage of early 1st-century Palestine, he has had in mind an audience seated in the dark-

> ened theater of the future, silently viewing what Jesus was saying and doing. True to the limitations and logic of the stage drama imposed by the Gospel form, the Johannine Jesus could address that audience only indirectly through the disciples who shared the stage and gave voice to sentiments and reactions that were shared by the audience as well. But now, as the curtain is about to fall on the stage drama, the lights in the theater are suddenly turned on. Jesus shifts his attention from the disciples on the stage to the audience that has become visible and makes clear that his ultimate concern is for them—those who have come to believe in him through the word of his disciples.[3]

Paul never described his experience of the risen Christ. The Gospel of John might seem much more descriptive in presenting all these resurrection narratives. But in the telling, the boundary between past and present becomes indistinct. One cannot tell stories about the risen Jesus without them becoming also stories about how to follow him.

A bit earlier in John's Gospel, Jesus appears to the disciples on an evening when Thomas is absent, and doubting Thomas does not believe it happened. Jesus appears again a week later, and Thomas can only exclaim, "'My Lord and my God!' 'Have you believed because you have seen me?' Jesus asks. 'Blessed are those who have not seen and yet have come to believe.' " (John 20:28–29). Once again, the story slips out of its own frame, for there is no one in the story who has come to believe without seeing. The reference seems to be directed to future readers, and it makes a point common to resurrection stories.

Mysterious Endings

"How lucky we were," the first disciples might have said. "We witnessed the risen Jesus Christ, and no one will ever do that again." But that is not the tone of the Gospels. They keep making the appearances themselves (which were unique to that time) enigmatic and emphasizing the value of the Christian community's experience (which is still available to us) of Christ in the hearing of the word and the breaking of the bread.

The Gospel of Mark ends with three women meeting a young man at Jesus' tomb, who tells them that he has been raised:

> So they went out and fled from the tomb, for terror
> and amazement had seized them; and they said nothing to
> anyone, for they were afraid.
>
> (Mark 16:8)

And there the Gospel ends, on a note so odd that even in the early church Christians kept tacking on additional verses to reach a more positive conclusion.

Luke offers a much more detailed account of resurrection witness, but in his version the risen Christ produces an odd set of reactions. The women who are the first to find the tomb empty are initially perplexed, and then, when two men in dazzling clothes appear to them, they are terrified (Luke 24:4–5). The apostles dismiss their news as "an idle tale, and they did not believe them" (24:11). Peter goes to the tomb, and is amazed, astonished. All the verbs of reaction are ambivalent at best. Later, when Jesus appears to the eleven remaining apostles, "they were startled and terrified, and thought they were seeing a ghost" (24:37). Matthew might seem to present a more positive account, but at its climax, when the eleven go to a mountaintop in Galilee for their final vision of Jesus, the most dramatic moment of all, "they worshiped him, but some doubted" (Matt. 28:17).

The point seems clear enough: Don't think that if you had been there to witness the risen Jesus, everything would have been clear and reassuring. Whatever happened, it was frightening, strange, and ambiguous. To those who believed (and Matthew says that not everyone did), it transformed their lives and gave them a call to do something, just as it did for Paul on the road to Damascus. For Paul, the call was "to proclaim him among the Gentiles" (Gal. 1:16). At the end of Matthew's Gospel, Jesus tells the assembled disciples to "go . . . and make disciples of all nations" (Matt. 28:19). At the beginning of Acts, Luke has Jesus tell his followers that they "will be my witnesses in Jerusalem, in all Judea and Samaria, and to the ends of the earth" (Acts 1:8). Even in Mark's truncated, enigmatic ending, the young man tells the women, "go, tell his disciples and Peter" (Mark 16:7). The experience of the resurrected one is shrouded in mystery, but the message is clear: Go. Tell. Be witnesses. Proclaim. Feed my sheep.

24

Baptism

Those who believed that they had encountered the risen Christ wanted not only to become his followers but to invite others to join them. Following Jesus Christ, however, was not something people just did on their own; it involved joining the community that was becoming the church—and being baptized is the way one joins the church community.

In Acts, when Peter preaches the first Christian sermon and the crowd asks, "What should we do?" he immediately replies, "Repent, and be baptized every one of you in the name of Jesus Christ" (Acts 2:37–38). Matthew's Gospel ends with the risen Jesus commanding his followers, "Go therefore and make disciples of all nations, baptizing them in the name of the Father and of the Son and of the Holy Spirit" (Matt. 28:19).

For the first Christians baptism symbolized death and rebirth. Paul writes to the Romans,

> Do you not know that all of us who have been baptized into Christ Jesus were baptized into his death? Therefore we have been buried with him by baptism into death, so that, just as Christ was raised from the dead by the glory of the Father, so we too might walk in newness of life. For if we have been united with him in a death like his, we will certainly be united with him in a resurrection like his.
>
> (Rom. 6:3–5)

When Nicodemus the Pharisee visits Jesus in John's Gospel, Jesus tells him he must be born again. "How can anyone be born after having grown old?" Nicodemus asks. "Can one enter a second time into the mother's womb and be born?" Jesus replies that it is not that kind of birth he means, but the new birth one receives in baptism: "No one can enter the reign of God without being born of water and the Spirit" (John 3:4–5).

The three marks of the church are thus linked: just as preaching fits with Jesus' ministry and Lord's Supper with his cross, so baptism is related to new life and resurrection.

The Backgrounds of Christian Baptism

The word "baptism" comes from a Greek word meaning "to dip" or "to plunge." The symbolism of washing away the old life or one's sins is sufficiently obvious that it appears in many cultures. Sin renders us dirty; to get rid of its consequences, we need to partake in a ritual in which we are washed clean. Baptism was less central to Judaism than was circumcision or anointing, but Gentiles who wanted to become Jews went through a ritual baptism, and the Qumran community that wrote the Dead Sea Scrolls required ritual washings. John the Baptist went out to the Jordan, "proclaiming a baptism of repentence for the forgiveness of sins" (Mark 1:4). So the idea was not entirely new to Judaism by Jesus' time.

Jesus' baptism by John is one of the most historically well-established events of his life. The first three Gospels all describe it, and the fourth alludes to it. Moreover, the early Christians seem to have been a bit embarrassed by the incident—if baptism washes away sins, then why would Jesus, who was without sin, be baptized? Their very discomfort with the episode makes it unlikely that early Christians would have invented it.

Christians concluded that, when Jesus was baptized, the water didn't purify him, but he purified the water. Jesus was baptized, Ignatius of Antioch said, "that he might hallow water."[1] In many of Jesus' healings, where we might expect that the touch of an unclean person would pollute Jesus, instead he "cleansed" the person he healed. So in being baptized, he cleansed the water so that it can in turn cleanse us of our sins. As Athanasius put it, "For when the Lord, as human, was washed in Jordan, it was we who were washed in him and by him."[2]

Christians soon came to think of baptism, whether Jesus' or ours, as related to a number of key events in the Old Testament, in which water has conflicting meanings.[3] For example, in Genesis 1:2 the Spirit of God "swept over the face of the waters." In the story of Noah, the flood destroyed all living things except for those saved in the ark. When the Hebrew people escaped from Egypt, closely pursued by an Egyptian army, the Lord sent a great wind ("wind" is the same word as "spirit"), divided the waters, and turned the sea into dry land (Exod. 14:21). After forty years of wandering in the wilderness, when the people at last prepared to enter the promised land, they formed a procession led by the ark of the covenant, and the flow of the Jordan stopped, and all the people crossed it on dry land (Josh. 3:14–17).

The author of First Peter reminded his readers how, in the time of Noah, "a few, that is, eight persons, were saved through water. And baptism, which this prefigured, now saves you" (1 Pet. 3:20–21). Similarly, Paul wrote to the Corinthians that "our ancestors . . . passed through the sea," and were "baptized into Moses . . . in the sea. . . . Now these things occurred as examples to us." (1 Cor. 10:1–2, 6).

In these stories, water functions as a double-edged symbol. On the one hand, it gives life—it symbolizes creation, whether of the world or the Hebrew people or newly baptized Christians. On the other hand, it threatens. Whether at the Red Sea or the Jordan, the Israelites move through water that could drown them at any minute if not held back by the hand of God. Baptism among Christians had something of the same function that these dramatic events or, for that matter, circumcision had among Jews—and circumcision drew blood, hurt, and could even kill a person if infection set in. Crossing through the water, risking your life, takes faith.

Baptism in the Early Church

The drama of the early church's services for the baptism of adults conveyed both hope and danger. After three years of study and participation in the life of the community, those who wanted to be baptized would undergo a period of prayer and fasting after which, often in the dark of early Easter morning, they would strip naked and be baptized by total immersion. Then they would be clothed in white garments to symbolize their purity, and be welcomed into the church.

In an age when Christians risked martyrdom, such a ceremony conveyed the dangers involved in Christian faith. One comes to new life through at least a symbolic risk of death. "For in the water," Ambrose wrote in the fourth century, "is the representation of death . . . that the body of sin may die through the water, which encloses the body as it were in a kind of tomb, that we, by the power of the Spirit, may be renewed from the death of sin, being born again in God."[4] The old person has to die so that the new one can be born. Everything has to be given away to start afresh. Only those willing to lose their lives will find them.

Many churches today perform baptism in ways that lose most of this symbolism. They require little by way of preparation, either of adults seeking baptism or of parents seeking to have their children baptized. The smallest dab of water suffices, hardly enough to wash away serious sins, and certainly not enough to threaten drowning.

I do not propose a return to the practice of full immersion even for infants, but when a church was willing to risk an occasional case of pneumonia from baptismal water its members better understood the seriousness of this business. Baptism, as many great theologians remind us, should involve plenty of water—splashing, pouring, and dunking.[5] If a baby howls or an adult's hair is messed up, that at least might suggest that what has just happened is not trivial.[6]

Baptism washes away sin and moves the one baptized through a symbolic death to new life. In baptism, Christians share in Christ's resurrection. It also involves joining a community: through baptism we become part of the church, united not only to Christ but also to all those who are also united to Christ. "For just as the body is one and has many members, and all the members of the body, though many, are one body, so it is with Christ. For in the one Spirit we were all baptized into one body—Jews or Greeks, slaves or free" (1 Cor. 12:12–13).

In the first baptism of new Christians that the New Testament reports, at the beginning of Acts, the story emphasizes that people from different nations came and received baptism together. Now they were one in Christ, and therefore one with each other.

> I therefore . . . beg you to lead a life worthy of the calling to which you have been called, with all humility and gentleness, with patience, bearing with one another in love, making every effort to maintain the unity of the Spirit in the bond of peace. There is one body and one Spirit, just as you were called to the one hope of your calling, one Lord, one faith, one baptism, one God and Father of all.
>
> (Eph. 4:1–6)

Churches in which some are excluded from baptism, for whatever reason, have not understood the meaning of baptism. When we exclude some kinds of people from baptism, or some kinds of baptized people from our fellowship, we exclude ourselves from fellowship with Christ, who stands with those who are excluded.

Some Questions about Baptism

In the case of babies who are born into the church, two of the meanings of baptism, in combination, lead to a puzzle. Baptism represents the moment when we boldly put aside the old life and sin and risk the new life of following Jesus in Christian community. It is also the sign of entrance into the Christian community. For adult converts, both those events happen at the same time.

But infants in Christian families, who are being raised in the faith, are not in a position to make a bold confession of their faith or commitment of their lives; yet, held in their parents' arms or running around the church building, they seem so obviously part of the Christian community. Should they be baptized?[7]

The New Testament mentions by name only adults as baptized but refers twice to people baptized with their "households" or "families" (Acts 16:15 and 16:33). Scholars have regularly debated whether those families and households included small children. We know that by the second century Christians were baptizing infants, but debates about infant baptism have continued ever since. In the Reformation, and again in the seventeenth century, some Christians insisted that only adults who could confess their faith and understand the commitment they were making should be baptized, and they founded "Baptist" and other Christian communities where they rebaptized adults who had been baptized as infants. The greatest theologian of the twentieth century, Karl Barth, described infant baptism as "a wound in the body of the Church," which has badly distorted our sense of what it means to be a Christian.[8]

In short, infant baptism is an issue on which Christians continue to differ. Those of us who believe in baptizing infants offer several arguments.[9] It is a wonderful symbol of God's grace that, when we are too young to know what is going on and utterly powerless, we can nevertheless be made one with Christ in baptism. Infant baptism also recognizes the reality that our families and our congregations have the responsibility of raising us in Christian faith. And it symbolizes that, before all our wanderings and errors, we were already related to God.

In his moments of doubt and fear, Luther used to repeat over and over to himself, as something to which he could cling, that he had been baptized.[10] Likewise Calvin recommended,

> All pious folk throughout life, whenever they are troubled by a consciousness of their faults, may venture to remind themselves of their baptism, that from it they may be confirmed in assurance of that sole and perpetual cleansing which we have in Christ's blood.[11]

If the remembrance of baptism is to have that power, then those of us who believe in infant baptism have an obligation to make it more serious than it has become in most of our churches. Adult baptism should include some of the drama it had in earlier centuries. The baptism of infants should avoid all-too-common cuteness. Parents of the baptized child should have sought disciplined preparation for raising a child in the faith. If they have no intention of raising the child in a Christian church, then the child ought not to be baptized, no matter the resulting hurt feelings of doting grandparents. The rite of baptism might well remind both parents and congregation of the risks and dangers that may follow from Christian life.

What about the unbaptized? Baptism is not magic. It welcomes us into Christian community and calls us to a Christian life; it offers no guarantee that we will live up to our responsibilities as Christians. Conversely, many theologians of the Christian tradition have acknowledged that baptism is not necessary for salvation. Did not Christ, Aquinas asked, assure the (unbaptized!) thief who spoke kindly to him on the cross, "Today you shall be with me in Paradise"? More generally, anyone can receive "the effect of Baptism by the power of the Holy Ghost . . . without Baptism of water . . . as his heart is moved by the Holy Ghost to believe in and love God and to repent of his sins."[12]

So why bother with baptism at all? Well, we sinners need all the help we can get. We need the comfort and the challenge that this rite provides: the special assurance that we are under God's care, and the call to live up to our identity as baptized in Christ. To live out our lives as Christians, we need to be part of a Christian community and to acknowledge that we are at one with all the diverse folk who make up that community, and, like them, in need of forgiveness. We need to be willing to identify ourselves publicly as Christians, even as others have done for whom that declaration led to martyrdom—not only for our own sake, but above all to God's glory.

Perhaps most of all, we need the help that comes, in ways we cannot understand, through God's grace in the water of baptism. Baptism is not something we do or the church does, but something God does, and our assurance as baptized Christians therefore rests not on the purity of our own faith or the sanctity of the church community, but on the love of God. As Luther put it:

> Assuredly nothing in us effects salvation but faith. . . . But . . . faith must have something to believe—something to which it may cling and upon which it may plant its feet and take root. Thus faith clings to the water and believes it to be baptism which effects pure salvation and life, not through the water . . . but through the fact that the Word and institution of God are embodied in it and God's name is joined to it. Now, when I believe this, what else does it mean but to believe in God.[13]

25

The Christ Who Reigns

Our baptism into Christ promises us victory over death. Resurrection is, among other things, about victory—victory over death, and victory over all the forces that can kill. In this final chapter on resurrection I therefore discuss three interrelated topics. First, in earlier chapters we considered Christ's "offices" as prophet and priest; in this one we address his office as monarch. He turns out, as we have already seen, to be an unusual kind of monarch, and thinking about the sort of monarch he is leads, second, to reflection about how Christians should think about nations and wars between nations (the ethical issue that parallels the analyses of sexual orientation and prisons in earlier parts). Thinking about Christ as a monarch also leads, third, to questions about what happened to Christ after his resurrection, for it is after his resurrection victory that he most clearly "reigns." The section of the Apostles' Creed on Jesus Christ ends like this:

> On the third day he rose again;
> he ascended into heaven,
> he is seated at the right hand of the Father,
> and he will come to judge the living and the dead.

The resurrection, then, is not the end of Jesus' story. Thinking about the rest of that story as the creed lays it out—ascension, sitting at the right hand, coming in judgment—helps us think about what it means to call Christ "monarch" and what that means for the relation of Christians to earthly authorities and the violence those authorities sometimes use to get things done.

Ascended to the Right Hand of the Father

So first the ascension. In the New Testament it marks the break between the time of Jesus' appearances among his disciples and the rest of history. "There is no sense," Karl Barth once wrote, "in trying to visualize the ascension as a literal event, like going up in a balloon."[1] In some special but mysterious way Christ was present among his followers for a brief time after his death. He did not then abandon us, but the New Testament authors recognize that he is no longer with us in the same way that he was for a time with them. How to express the difference? "He was lifted up," Luke says, "and a cloud took him out of their sight" (Acts 1:9).

It is easy to be condescending today and say, "People used to think that God was 'up in the sky'—but we know better." But people recognized the metaphorical character of such language long before the advent of modern astronomy. What does it mean that Jesus "ascended" to "the right hand of the Father"? "We do not hold that the right hand of the Father is an actual place," John of Damascus wrote in the eighth century. "For how could God, who is uncircumscribed, have a right hand limited by place?"[2] "When Christ is said to be in heaven," Calvin remarked sarcastically, "we must not view him as dwelling among the spheres and numbering the stars,"[3] as if we needed to "build a cottage for him among the planets."[4] Rather, Christ's "ascension" has traditionally meant two things: first, he went clean out of any realm we can reach, get access to, or understand, and, second, he went to be with God.[5]

More precisely, the creed says he went to be "at the right hand of the Father." The seat at the right hand of the person in charge, in biblical times as today, is a position of special power and influence. To say that Christ is there indicates metaphorically that in the highest level of whatever decision-making processes guide the universe, there is someone who is the advocate not only for our sins but for the sins of the whole world (1 John 2:1–2), and who can sympathize with our weaknesses, for he has been tested in every way that we are (Heb. 4:15).

When we meditate on our guilt, we can feel overwhelmed at the thought of facing divine judgment. When we think about the vastness of the universe, we can conclude that our small planet is of the most trivial significance in the grand scheme of things. But if Christ sits at the "right hand of the Father," then Jesus, our friend and brother, who knows the beauties and sorrows of this earth so intimately, is there in the highest place of honor and influence. "Let us therefore approach the throne of grace with boldness, so that we may receive mercy and find grace to help in time of need" (Heb. 4:16).

Christ "sits on the right hand of the Father," the Creed says. Does even such an exalted position for Christ imply a kind of subordination at odds with the perfect equality of the Persons of the Trinity? If this were a book about the Trinity, it would be important to explore the relations of equality and mutual glorification among its Persons. For present purposes, let this suffice: the Persons of the Trinity are equal, but they do not share an equality of carefully assigned rights, jealously guarded. Rather, each celebrates the uniquenesses of the others in mutual glorification.

This is one of the special themes of the Gospel of John. Jesus says, "If I glorify myself, my glory is nothing. It is my Father who glorifies me" (8:54). But in turn he says that the Father will be "glorified in the Son" (14:13). "Glorify your Son," he prays, "so that the Son may glorify you" (17:1). And one could develop similar ideas with respect to the Holy Spirit. The equality within the Trinity is expressed in the ways its three Persons defer to one another.

Questions about mutual deference within the Trinity, indeed, provide an entry point for thinking about the kind of power Christ has, "seated at the right hand of the Father." Christ reigns over all the world. And yet, even after the resurrection, he is recognized by the marks of the nails on his hands and feet and the wound in his side. He is a monarch who died on a cross, a ruler who serves, a leader who calls his followers not servants but friends (John 15:15).

Christ as Monarch

The theologian Paul Tillich used to warn about the dangers of using symbols for God—they shape, he said, not only the way we think about God, but the way we think about whatever we use as a symbol.[6] When we call God a king, we think not only about God but also about kings in a different way. So, down through history, rulers had to be obeyed, could not be challenged, deserved every measure of pomp and glory—after all, they were like God.

But a Christian can also push the argument in the other direction. Beneath all its gold and jewels, the crown of the French monarchs supposedly contained a fragment of the crown of thorns placed on Jesus' head.[7] No doubt the crown of thorns was buried deep beneath layers of gold, and most French kings lived lives with little in common to that of Jesus. Yet from its hiding place, might a fragment of thornwood, authentic or not, call rulers to an ideal at odds with the world's general pattern of things?

Sometimes it happens. On a small scale even fairly often. We see the town mayor or the charity president who really does hold an office for the good of others, and at personal sacrifice. Even on a national scale—Gandhi liberated India, Mandela held South Africa together, and no one could doubt that a different sort of life would have been easier for them. In different ways they gave their lives for the good of their peoples. But the temptations are great—wealth and attention can come so easily to those who have power, and the excuses come just as easily. For the sake of public order, after all, surely one must have proper respect for the nation's ruler, and a little pomp encourages respect. But, once one starts down that road, it is hard to stop.

Jesus offers a different model of one who reigns. Even legitimate power, the great twentieth-century Catholic theologian Karl Rahner wrote, is "something to be gradually modified and absorbed by love." But too often

> [i]t is used in order to rule, and not because one wishes to serve; it is used as a means of self-assertion and not as the sword of God with which one is entrusted. Rulers deceive themselves and believe that they are in the right because they are in power; they claim they have the better arguments because they have reduced the others to silence. They are tempted to claim their rights by force, where justice itself would have enforced their claims, if they themselves were more just: but it is simpler and easier the other way.[8]

Power is not itself sin, but it is so full of temptations to sin that it must constantly judge itself by the light of the cross. Power often involves many burdens, and so those with power find it hard to give up any accompanying perquisites. What begins as service can too easily come to center on privilege.

Kings in Ancient Israel

Most cultures of the ancient world identified the monarch with the divine and unhesitatingly celebrated royal power. But Israel had always been ambivalent about its kings. The book of Judges tells how the first person who tried to be king, Abimelech, killed all but one of his seventy brothers to secure unchallenged power, and later died when a woman threw an upper millstone onto his head and crushed his skull (Judg. 9). In such a male-oriented society, to be killed by a woman was particularly shameful, but even apart from that, the story of Abimelech was not an auspicious beginning for attempts at monarchy.

For a good long while, the Israelites apparently rejected the idea of having a king, insisting that they had no king but the Lord.[9] But over time they came to envy the elaborate courts and concentrated power of their neighbors, and began to demand a king. Israel's historians report how the prophet Samuel warned them against the idea:

> These will be the ways of the king who will reign over
> you: he will take your sons and appoint them to his
> chariots and to be his horsemen, and to run before his
> chariots; and he will appoint for himself commanders of
> thousands and commanders of fifties, and some to plow his
> ground and to reap his harvest, and to make his
> implements of war and the equipment of his chariots. He
> will take your daughters to be perfumers and cooks and
> bakers. He will take the best of your fields and
> vineyards and olive orchards and give them to his courtiers.
> (1 Sam. 8:11–14)

In short—he will spend your sons in warfare and your money in high living, and you don't want a king. But they still did.

Other Old Testament texts, to be sure, offer a much more positive picture of monarchy. Many of the Psalms, for instance, come from rituals honoring the monarch, and they celebrate the monarch as the Lord's anointed. Psalm 2 declares:

> I will tell of the decree of the Lord:
> He said to me, "You are my son;
> today I have begotten you.
> Ask of me, and I will make the nations your heritage,
> and the ends of the earth your possession."
> (Ps. 2:7–8)

In another Psalm, the Lord even invites David the king to "sit at my right hand" (110:1). The monarch is the source of justice, righteousness, and prosperity for the people:

> For he delivers the needy when they call,
> the poor and those who have no helper.
> He has pity on the weak and the needy,
> and saves the lives of the needy.
> From oppression and violence he redeems their life.
> (Ps. 72:12–14)

Israel's prophets and people struggled with the question of whether the monarch was always the Lord's representative, or only if he lived up to this ideal of the king as dispenser of justice.[10] After all, prophets had been ambivalent about the monarchy from the start, and the oldest strand of Israelite thought held that the Lord alone was king.

The scriptures present David's and Solomon's faults in remarkably frank terms, yet both clearly had a special covenant with the Lord. The people of Israel looked back on their reigns as a time of great prosperity and power and were willing to forgive a lot. But over time, as more corrupt and less successful kings came to power, they began to wonder if the bad kings who ruled them could really be God's representatives. They hoped for a better king, but those hopes came to be stated less in terms of practical expectations, and pushed ever farther into the future.

Israel gradually came to live in the tension between the ancient dream of the Lord alone as king and an increasing dissatisfaction with, first, corrupt and earthly kings and then (after Israel's independence had ended) one conquering empire after another. If there were to be a good ruler at all, Israelites came to believe, such a person would have to be wildly unlike any of the models they had seen. Out of that tension came the various hopes for Messiahs, divinely installed rulers who would be radically different from the powers and principalities known in this world.

Either Jesus himself or his earliest followers reinterpreted the hope for a Messiah in terms of the suffering servant of Second Isaiah. That anonymous prophet from the time of Israel's exile, whose words are included in the book of Isaiah, wrote of this haunting figure who

> had no form or majesty that we should look at him,
> nothing in his appearance that we should desire him.
> He was despised and rejected by others;
> a man of suffering and acquainted with infirmity. . . .
> But he was wounded for our transgressions,
> crushed for our iniquities;
> upon him was the punishment that made us whole,
> and by his bruises we are healed. . . .
> He was oppressed, and he was afflicted,
> yet he did not open his mouth;
> like a lamb that is led to the slaughter,
> and like a sheep that before its shearers is silent,
> so he did not open his mouth.
> By a perversion of justice he was taken away.
> (Isa. 53:2–3, 5, 7–8)

Whoever or whatever the original author meant by this text, Christians could hardly avoid interpreting it as referring to the crucified Jesus.

Caesar and Christ

What an odd sort of ruler Second Isaiah described! Such an image certainly ran squarely into conflict in the Greco-Roman world where the "lords" and "saviors" were military victors and emperors who lived in luxury.[11] In the Gospel of John the choice is defined when the crowd that is urging that Jesus be crucified cries out, "We have no king but Caesar" (John 19:15)—imperial Caesar versus the crucified one.

Rome was not a bad empire, as empires go. It brought peace to a good bit of the world, was usually tolerant of local religions, and for the most part left people alone if they paid their taxes and did not rebel. Just as we can understand the Gospels' critique of the Pharisees only if we realize that the Pharisees represented religious faithfulness at its best, so we can understand Christ's implied judgment of Caesar only if we recognize how good an empire Rome provided.

But, like any empire, it was based on military conquest, and it had a luxurious and sometimes decadent court supported by taxing the conquered. Augustine admired the Romans and knew how much he owed their culture. Still, he wrote,

> Is it reasonable and wise to glory in the extent and greatness of the empire when you can in no way prove that there is any real happiness in people perpetually living amid the horrors of war, perpetually wading in blood? Does it matter whether it is the blood of their fellow citizens or the blood of their enemies? It is still human blood, in people perpetually haunted by the bloody spectre of fear and driven by murderous passions. The happiness arising from such conditions is a thing of glass, of mere glittering brittleness. One can never shake off the horrible dread that it may suddenly shiver into fragments.[12]

Nations as we know them rest on blood: the blood of warfare, and sometimes the blood of executed criminals. Christians therefore can never be unquestioningly loyal citizens of any state. For those whose "minds are set on earthly things," "their end is destruction; their god is the belly; and their glory is in their shame. . . . But our citizenship is in heaven" (Phil. 3:19–20).

The unknown author of the Letter to Diognetus, one of the earliest Christian works outside the New Testament, put it this way:

> Christians are distinguished from other people neither by country, nor language, nor the customs which they observe. . . . But, inhabiting Greek as well as barbarian cities . . . they dwell in their own countries, but simply as sojourners. . . . Every foreign land is to them like their native country, and the land of their birth is like a land of strangers.[13]

We encounter the true monarch of such sojourners in the one who enters Jerusalem riding a donkey, and in the book of Revelation's picture of a slaughtered lamb who accomplishes God's triumph.

How could God not be like this if Jesus the Lamb of God "sits on the right hand of the Father"? In spite of the fact that our world seems too often to be under the control of brutal power and cynical corruption, this clause of the creed affirms that we already secretly live in the reign of the one who was crucified. Someday, we also believe, that reign will be more visibly manifest in our world in ways we cannot imagine. Christ "will come again to judge the living and the dead." We really cannot imagine the form of that "coming," but in affirming it we affirm that the powers of this world do not have the last word.

Christians and Violence

At least to some degree, the earliest Christians tried to live out this ideal by rejecting violence. Justin Martyr, writing in the second century, quotes Isaiah's prophecy of the day when people will "beat their swords into plowshares and their spears into pruning hooks; nation shall not lift up sword against nation, neither shall they learn war any more" (Isa. 2:4). As Christians, he then announces,

> We can show you that this has really happened. For a band of twelve men went forth from Jerusalem, and they were common men, not trained in speaking, but by the power of God they testified to every race of humankind that they were sent by Christ to teach to all the Word of God; and now we who once killed each other . . . do not make war on each other.[14]

Justin takes for granted that his readers will know that Christians are pacifists. Indeed, we have no clear evidence that there were any Christian soldiers before 170, and as late as 295 Maximilianus, a Numidian Christian 21 years old, was killed by the proconsul of Africa for refusing military service. "I cannot serve as a soldier," he declared. "I cannot do evil. I am a Christian."[15]

Admittedly the issues are complicated. Roman soldiers usually had to swear allegiance to the emperor and even participate in the imperial cult, and those would be reasons, quite independent of general questions about war and pacifism, for Christians to refuse service. But Maximilianus went to his death, his story indicates, not for such reasons as this, but because he was unwilling to kill people.

In the second century, Clement of Alexandria reminded Christians, "If you enroll yourself as one of God's people, heaven is your country, God your lawgiver. And what are the laws? 'You shall not kill . . . ' "[16] Even the testimony of its critics indicates the pacifism of early Christianity. Celsus, a critic of Christianity who lived a generation later than Clement, demanded of Christians, "If all were to do the same as you . . . the affairs of earth would fall into the hands of the wildest and most lawless barbarians."[17] Christians, evidently, were known to be unwilling to fight to defend the empire.

Such Christian ideals have never entirely disappeared, but they have, since those first centuries, usually represented a minority view. If we tried to live them out, most Christians have concluded, this tough world of ours would just chew us up: the world's bullies would kill us if we resisted nonviolently and steal everything we own if we did not resist at all.

Should we not seek to defeat the Hitlers of this world? Do not the unjustly oppressed at least have the right to resist their oppressors by whatever means are at hand? If good people turn away from violence, then won't bad people end up running everything? Those who oppose violence have to address such questions.

First of all, distinguishing good people from bad, oppressed from oppressors, often turns out to be complicated. Miroslav Volf, a contemporary theologian who grew up in Croatia, points out the problems that arise in the former Yugoslavia.[18] Look back far enough into history, and every group can find reason to claim to be a victim. One could make a similar case with Arab-Israeli conflicts, in Northern Ireland, and in many other places: our violence is justified because of your bombing last week, or the way you treated us a generation ago, or because of that terrible persecution several centuries ago. Furthermore, even when one side is rather clearly "in the right," any violent action against those in the wrong almost inevitably harms innocent bystanders or conscripted soldiers, thereby compromising the originally just cause. The cycle of violence can go on forever.

Or at some point, could it stop? A white South African talked to me about the transforming power of going to a church meeting with black people, after the end of apartheid, and realizing "that they had forgiven us." In the work of the Truth and Reconciliation Commission, that nation made an end to violence part of national policy: those who were willing to confess their deeds in public, however horrible, would not be prosecuted. This sounds like an easy way out for people who had committed appalling acts, but truth has its own power. When those who have lived their lives with authority and privilege have to recount their dreadful acts in detail on national television, their society changes forever. This is not and has not been a perfect solution, and it has not always been carried out consistently. But at least the South Africans have a vision of how violence might end.[19] Jesus offered a similar answer.

> You have heard that it was said, "An eye for an eye and a tooth for a tooth." But I say to you, do not resist an evildoer. But if anyone strikes you on the right cheek, turn the other also; and if anyone wants to sue you and take your coat, give your cloak as well."
>
> (Matt. 5:38–39)

As he died on the cross, Luke tells us, Jesus lived out that injunction, praying for those who were killing him (Luke 23:34).

Could we live that way? Is it only a road to destruction? Consider some examples that challenge our instinct to make our lives easier by ruling out that kind of commitment to nonviolence:

The civil rights struggle in the American South, led by Martin Luther King Jr. and others, and dedicated in Christian faith to peaceful protest and love toward their oppressors, accomplished more social change in America than any other movement in my lifetime.

During World War II the French village of Le Chambon, under the leadership of its pacifist pastor, hid escaping Jews by the thousands and helped them escape throughout the Nazi terror.[20] With very few exceptions, the villagers kept their commitment never to lie and never to use violence, and neither they nor those they helped were killed or imprisoned in large numbers.

When the regime of the unspeakable Ceaucescu was collapsing in Romania, he sent out his army to kill the protesters, but the priests stood at the front of the crowds holding the sacred icons, and the soldiers refused to fire.

Among all the tragedy of the twentieth century, there is this: with Gandhi and then with Martin Luther King, movements that rejected violence had greater political success than such efforts have ever had, throughout history. Can we take some hope from that?

I was meeting with some southern Presbyterian pastors just after American troops had been sent into Kosovo. The situation there had raised hard questions. Could we simply stand by as a whole people began to be murdered? Should we pursue a military policy in which we would try to force guilty rulers to withdraw by killing their innocent subjects? "Well, what we ought to do," one pastor said, "is go in, but unarmed, and led by our civic and religious leaders."

Well, why not? In chapter 3, I proposed that the obedience and love to which Jesus calls us require imagination. Thinking about alternatives to violence makes that particularly clear. If we lack sufficient imagination to envision nonviolent responses that make a difference, then we can find ourselves facing a choice between violence and inaction. It can be hard to judge which would be worse in a given situation. I concede that violence can sometimes be the lesser of these two evils, and that a series of failures of imagination can bring us to the point where we can envision no alternative. But we must concede this hesitantly, for sin leaves us too eager to choose violence as the alternative to inaction, and we need to be clear that such forced choices are always the result of previous sins.

To propose that we cultivate nonviolent imagination is not to invite withdrawal from our political responsibilities but is rather a radically different way in which we might enact those responsibilities. It would seem crazy and certainly be risky in this world of sin. We might get killed—isn't that the ultimate threat of the powers of this world? But Christians are supposed to have a faith in resurrection that frees us from the fear of death. Historians justifiably look back with horror at the religious wars of the seventeenth century and wonder how Christians could kill each other in such numbers in the name of their religion. But we take it for granted that we should kill and be killed in the name of our nations. Christians should at least dream of a time when that too will seem part of a horrible past.

This life, Calvin once wrote, is for Christians full of "contempt, reproaches, and other troubles," yet "we may patiently pass through this life . . . content with this one thing: that our King will never leave us destitute, but will provide for our need until, our warfare ended, we are called to triumph."[21] Holding such a faith requires redefining our "need" and discovering how many luxuries we could live without, as well as planning different kinds of "warfare," and expecting a different kind of "triumph." But, if the crucified Christ is raised from the dead and sits at the right hand of God, then it seems that this is what it means to follow him.

After all, if Christ has united humanity with divinity, then every single human being is through Christ united to God. Dare we risk killing any of them? In his ministry Christ taught those who would follow him to turn the other cheek, to go two miles when a Roman oppressor demands you carry his gear for one mile, to give your coat as well when someone asks for your shirt. Dying on a cross, Christ redeems the guilty from their entrapment in evil and reconciles us all to God. In the triumph of the resurrection, Christ establishes that even those who have the power to kill us are not our lords. In the whole course of his obedience, then, Christ invites us to follow him in love, and offers us eternal life.

But it isn't easy. Resurrection lies on the other side of the cross, and hope follows only on the risks of love. Hans Urs von Balthasar writes with eloquent irony,

> If you have a fire in the house, guard it well in a fireproof hearth. . . . Cover it up, for if even but one spark escapes and you fail to see it, you and everything that is yours will fall victim to the flames. If you have the Lord of the World in you, in your fireproof heart, fence him in well, be careful as you carry him about, lest he begin to make demands on you and you no longer know whither he pushes you. Hold the reins tightly in your hand. Don't let go of the rudder. God is dangerous.[22]

This book began with the invitation to searchers and pilgrims who do not share Christian faith to take a fresh look at Jesus. It is fitting that the book should end with a warning. This Jesus can capture your heart and not let go, and he calls us to a dangerous discipleship. Yet our hearts are restless till they find their rest in God; we seek to make sense of a world that doesn't seem to make sense on its own; we want a way of living that does not keep turning ourselves in on ourselves. When we truly encounter Jesus—incarnate and ministering among us, crucified and resurrected—our fireproof hearts catch fire, and in following him we come to that obedience to God which is perfect freedom, and we begin to find our way home.

A Note on Language

One of the most perplexing problems facing those of us who write about Christian faith today, especially in the United States, concerns language and gender. It's a real dilemma. On the one hand, male language can feel to many women that it excludes them—or worse. If Jesus came "to men of good will," then what about women? If the Bible sometimes calls him "the Son of Man," does that mean he wasn't the son of a woman? For that matter, do we have to keep being reminded that he was a son and not a daughter? If my earthly father beat me up and sexually abused me, then does it really help me understand God's love to call God "Father"?

On the other hand, I believe that in Jesus we come to know who God is more fully than we could in any other way. I also believe that through the Bible we best come to know who Jesus is. How can I then discard language the Bible uses about God or Jesus even when it seems most problematic? If I think that the Bible has a special authority, I can't just pick and choose the parts I like.

I wish I had a clear and dramatic solution to this problem. Instead, I have a series of compromises.

When English translations introduce an element of distinctive "maleness" that isn't present in the Hebrew or Greek, then we ought to get rid of it and get back closer to the original. For example: queens rarely ruled in the ancient Mediterranean world, but, when they did, what they ruled would still be called a "*basileia*." So it seems better to translate *basileia* by the inclusive term "reign" rather than use the traditional translation, "kingdom." I have also usually referred to "monarchs" rather than "kings," though I have also spoken of the "kings" of ancient Israel, where all the monarchs were in fact male.

Christian theology has sometimes adopted a few key concepts from the rich diversity with which the Bible speaks of Jesus and of God. For instance, the New Testament talks about Jesus as "the Son of God" and "the Wisdom of God." "Son" is obviously a male term; "Wisdom," as noted in chapter 2, had feminine connotations. Christian theologians have talked a great deal more about "Son" than about "Wisdom." It seems both faithful to the Bible and sensitive to contemporary concerns to look at "Wisdom" again.

In contrast, I have not found my way around a good many traditionally "male" terms. I wrote drafts of complete chapters using "Offspring of

God" and "Offspring of a Human Being" instead of "Son of God" and "Son of Man," but the results just ended up sounding, to my ear, too self-conscious and distracting. The story of Jesus is just so important that one wants desperately to avoid language that, for whatever reason, gets in the way of telling it most effectively. Ways of avoiding stumbling blocks for some create stumbling blocks for others, and writers have to make their best judgments about which path works best.

"Father" is the hardest case. In the New Testament, Jesus regularly calls God "Father."[1] Most scholars agree that this usage goes back to the historical Jesus. A few New Testament passages use the term "Abba," which may have a more informal meaning, something like "Daddy," but how to translate it best and whether it can be traced back to Jesus himself remain matters of controversy.[2]

What the Bible mostly means to convey by calling God "Father," I am convinced, is that this divine, holy, omnipotent Creator of the universe loves us, cares for us, and forgives us.[3] In terms of traditional cultural stereotypes, this use of "Father" comes closer to evoking a gentle mother than a stern father, a nurturer who gathers her children "together as a hen gathers her brood under her wings" (Matt. 23:37). Yet Jesus did in fact call the one to whom he prayed "Father" rather than "Mother."

In some ways, the best solution would be to translate these terms as "Parent," but "parent" has the crucial weakness that we never use it as a term of address. I never call, "Parent, please, I need your help." Thus such a translation loses the element of personal connection which is so central to what the Bible means by calling God "Father." So I've mostly stayed with "Father," though I've sometimes flagged it (as for instance, "the One Jesus called 'Father' ") in ways that may remind both author and readers of the problems.

Christians ought to use God as the model for what a "father" ought to be, in a way that shows how much all human fathers fall short, rather than taking human fathers as a starting point for our understanding of God,[4] but doing that requires keeping ourselves just a little uncomfortable with the language of God as "Father."

Notes

Introduction: Even His Name Means Salvation

1. Frederick Buechner, *The Hungering Dark* (New York: Seabury Press, 1969), 12–13.
2. For a much more developed presentation of this argument, see Luke Timothy Johnson, *The Real Jesus* (San Francisco: Harper San Francisco, 1997).
3. John Calvin, "Commentary on a Harmony of the Evangelists," trans. William Pringle, vol. 2, *Calvin's Commentaries* (Grand Rapids: Baker Book House, 1989), 16:89, on Luke 8:19.
4. Hans W. Frei, *The Identity of Jesus Christ* (Philadelphia: Fortress Press, 1975), 8.
5. Jack Dean Kingsbury, *Matthew as Story* (Minneapolis: Augsburg Fortress, 1988), 45.
6. Philipp Melanchthon, *Loci Communes Theologici*, trans. Lowell J. Satre, *Melanchthon and Bucer*, ed. Wilhelm Pauck (Philadelphia: Westminster Press, 1969), 21.
7. John Calvin, *Institutes of the Christian Religion* 2.16.5, trans. Ford Lewis Battles (Philadelphia: Westminster Press, 1960), 507, emphasis added.
8. Ibid., 2.15.1–6, 494–503.
9. Ibid. 4.1.9, 1023.

Part 1: Incarnation

1. "The So-called Second Letter of Clement" 1, in *The Apostolic Fathers*, trans. Edgar J. Goodspeed (New York: Harper and Brothers, 1950), 85.
2. Pliny the Younger, *Letters* 10.96, in J. Stevenson, *A New Eusebius* (London: S.P.C.K, 1968), 14.

Chapter 1: Truly God

1. John Calvin, *Commentary on the Epistle to the Colossians* (on Col. 1:15), trans. William Pringle, *Calvin's Commentaries* (Grand Rapids: Baker Book House, 1989), 21:149–50, translation altered.
2. John Calvin, *Congregation on Eternal Election*, in Philip C. Holtrup, *The Bolsec Controversy on Predestination from 1551 to 1555* (Lewiston, Maine: Edwin Mellen, 1993), vol. 1, book 2, 717. Luther makes much the same point:

> Those who want to ascend advantageously to the love and knowledge of God should abandon the human metaphysical rules concerning knowledge of the divinity and apply themselves first to the humanity of Christ. For it is exceedingly godless temerity, where God has humiliated Himself in order to become recognizable, to seek for oneself another way.

Martin Luther, *Lectures on Hebrews* (on Heb. 1:2) trans. Walter A. Hansen, *Luther's Works*, vol. 29 (St. Louis: Concordia Publishing House, 1968), 111, translation altered.

3. The best recent account of the strangeness of this biblical God comes in Walter Brueggemann, *Theology of the Old Testament* (Minneapolis: Augsburg Fortress, 1997).

4. See Dietrich Bonhoeffer, *Letters and Papers from Prison*, trans. Reginald Fuller et al. (New York: Macmillan, 1972), 360; Karl Rahner, "The Concept of Mystery in Catholic Theology," in *Theological Investigations*, vol. 4, trans. Kevin Smyth (Baltimore: Helicon Press, 1966), 36–73.

5. Gregory of Nyssa, *The Life of Moses* 163 (New York: Paulist Press, 1978), 95.

6. Acts of John 88–89, *The Apocryphal Jesus*, ed. J. K. Elliott (Oxford: Oxford University Press, 1996), 57–58.

7. See Franz Rosenzweig, *The Star of Redemption*, trans. William W. Hallo (New York: Holt, Rinehart, and Winston, 1971), 409–10.

8. Aristotle, *Metaphysics* 12.9.1074b20–34, *Introduction to Aristotle*, ed. Richard McKeon (New York: Modern Library, 1947), 291–92.

9. Gregory of Nyssa, *Address on Religious Instruction* 24, trans. Cyril C. Richardson, in *Christology of the Later Fathers*, ed. E. R. Hardy (Philadelphia: Westminster Press, 1954), 301.

It is not true that God lacks all passions. God "has the passion of love" and is therefore "long-suffering, merciful, and full of pity." Origen, *Homilies on Ezekiel* 6.6; quoted in Charles Bigg, *The Christian Platonists of Alexandria* (Oxford: Clarendon Press, 1913), 197.

10. Karl Barth, *Church Dogmatics* 4/1, trans. G. W. Bromiley (Edinburgh: T. & T. Clark, 1956), 159.

11. Thomas F. Torrance, *Preaching Christ Today* (Grand Rapids: Eerdmans, 1994), 55.

Chapter 2: Wisdom, Word, Son

1. "The origin of the doctrine of the incarnation is in a Wisdom Christology." James Dunn, *Christology in the Making* (Grand Rapids: Eerdmans, 1996), 212. See also Raymond Brown, *The Gospel of John I–XII* (Garden City, N.Y.: Doubleday, 1966), 519–24; Eduard Schweizer, "Zur Herkunft der Präexistenzvorstellung bei Paulus," *Evangelische Theologie* 19 (1959): 109.

2. Sirach 24:9; Proverbs 3:19; Wisdom of Solomon 7:12, 7:25–26, 9:1–2; Proverbs 8:15; Wisdom of Solomon 9:18.

3. For a review of positions see Elizabeth A. Johnson, "Wisdom Was Made Flesh and Pitched Her Tent Among Us," in Maryanne Stevens, *Reconstructing the Christ Symbol: Essays in Feminist Christology* (New York: Paulist Press, 1993), 99.

4. See Gerhard von Rad, *Old Testament Theology*, vol. 1 (New York: Harper and Row, 1962), 428; John J. Collins, *Jewish Wisdom in the Hellenistic Age* (Louisville: Westminster John Knox Press, 1997), 2.

5. Wisdom of Solomon 9:18.

6. See Sirach 24:1–34, 39:1–11, Baruch 3:9–4:4.

7. In New Testament texts, most clearly in Colossians 1:16–17 and 2:3, but see also Philippians 2:6–11 and Matthew 11:25–30.

8. See Brown, *The Gospel according to John I–XII*, cxxii–cxxvii, 3–37, 519–24; John Ashton, "The Transformation of Wisdom: A Study of the Prologue of John's Gospel," *New Testament Studies* 32 (1986): 161–86. The range of parallels between what is said of the Word in John 1 and of Wisdom in Jewish texts is extraordinary (with Wisdom references in parentheses):

Pre-existent 1:1 (Proverbs 8:22)
"With God" 1:1 (Proverbs 8:30)

Divine 1:1 (Wisdom of Solomon 7:25–26)
Instrument of creation 1:3 (Proverbs 8:30, 3:19)
Source of life 1:4 (Proverbs 8:35)
Cannot be overcome by darkness 1:5 (Wisdom of Solomon 7:29–30)
Continually comes into the world 1:9 (Wisdom of Solomon 6:13, 7:27)
Rejected by humans 1:10–11 (Baruch 3:20–21)
Creates a relation to God among receptive 1:12–13 (Wisdom of Solomon 7:27)
Lived among humans on earth 1:14 (Baruch 3:37)
Possesses a unique glory 1:14, 18 (Wisdom of Solomon 7:25)
Knows God and makes God known 1:18 (Wisdom of Solomon 8:4, 9:9–10)

Charles H. Talbert, *Reading John* (New York: Crossroad, 1994), 69–70.

9. See for instance Wisdom of Solomon 9:1–2; Sirach 24:3; Philo, *Allegorical Interpretation* 1:65, *Philo*, trans. F. H. Colson and G. H. Whitaker (Cambridge, Mass.: Harvard University Press, 1949), 189; and Philo, *On Dreams* 2:242–45, *Philo*, vol. 5, 551.

10. Heraclitus, frag. 1 and 2, *The Presocratics*, ed. Philip Wheelwright (New York: Odyssey Press, 1966), 69.

11. For a summary, see A. A. Long, *Hellenistic Philosophy*, 2d ed. (Berkeley: University of California Press, 1986), 144–54.

12. Philo, *The Confusion of Tongues* 146, *Philo*, vol. 4, 89.

13. Philo, *Questions and Answers on Genesis* 2.62, *Philo*, supp. vol. 1 (1953), 150.

14. Philo, *Allegorical Interpretation* 1.38, *Philo*, vol. 1, 171; for all of this discussion, see Dunn, *Christology in the Making*, 224–26.

15. Philo, *The Confusion of Tongues* 62, *Philo*, vol. 4, 45.

16. Irenaeus, *Against Heresies* 3.18, *Ante Nicene Fathers*, vol. 1, 446, translation altered.

17. See for instance Athanasius, *On the Incarnation of the Word* 54, *Nicene and Post Nicene Fathers* 2d ser., vol. 4, 65; Origen, *On First Principles* 3.5.6, trans. G. W. Butterworth (New York: Harper and Row, 1966), 242.

18. For example: Justin Martyr, *Dialogue with Trypho* 61, *Ante Nicene Fathers*, vol. 1, 227; Athanasius, *Discourses against the Arians* 1.19, *Nicene and Post Nicene Fathers*, 2d ser., vol. 4, 317; Tertullian, *Against Praxeas* 6, *Ante Nicene Fathers*, vol. 3, 601.

19. J. W. C. Wand, *The Atonement* (London: S.P.C.K., 1963), 83.

20. See for instance Elizabeth Schüssler Fiorenza, *Jesus: Miriam's Child, Sophia's Prophet* (New York: Continuum, 1995); Johnson, "Wisdom Was Made Flesh and Pitched Her Tent Among Us."

21. In the Jewish text Enoch 48:1–7, Son of Man and Wisdom seem to be equated.

22. N. T. Wright, *Jesus and the Victory of God* (Minneapolis: Augsburg Fortress, 1993), 513.

23. Josephus, *The Jewish War* 6.312, *Josephus*, vol. 3, trans. H. St. J. Thackery (Cambridge, Mass.: Harvard University Press, 1957), 467.

24. Oscar Cullmann, *The Christology of the New Testament*, rev. ed. (Philadelphia: Westminster Press, 1959), 155.

25. Irenaeus, *Against Heresies* 3.19, *Ante Nicene Fathers*, vol. 1, 448.

26. Dunn, *Christology in the Making*, 14–15.

27. See the Letter of Alexander, bishop of Alexandria, summarizing the Arian position, in Socrates, *Ecclesiastical History* 1.6, *Nicene and Post Nicene Fathers*, 2d ser., vol. 2, 4.

28. Who had taught the Arians, he demanded, to abandon the worship of the creator, and then worship a creature? Athanasius, *Discourses against the Arians* 2.14 and 3.16, *Nicene and Post Nicene Fathers*, 2d ser., vol. 4, 355 and 402.

29. The Creed of Nicaea, John H. Leith, *Creeds of the Churches*, 3d ed. (Atlanta: John Knox Press, 1982), 30–31.

Chapter 3: Truly Human

1. For accounts, see Irenaeus, *Against Heresies* 1.6.1, *Ante Nicene Fathers*, vol. 1, 324; 1.7.2, 325; 3.16.5, 442; Tertullian, *On the Flesh of Christ* 5, *Ante Nicene Fathers*, vol. 3, 525.

2. Ignatius of Antioch, "To the Smyrnaeans," 4.2, *Early Christian Fathers*, trans. Cyril C. Richardson (Philadelphia: Westminster Press, 1953), 113.

3. Ignatius of Antioch, "To the Trallians" 9, *Early Christian Fathers*, 100. "This is how you can recognize the Spirit of God: every spirit that acknowledges that Jesus Christ came in the flesh is from God" (1 John 4:2).

4. Martin Luther, *Sermons on the Gospel of St. John*, 7th sermon on chapter 1, ed. Jaroslav Pelikan, *Luther's Works*, vol 22 (St. Louis: Concordia Publishing House, 1957), 113.

5. Friedrich Schleiermacher, *The Christian Faith*, trans. H. R. Mackintosh and J. S. Stewart (Edinburgh: T. & T. Clark, 1989), 382.

6. "The tools of his thinking came from local stock; only he made a divinely perfect use of them." Austin Farrer, *Saving Belief* (New York: Morehouse and Barlow, 1965), 71. "The paradigm is Christ's ability to play his part with the mental furniture acquired from his village rabbi." Austin Farrer, *Faith and Speculation* (New York: New York University Press, 1967), 103.

7. These debates took particularly clear form among seventeenth-century Lutherans. For reviews of the issues, see Karl Barth, *Church Dogmatics* 4/1, trans. T. F. Torrance (Edinburgh: T. & T. Clark, 1956), 181–83; Wolfhart Pannenberg, *Systematic Theology* vol. 2, trans. G. W. Bromiley (Grand Rapids: Eerdmans, 1994), 377–79.

8. Karl Rahner, "Dogmatic Reflections on the Knowledge and Self-Consciousness of Christ," *Theological Investigations*, vol. 5, trans. Karl-H. Kruger (Baltimore: Helicon Press, 1966), 193–215.

9. For a particularly powerful account of this, see Feodor Dostoevsky, *The Brothers Karamazov*, book 6, chapter 2, trans. Constance Garnett (New York: W. W. Norton, 1976), 266–91.

10. One of the reasons, I think, why Augustine's *Confessions* is such a profound autobiography is that Augustine is speaking to God and not just to himself.

11. Irenaeus, *Against Heresies*, 3.22.3, *Irenaeus of Lyons*, ed. Robert M. Grant (London: Routledge, 1997), 140.

12. For views along these lines from quite different periods, see Bonaventure, *Commentarii in quatuor libros Sententiarum Petri Lombardi* (Quaracchi edition), vol. 2, 394, 447; Karl Rahner, "Christology within an Evolutionary View of the World," *Theological Investigations*, vol. 5, 157–92.

Chapter 4: The Man Jesus

1. "Of all the doctrines of the church, Christology is the one most used to suppress and exclude women." Elizabeth A. Johnson, *She Who Is: The Mystery of God in Feminist Theological Discourse* (New York: Crossroad, 1992), 151.

2. See Leo Steinberg, *The Sexuality of Christ in Renaissance Art and in Modern Oblivion*, 2d rev. ed. (Chicago: University of Chicago Press, 1996).

3. Krister Stendahl, *Paul among Jews and Gentiles* (Philadelphia: Fortress Press, 1976), 1, 3.

4. "The priest in his ministry represents Christ, especially in the eucharist when he acts in the very person of Christ. The priest in the specific and unique act of presiding at the eucharist is a sacramental sign in and through which the presence of Christ, who was and remains a man, is shown forth. This is in accord with the nature of sacramental signification, which requires that there be a natural resemblance between the sign and the person or thing signified." "Declaration on the Question of the Admission of Women to the Ministerial Priesthood," Congregation for the Doctrine of the Faith, October 15, 1976, quoted in Rosemary Radford Ruether, *Sexism and God-Talk: Toward a Feminist Theology* (Boston: Beacon Press, 1983), 126.

5. Patricia Wilson-Kastner, *Faith, Feminism, and the Christ* (Philadelphia: Fortress Press, 1983), 72.

6. Anselm, "Prayer to St. Paul," *The Prayers and Meditations of St. Saint Anselm*, trans. Benedicta Ward (Harmondsworth: Penguin Books, 1973), 153–56.

7. Julian of Norwich, *Showings* (long text) 58, trans. Edmund Colledge and James Walsh (New York: Paulist Press, 1978), 293–94.

8. See Caroline Walker Bynum, *Jesus as Mother* (Berkeley: University of California Press, 1982), 110–69.

9. "It was suitable," Aquinas wrote (quoting Augustine) "that human liberation should be made manifest in both sexes. Consequently, since it behooved a man, being of the nobler sex, to assume, it was becoming that the liberation of the female sex should be manifested in that man being born of a woman." Thomas Aquinas, *Summa Theologica* 3.31.4, trans. Fathers of the English Dominican Province, vol. 2 (New York: Benzinger Brothers, 1947), 2187–88.

10. See Rosemary Radford Ruether's talk of the "kenosis of patriarchy" in *Sexism and God-Talk*, 137.

Chapter 5: Human *and* Divine

1. Gregory of Nyssa, *Against Eunomius* 12.1, *Nicene and Post Nicene Fathers*, 2d ser., vol. 5, 241.

2. Cyril of Alexandria, *On the Incarnation of the Only Begotten*, quoted in Jaroslav Pelikan, *The Emergence of the Catholic Tradition* (Chicago: University of Chicago Press, 1971), 233.

3. Athanasius, *On the Incarnation of the Word* 9, *Christology of the Later Fathers*, ed. and trans. E. R. Hardy (Philadelphia: Westminster Press, 1954), 63.

4. Gregory of Nazianzus, Oration 30.6, *Nicene and Post Nicene Fathers.*, 2d ser., vol. 7, 311.

5. "Because of his immeasurable love," the Word of God "became what we are in order to make us what he is." Irenaeus, *Against Heresies* 5, pref., trans. Robert M. Grant, *Irenaeus of Lyons* (London: Routledge, 1997), 164. " . . . the Word was made flesh in order . . . that we, partaking of his Spirit, might be deified." Athanasius, *Defence of the Nicene Definition* 3.14, *Nicene and Post-Nicene Fathers*, 2d. ser., vol. 4, 159.

6. J. N. D. Kelly, *Early Christian Doctrines* (London: Adam and Charles Black, 1958), 173–74.

7. "Let us become like Christ, since Christ became like us. Let us become God's for His sake, since He for ours became human. He assumed the worse that He might give us the better; He became poor that we through His poverty might be rich; He took

upon Him the form of a servant that we might receive back our liberty." Gregory of Nazianzus, Oration 1.5, *Nicene and Post Nicene Fathers*, 2nd ser., vol. 7, 203.

8. Supposedly quoting Antony in Athanasius, *Life of Antony* 74, *Nicene and Post Nicene Fathers*, 2d ser., vol. 4, 215.

9. See Aloys Grillmeier, *Christ in Christian Tradition*, vol. 1, trans. John Bowden (Louisville: Westminster John Knox, 1975), 328.

10. "When the flesh suffered, the Word was not external to it, and therefore is the passion said to be His." Athanasius, *Discourses against the Arians* 3.32, *Nicene and Post Nicene Fathers*, 2d ser., vol. 4, 411.

11. Apollinaris, *Letter to the Bishops Exiled at Diocaesarea* 2, quoted in G. L. Prestige, *Fathers and Heretics* (London: S.P.C.K., 1940), 111.

12. See Theodore of Mopsuestia, *Catechetical Homilies* 5.8, quoted in Grillmeier, *Christ in Christian Tradition*, vol. 1, 426.

13. Apollinaris could live with this problem, since he believed that the human spirit has a natural tendency to good, and the body is the only source of human corruption. See Richard A. Norris, *Manhood and Christ* (Oxford: Clarendon Press, 1963), 119.

14. Gregory of Nazianzus, Letter 101, *Nicene and Post-Nicene Fathers*, 2d ser., vol. 7, 441.

15. Ibid., 440.

16. Theodore of Mopsuestia, *Catechetical Homilies* 8.9, quoted in Jaroslav Pelikan, *The Emergence of the Catholic Tradition* (Chicago: University of Chicago Press, 1971), 254.

17. Quoted in Prestige, *Fathers and Heretics*, 115.

18. Ibid.

19. Leith, *Creeds of the Churches*, 35–36, for an alternative translation.

20. "Who knows how God is made flesh and yet remains God? This only faith understands, adoring the Logos in silence." Maximus Confessor, *Ambigua* 5 (PG 91:1057), quoted in Jaroslav Pelikan, "Introduction" to Maximus, *Selected Writings*, ed. George C. Berthold (New York: Paulist Press, 1985), 9.

21. See David S. Yeago, "Jesus of Nazareth and Cosmic Redemption: The Relevance of St. Maximus the Confessor," *Modern Theology* 12 (1996): 167.

22. "It is impossible to listen to the two statements at the same time, Jesus of Nazareth is God's Son and God's Son is Jesus of Nazareth. Here we listen to either the one or the other, or we listen to nothing at all." Karl Barth, *Church Dogmatics* 1/1, trans. T. F. Torrance (Edinburgh: T. & T. Clark), 206.

23. "God Himself in person is the Subject of a real human being and acting. And just because God is the subject of it, this being and acting are real. They are a genuinely and truly human being and acting." Karl Barth, *Church Dogmatics* 1/2, trans. G. T. Thomson and Harold Knight (Edinburgh: T. & T. Clark, 1956), 151. I am indebted throughout this section to conversations over the years with George Hunsinger. See particularly George Hunsinger, "Karl Barth's Christology: Its Basic Chalcedonian Character," *Disruptive Grace* (Grand Rapids: Eerdmans, 2000), 131–47.

Chapter 6: Christmas

1. Roland H. Bainton, *The Martin Luther Christmas Book* (Philadelphia: Westminster Press, 1948), 39–40. Mr. Bainton was the greatest American Luther scholar of his generation, but in this *Christmas Book* he does not cite his sources and may sometimes have interpreted Luther rather freely.

2. Raymond E. Brown, *The Birth of the Messiah* (Garden City, N.Y.: Doubleday, 1977), 575.

3. Bainton, *The Martin Luther Christmas Book*, 30.

4. Barth, *Church Dogmatics* 1/2, 184.

5. The Reformation leader Ulrich Zwingli said that, in showing how the unworthy are part of God's plan, the genealogies contained the essential theology of the Reformation. Brown, *The Birth of the Messiah*, 596.

6. Josephus, *The Jewish War* 6.289, *Josephus*, trans. H. St. J. Thackeray, vol. 3 (Cambridge, Mass.: Harvard University Press, 1958), 261.

7. Josephus, *The Jewish War* 1.659–60, *Ibid.*, vol. 2, 313–14.

8. Rudolf Schnackenburg, *Jesus in the Gospels*, trans. O. C. Dean, Jr. (Louisville: Westminster John Knox, 1995), 77.

9. Richard A. Horsley, *The Liberation of Christmas* (New York: Continuum, 1993), 107–8.

10. Ernesto Cardenal, *The Gospel in Solentiname*, vol. 1, trans. Donald D. Walsh (Maryknoll, N.Y.: Orbis, 1976), 15, 73.

11. Charles H. Talbert, *Reading Luke* (New York: Crossroad, 1982), 190–91.

12. Thucydides, *History of the Peloponnesian War*, trans. R. Crawley (New York: Modern Library, 1951), 331.

13. Sanhedrin 25b, *The Talmud: The Steinsaltz Edition*, vol. 16, trans. David Strauss (New York: Random House, 1998), 115.

14. Bainton, *The Martin Luther Christmas Book*, 38.

Part 2: Ministry

1. John Calvin, "Catechism of the Church of Geneva," *Tracts and Treatises*, vol. 2, trans. Henry Beveridge (Grand Rapids: Eerdmans, 1958), 45.

2. Erich Auerbach, *Mimesis*, trans. Willard R. Trask (Princeton: Princeton University Press, 1953), 40–49.

3. Ched Myers, *Binding the Strong Man* (Maryknoll, N.Y.: Orbis Books, 1990), 123.

Chapter 7: Jesus and the Prophets

1. 1 Maccabees 4:46 and 14:41.

2. Kenan B. Osborne, *The Resurrection of Jesus* (New York: Paulist Press, 1997), 148.

3. Paul Ricoeur, *The Conflict of Interpretations*, trans. Peter McCormick et al. (Evanston, Ill.: Northwestern University Press, 1974), 350.

4. Abraham J. Heschel, *The Prophets*, vol. 1 (New York: Harper and Row, 1962), ix.

5. Ibid., 10.

6. Robert R. Wilson, *Prophecy and Society in Ancient Israel* (Philadelphia: Fortress Press, 1980), 46–47.

7. For instance, Miriam in Exodus 15:20, Deborah in Judges 4:4–7, and Huldah in 2 Kings 22–23 and 2 Chronicles 34–35.

8. Gerhard von Rad, *Old Testament Theology*, vol. 2, trans. G. M. G. Stalker (New York: Harper and Row, 1965), 36.

Chapter 8: Message: The Surprising Reign of God

1. "Reign" or "kingdom" of God was, however, for reasons still mysterious to scholars, a term the Essenes almost never used.

2. For classic statements of each position, see Johannes Weiss, *Jesus' Proclamation of the Kingdom of God*, trans. Richard Hyde Hiers and David Larrimore Holland (Philadelphia:

Fortress Press, 1971) and C. H. Dodd, *The Parables of the Kingdom*, rev. ed. (New York: Charles Scribner's Sons, 1961).

3. Joachim Jeremias, *The Parables of Jesus*, trans. S. H. Hooke (New York: Scribner, 1963), 148.

4. Indiana farmers still like the image, and enjoy singing the old hymn:

> First the blade, and then the ear,
> Then the full corn shall appear:
> Lord of harvest, grant that we
> Wholesome grain and pure may be.

Henry Alford, "Come, Ye Thankful People, Come," *The Presbyterian Hymnal* (Louisville: Westminster John Knox Press, 1990), #551.

5. Jeremias, *The Parables of the Kingdom*, 152, though to my mind Jeremias over-emphasizes continuities.

6. See Jürgen Moltmann, *The Crucified God*, trans. R. A. Wilson and John Bowden (New York: Harper and Row, 1974), 140, though Moltmann at that point puts less emphasis on Jesus' commitment to nonviolence.

7. Most systematically in Martin Werner, *The Formation of Christian Dogma*, trans. S. G. F. Brandon (New York: Harper and Brothers, 1957). Recently N. T. Wright has proposed a quite different solution. Jesus' expectations of the end of the current order of things, he says, were for the destruction of the Jerusalem Temple. Therefore, he wasn't wrong, since the Temple was in fact destroyed in 70 A.D. See N. T. Wright, *Jesus and the Victory of God* (Minneapolis: Fortress Press, 1996). Wright is a brilliant scholar and a devout believer, but I remain puzzled by the sheer oddity of a Christian faith that would make the destruction of the Temple the core of Jesus' message.

8. Dice players, usurers, managers of pigeon races, dealers in Sabbath year produce, shepherds, tax collectors, and toll collectors could not serve as witnesses in trials or be admitted to a Pharisaic gathering. b. Sanhedrin 25b, *The Babylonian Talmud*, Seder Nezikin, vol. 3, trans. Isidore Epstein (London: The Soncino Press, 1935), 148. If a tax collector entered a house, everything in it became unclean. Tohoroth 7.6, *The Mishnah*, trans. Herbert Danby (Oxford: Oxford University Press, 1932), 726.

9. It is indecent to listen to a woman's voice. One must not inquire after a woman's welfare. b. Kiddushim 70a, *The Babylonian Talmud*, Seder Nashim, vol. 4, trans. Isidore Epstein (London: Soncino Press, 1936), 356. "He that eats the bread of the Samaritans is like to one that eats the flesh of swine." Shebiith 8.10, *The Mishnah*, 49.

10. See Jacques Ellul's devastating distinction between the "interesting" and "uninteresting" poor. Jacques Ellul, *Violence* (New York: Seabury Press, 1969), 66–67. Amnesty International is a generally admirable exception in its opposition to injustices from any ideological source—but it is admirable in part because it is so unusual.

11. Washing a guest's feet might have been more natural in Jesus' time, but it was disgraceful for a woman to let down her hair in public—so the scandal, all in all, may have been as great then as now.

12. Martin Luther, *Lectures on Galatians* (1535) (on Gal. 3:19), trans. Jaroslav Pelikan, *Luther's Works*, vol. 27 (St. Louis: Concordia Publishing House, 1964), 314.

13. Martin Luther, "Heidelberg Disputation," trans. Harold J. Grimm, *Luther's Works*, vol. 31 (Philadelphia: Muhlenberg Press, 1957), 57.

14. Plato, *Symposium* 202c–d, trans. Alexander Nehamas and Paul Woodruff (Indianapolis: Hackett Publishing, 1989), 46–47.

15. Alfred North Whitehead, *Process and Reality* (New York: Free Press, 1969), 404.

16. John Calvin, *Institutes of the Christian Religion*, 3.19.4, trans. Ford Lewis Battles (Philadelphia: Westminster Press, 1960), 836.

17. Ibid. 3.19.5, 837.

18. See Walter Brueggemann, *Theology of the Old Testament* (Minneapolis: Fortress Press, 1997), 190.

Chapter 9: Messenger: Who Do You Say that I Am?

1. Dietrich Bonhoeffer, *The Cost of Discipleship*, trans. R. H. Fuller (New York: Macmillan, 1963), 61–63.

2. J. Louis Martyn argues that John's Gospel was written in the context of Christians just having been expelled from Jewish synagogues, so that the issue of alternative places and ways of worship was critical for the author and his readers. See J. Louis Martyn, *History and Theology in the Fourth Gospel* (New York: Harper and Row, 1968), 18–21.

3. See, for instance, Luke 4:31–5:11; Acts 3:1–4:4; 5:12–14; 8:6–8; 13:4–12. For this and what follows, see Charles H. Talbert, *Reading John* (New York: Crossroad, 1992), 104.

4. See Benedicta Ward, *Miracles and the Medieval Mind* (Philadelphia: University of Pennsylvania Press, 1982), 3–20.

5. For a fine set of typical popular stories, see for instance Lucian of Samasota, "The Liar" 11–12, *The Works of Lucian of Samasota*, trans. H. W. Fowler and F. G. Fowler, vol. 3, (Oxford: Clarendon Press, 1905), 235–36.

6. Tacitus, *The Histories* 4.81, trans. Clifford H. Moore, *Tacitus*, vol. 3 (Cambridge, Mass.: Harvard University Press, 1969), 159–60.

7. For this and other points, see Wright, *Jesus and the Victory of God*, 186–96.

8. Augustine, *The City of God* 21.8, trans. Henry Bettenson (Harmondsworth: Penguin Books, 1972), 980.

9. See Thomas F. Tracy, "Divine Action, Created Causes, and Human Freedom," in Thomas F. Tracy, *The God Who Acts* (University Park, Pa.: Pennsylvania State University Press, 1994), 77–102.

Chapter 10: Controversies

1. See Josephus, *Jewish Antiquities* 18.11–16, *Josephus*, vol. 9, trans. Louis H. Feldman (Cambridge, Mass.: Harvard University Press, 1965), 11–13. The shortest definition I know: "The Pharisees were Jews who believed one must keep the purity laws outside of the Temple." Jacob Neusner, *From Politics to Piety* (New York: Ktav Publishing House, 1979), 83.

2. Acts has Paul, himself trained as a Pharisee, describe them as "the strictest party of our religion" (Acts 26:5).

3. They were "the people's party." Joachim Jeremias, *Jerusalem in the Time of Jesus*, trans. C. H. Cone and F. H. Cone (Philadelphia: Fortress Press, 1979), 266.

4. Such distinctions, alas, also appear in the scholarly literature. The well-known New Testament scholar C. K. Barrett defined the issue Jesus posed to his contemporaries as "whether grace or legalism represented the truth about God." C. K. Barrett, *Jesus and the Gospel Tradition* (Philadelphia: Fortress Press, 1968), 67.

5. Karl Barth, *Church Dogmatics* 4/2, trans. G. W. Bromiley (Edinburgh: T. & T. Clark, 1958), 176.

6. John Cotton, "Mr. Cottons Rejoynder," in *The Antinomian Controversy*, ed. David D. Hall (Durham, N.C.: Duke University Press, 1990), 134.

7. John Cotton, *The Way of Life* (London: L. Fawne and S. Gellibrand, 1641), 109, spelling modernized.

Chapter 11: Homosexuality

1. On this whole topic, see Eugene F. Rogers, Jr., *Sexuality and the Christian Body* (Oxford: Blackwell, 1999).

2. See, for instance, George R. Edwards, *Gay/Lesbian Liberation: A Biblical Perspective* (New York: Pilgrim Press, 1984), 64–69.

3. Victor Paul Furnish, "What Does the Bible Say about Homosexuality?" in *Caught in the Crossfire*, ed. Sally B. Geis and Donald E. Messer (Nashville: Abingdon Press, 1994), 60–61.

4. See Richard B. Hays, *The Moral Vision of the New Testament* (San Francisco: Harper San Francisco, 1996), 381.

5. Since I have just argued that the story of Sodom is not about homosexuality, it seemed inappropriate to follow the NRSV in translating *arsenokoitai* as "sodomites." "Men who have sex with other men" seemed as neutral an alternative as I could find.

6. For instance, Plato, *Symposium* 178e–179b, trans. Alexander Nehamas and Paul Woodruff (Indianapolis: Hackett Publishing, 1989), 10. The puzzling exception is Plato, *Laws* 1, 636c, trans. Thomas L. Pangle (New York: Basic Books, 1980), 15.

7. Roman writers on these topics saw lots of different sexual categories. Did a man like women or other men? Adults or boys? Did he prefer being the passive or active partner in the sexual act? Similar questions were posed about women. The categories "heterosexual" and "homosexual" would have seemed simplistic. Bernadette J. Brooten, *Love Between Women* (Chicago: University of Chicago Press, 1996), 242.

8. Hays, *The Moral Vision of the New Testament*, 382–83.

9. See John Boswell, *Christianity, Social Tolerance, and Homosexuality* (Chicago: University of Chicago Press, 1980), 106–8. Here and elsewhere Boswell stated conclusions with more confidence than I can muster, but no one thinking about the topic can ignore his remarkable scholarship.

10. Gerald D. Coleman, *Homosexuality: Catholic Teaching and Pastoral Practice* (New York: Paulist Press, 1995), 65.

11. Stanley Grenz, *Welcoming but Not Affirming* (Louisville: Wesminster John Knox Press, 1998), 62.

12. Margaret Davies, "New Testament Ethics and Ours: Homosexuality and Sexuality in Romans 1:26–27," *Biblical Interpretation* 3 (1995), 318.

13. See Robin Scroggs, *The New Testament and Homosexuality* (Philadelphia: Fortress Press, 1983), 115–18; Victor Paul Furnish, *The Moral Teaching of Paul* (Nashville: Abingdon, 1979), 52–83.

14. See Brooten, *Love Between Women*, 244–45.

15. Augustine, *De Genesi ad Litteram* 10.13.23, *Sancti Aurelii Augustini Operum*, vol. 5 (Paris: Parent-Desbarres, 1836–40), 492.

16. It is sometimes argued that the difference is that people who have remarried after divorce can repent, whereas homosexuals who continue in sexual relations are presumably unrepentant. This argument tends to trivialize the meaning of "repentance," given the form pastoral counselling for divorce and remarriage usually takes. If homosexuals are counselled to lives of celibacy, it would seem appropriate to invite those who have divorced to consider committing themselves to celibacy as well. In any event, the

differences in our practices in these cases have more to do with contemporary social attitudes to divorce and homosexuality than to the biblical passages in question.

17. An analogy to the proper behavior would be Karl Barth's condemnation of Nazism in the 1930s and then refusal to condemn, on theological grounds, Communism in the same tones in the 1950s. German Christians, he said, had found the Nazis a real temptation but were quite clear about the dangers of Communism. So anti-Communism was *not* the critical place to draw the line.

Chapter 12: Preaching

1. See Hughes Oliphant Old, *The Reading and Preaching of the Scriptures in the Worship of the Christian Church*, vol. 2 and 3 (Grand Rapids: Eerdmans, 1998, 1999).

2. I am indebted for my discussion of these sermons to Hughes Oliphant Old, *The Reading and Preaching of the Scriptures in the Worship of the Christian Church*, vol. 1 (Grand Rapids: Eerdmans, 1998).

3. Since Jesus' exposition culminates in the breaking of bread with them in a way that at least evokes the idea of communion, this is the interpretation of Scripture in the context of a worship that includes sacrament.

4. Karl Barth, *Homiletics*, trans. Geoffrey W. Bromiley and Donald E. Daniels (Louisville: Westminster John Knox, 1991), 80.

5. Jean Jacques von Allmen, *Preaching and Congregation*, trans. B. L. Nicholas (Richmond: John Knox Press, 1962), 26.

6. Karl Barth, *The Göttingen Dogmatics*, vol. 1, trans. Geoffrey W. Bromiley (Grand Rapids: Eerdmans, 1991), 71.

7. Ibid., 35.

8. John Calvin, *Institutes of the Christian Religion* 4.3.1, trans. Ford Lewis Battles (Philadelphia: Westminster Press, 1960), 1054. This seems a good occasion for leaving male nouns and pronouns in place!

9. John Calvin, from a sermon on Job, cited in Peter Adam, *Speaking God's Words* (Downers Grove, IL: InterVarsity Press, 1996), 132.

10. Calvin, *Institutes of the Christian Religion* 1.9.3, 95.

Part 3: The Cross

1. "To state the matter somewhat provocatively, one could call the Gospels passion narratives with extended introductions." Martin Kähler, *The So-Called Historical Jesus and the Historic, Kerygmatic Christ*, trans. Carl E. Braaten (Philadelphia: Fortress Press, 1964), 80.

2. Jürgen Moltmann, *The Crucified God*, trans. R. A. Wilson and John Bowden (New York: Harper and Row, 1974), 1–6.

3. Walter Brueggemann, "Editor's Foreword," Charles B. Cousar, *A Theology of the Cross* (Minneapolis: Fortress Press, 1990), viii.

4. See, for instance, Rita Nakashima Brock, in *Christianity, Patriarchy and Abuse*, ed. Joanne Carlson Brown and Carole R. Bohn (New York: Pilgrim Press, 1989), 4.

5. Joanne Carlson Brown and Rebecca Parker, "For God So Loved the World?" in ibid., 2.

6. Martin Luther King, Jr., "Letter from Birmingham Jail," *A Testament of Hope*, ed. James Melvin Washington (San Francisco: Harper, 1986), 300.

7. John Calvin, *Commentary on the Epistle of St. Paul to the Galatians* (on Gal. 2:21),

trans. William Pringle, *Calvin's Commentaries* (Grand Rapids: Baker Book House, 1989), vol. 21, 77.

8. *Book of Confessions*, Presbyterian Church (U.S.A.), 9.09.

Chapter 13: The Way to the Cross in the Passion Narratives

1. John Howard Yoder, *The Politics of Jesus* (Grand Rapids: Eerdmans, 1972), 129.

2. For a review of options, see Ched Myers, *Binding the Strong Man* (Maryknoll, N.Y.: Orbis, 1988), 325.

3. See Ibid., 366; Vincent Taylor, *The Gospel according to St. Mark* (New York: St. Martin's, 1963), 552.

4. Raymond E. Brown, *The Death of the Messiah* (New York: Doubleday, 1994), 34–35.

5. I am thinking of the logic of the story as the Gospel presents it, not making a historical claim about what Pilate may have written. But see Nils A. Dahl, *The Crucified Messiah* (Minneapolis: Augsburg, 1974), 23.

6. Helmut Koester, "Apocryphal and Canonical Gospels," *Harvard Theological Review* 73 (1980): 127; John Dominic Crossan, *The Cross that Spoke* (San Francisco: Harper and Row, 1988), 405.

Chapter 14: The Lord's Supper

1. See Robert M. Fowler, *Loaves and Fishes: The Function of the Feeding Stories in the Gospel of Mark* (Chico, Calif.: Scholars Press, 1981).

2. The image of this future banquet regularly appears in Jesus' parables: see, for instance, Luke 12:35–40; Matt. 25:10; Matt. 22:1–10.

3. "Of the Redeemer in the fullness of His offered Self, and work and life and death, perpetually accepted by the Father in the world to come." Dom Gregory Dix, *The Shape of the Liturgy* (New York: Seabury Press, 1982), 243.

4. Rabbi Gamaliel on Exodus 13:8, quoted in Horton Davies, *Bread of Life and Cup of Joy* (Grand Rapids: Eerdmans, 1993), 2.

5. C. H. Dodd, *The Apostolic Preaching and Its Development* (London: Hodder and Stoughton, 1936), 234–35.

6. Thomas Aquinas, *Summa Theologica* 3.60.3, trans. Fathers of the English Dominican Province (Westminster, Md.: Christian Classics, 1981), 2341.

7. Quoted in Walter Kasper, *Theology and Church* (New York: Crossroad, 1989), 182.

8. See Ignatius, "To the Smyrneans" 7.1, *Early Christian Fathers*, trans. Cyril C. Richardson (New York: Macmillan, 1970), 114; Justin Martyr, *First Apology* 66, Ibid., 286.

9. John Calvin, *Institutes of the Christian Religion* 4.17.32, trans. Ford Lewis Battles (Philadelphia: Westminster Press, 1960), 1403.

10. See Edward Schillebeeckx, *The Eucharist*, trans. N. D. Smith (New York: Sheed and Ward, 1968); "Transubstantiation, Transfiguration, Transignification," *Worship* 40 (1966): 334; Karl Rahner, *Theological Investigations*, vol. 4, trans. Kevin Smyth (Baltimore: Helicon Press, 1966), 287, 297, 303.

11. Joseph M. Power, *Eucharistic Theology* (New York: Herder and Herder, 1967), 177.

12. Wolfhart Pannenberg, *Systematic Theology*, vol. 3, trans. Geoffrey W. Bromiley (Grand Rapids: Eerdmans, 1998), 299. The American Lutheran theologian Robert

Jenson emphasizes thinking about how persons are present in a way analogous to the Catholic Schillebeeckx. See Robert W. Jenson, "The Supper," in Carl E. Braaten and Robert W. Jenson, *Christian Dogmatics*, vol. 2 (Philadelphia: Fortress Press, 1984), 359.

13. Didache 9.4, Richardson, *Early Christian Fathers*, 175, translation revised.

14. Augustine, Sermon 227, *Sermons on the Liturgical Seasons*, trans. Mary Sarah Muldowney (New York: Fathers of the Church, 1959), 196.

15. Calvin, *Institutes* 4.17.41, 1418.

16. "If Christ gives himself over to us in the bread and the cup, then crumbs and spills are part of the humiliation he assumes, and if he makes us brothers and sisters in the cup, then sharing one another's human messiness belongs to the humiliation *we* thereby assume." Robert W. Jenson, "The Supper," in Braaten and Jenson, *Christian Dogmatics*, vol. 2, 344.

The spirit of inclusiveness has led some to welcome the unbaptized to communion. It seems to me that, when those who want to share in life in Christ but have not been baptized come forward, the most natural thing would be, not to give them communion, but to baptize them.

17. Cyprian, "On Works and Alms," Treatise 8.15, *Ante Nicene Fathers*, vol. 5, 480.

18. Ignatius, "To the Smyrneans" 6.2, Richardson, *Early Christian Fathers*, 114.

19. *Baptism, Eucharist, and Ministry*, Faith and Order Paper No. 111 (Geneva: World Council of Churches, 1982), 15.

Chapter 15: Solidarity

1. Elizabeth A. Johnson, *She Who Is* (New York: Crossroad, 1993), 158.

2. Calvin, *Institutes of the Christian Religion* 2.16.12, 518.

3. Alfred North Whitehead, *Process and Reality* (New York: Free Press, 1969), 413.

4. Aquinas, *Summa Theologica* 3.46.11, 2270.

5. Jacquelyn Grant, "Come to My Help, Lord, for I'm in Trouble," in Maryanne Stevens, *Reconstructing the Christ Symbol* (New York: Paulist Press, 1994), 67.

6. Rowan Williams, *Resurrection* (Harrisburg, Pa.: Morehouse Publishing, 1994), 18.

7. For probably the earliest reference, see Clement of Alexandria, *Miscellanies* 6.6, *Ante Nicene Fathers*, vol. 2, 491.

8. See, for instance, Aquinas, *Summa Theologica* 3.52.2, 4–6, 8, 2297–2302.

9. Calvin, *Institutes of the Christian Religion* 2.16.11, 516. A few medieval thinkers, like Nicholas of Cusa, had already proposed this interpretation.

10. Ibid. 2.16.10, 516.

11. Hans Urs von Balthasar, *The Von Balthasar Reader*, ed. Medard Kehl and Werner Löser, trans. Robert J. Daly and Fred Lawrence (Edinburgh: T. & T. Clark, 1985), 153.

12. Peter Abelard, *Commentary on Romans* 3:26; *A Scholastic Miscellany*, ed. and trans. Eugene R. Fairweather (New York: Macmillan, 1970), 283.

13. Ibid., 284.

Chapter 16: Priest and Sacrifice

1. "The stench of blood and of roasting flesh can hardly have been drowned by the smoke of incense; nor can the cries of traders, or the uplifted voices of priests and pilgrims at prayer, have drowned the screeching of the beasts as they had their throats cut, and their blood scattered in the time-honored manner." A. N. Wilson, *Jesus: A Life* (New York: Norton, 1992), 174.

2. Calvin, *Institutes of the Christian Religion* 2.15.6, 501–2. See also 2.12.3, 466, and John Calvin, *Commentary on Isaiah* (Isaiah 53:6), trans. William Pringle, *Calvin's Commentaries*, vol. 8 (Grand Rapids: Baker Book House, 1989), 118.

3. Walter Brueggemann, *Theology of the Old Testament* (Minneapolis: Augsburg Fortress, 1997), 667.

4. Jacob Milgrom, *Leviticus 1–16* (New York: Doubleday, 1991), 175. See also Roland de Vaux, *Studies in Old Testament Sacrifice* (Cardiff: University of Wales Press, 1964), 37–38.

5. Milgrom, *Leviticus 1–16*, 253.

6. See Paul Ricoeur, *The Symbolism of Evil*, trans. Emerson Buchanan (Boston: Beacon Press, 1967), 25–26.

7. Rowan Williams, "Between the Cherubim: The Empty Tomb and the Empty Throne," in Gavin D'Costa, *Resurrection Reconsidered* (Oxford: Oneworld, 1996), 90. I am following Williams in his contemporary reading of this text. Bruce Marshall persuades me that for the ancient Israelites God *was* present there, without dialectic between is and is not.

8. Baruch Levine, *The JPS Torah Commentary: Leviticus* (Philadelphia: Jewish Publication Society, 1989), xxiv–xxv.

9. 4 Maccabees 17:20–22.

10. Anselm, *Cur Deus Homo*, *Basic Writings*, trans. S. N. Deane (LaSalle, Ill.: Open Court, 1966), 202.

11. Ibid., 227.

Chapter 17: Reconciliation

1. Peter Abelard, *Exposition of the Epistle to the Romans*, in Eugene R. Fairweather, *A Scholastic Miscellany* (Philadelphia: Westminster Press, 1956), 283.

2. Rita Nakashima Brock, "And a Little Child Will Lead Us: Christology and Child Abuse," in *Christianity, Patriarchy, and Abuse*, ed. Joanne Carlson Brown and Carole R. Bohn (New York: Pilgrim Press, 1989), 53.

3. Calvin, *Institutes of the Christian Religion* 2.16.4, 506.

4. "There is a cross in God before the wood is seen upon Calvary. . . . It is as if there were a cross unseen, standing on its undiscovered hill, far back in the ages, out of which were sounding always, just the same deep voice of suffering love and patience, that was heard by mortal ears from the sacred hill of Calvary." Horace Bushnell, *The Vicarious Sacrifice* (New York: Charles Scribner, 1866), 64.

5. Aquinas, *Summa Theologica* 3.47.3 ad 1, 2274.

6. Origen, *Homilies on Jeremiah* 18.6, quoted in Frances M. Young, *Sacrifice and the Death of Christ* (Philadelphia: Westminster Press, 1978), 74–75.

7. John Calvin, *Commentary on a Harmony of the Evangelists* (on Matt. 27:45), trans. William Pringle, *Calvin's Commentaries*, vol. 17 (Grand Rapids: Baker Books, 1989), 316–17.

8. Calvin, *Institutes* 2.16.4, 506.

9. John Calvin, *Commentaries on the Epistles of Paul the Apostle to the Corinthians* (on 1 Cor. 3:2), *Calvin's Commentaries* vol. 20, trans. William Pringle (Grand Rapids: Baker Books, 1989), 122. See also *Institutes* 1.17.12, 226 and 2.16.2–3, 504–506.

10. Calvin, *Institutes* 2.16.2, 504.

11. "Just as truly as sin is real . . . so also God's anger is real. . . . But the wrath of God is not the ultimate reality; it is the divine reality which corresponds to sin. But it

is not the essential reality of God. In Himself God is love." Emil Brunner, *The Mediator*, trans. Olive Wyon (Philadelphia: Westminster Press, 1947), 519.

12. Karl Barth, *Church Dogmatics*, 2/2, trans. G. W. Bromiley et al. (Edinburgh: T. & T. Clark, 1957), 164–65.

13. Barth, *Church Dogmatics*, 1/1, trans. G. T. Thomson and Harold Knight (Edinburgh: T. & T. Clark, 1956), 152, translation revised.

14. Gregory of Nazianzus, Theological Oration 30.5, *Nicene and Post Nicene Fathers*, 2d ser., vol. 7, 311.

15. John Calvin, *Commentary on the Gospel according to John* (on John 12:27), *Calvin's Commentaries*, vol. 18, trans. William Pringle (Grand Rapids: Baker Books, 1989), 32.

Chapter 18: Redemption

1. The contrast between "many" and "all" has occasioned a long debate in the history of Christian thought.

2. See Irenaeus, *Against Heresies* 3.21.10, *Ante Nicene Fathers*, vol. 1, 454.

3. Martin Luther, *Commentary on Galatians*, trans. Fleming H. Revell (Grand Rapids: Baker, 1988), 180.

4. Ibid., 184.

5. Ibid., 187.

6. See Elaine Pagels, *The Origin of Satan* (New York: Random House, 1995), 35–62.

7. Origen, *Der Kommentar zum Evangelium nach Mattäus*, trans. Hermann J. Voght, vol. 2 (Stuttgart: Anton Hiersemann, 1990), 179.

8. Gregory of Nyssa, *Catechetical Oration*, in *The Later Christian Fathers*, trans. Henry Bettenson (London: Oxford University Press, 1970), 142.

9. Ibid.

10. Gregory of Nazianzus, Oration 45.22, *Nicene and Post Nicene Fathers*, 2d ser., vol. 7, 431.

11. For the classic defense of this model, see Gustaf Aulén, *Christus Victor* (New York: Macmillan, 1969).

12. See Miroslav Volf, *Exclusion and Embrace* (Nashville: Abingdon Press, 1996).

13. Irenaeus, *Against Heresies* 5.1.1, *Ante Nicene Fathers*, vol. 1, 527.

14. Augustine, *On the Trinity* 13.4.17, *Nicene and Post Nicene Fathers*, 1st ser., vol. 3, 176.

15. Aquinas, *Summa Theologica* 3.41.1, 2235.

"Here we have a most pleasing vision not only of communion but of a blessed struggle and victory and salvation and redemption. Christ is God and man in one person. He has neither sinned nor died, and is not condemned, and he cannot sin, die, or be condemned; his righteousness, life, and salvation are unconquerable, eternal, omnipotent. By the wedding ring of faith he shares in the sins, death, and pains of hell which are his bride's. As a matter of fact, he makes them his own and acts as if they were his own and as if he himself had sinned; he suffered, died, and descended into hell that he might overcome them all. Now since it was such a one who did all this, and death and hell could not swallow him up, these were necessarily swallowed up by him in a mighty duel; for his righteousness is greater than the sins of all men, his life stronger than death, his salvation more invincible than hell." Martin Luther, *The Freedom of a Christian*, trans. W. A. Lambert, *Three Treatises* (Philadelphia: Fortress Press, 1970), 286–87.

16. "The cross is not a recipe for resurrection. Suffering is not a tool to make people come around nor a good in itself. But the kind of faithfulness that is willing to accept

evident defeat rather than complicity with evil is by virtue of its conformity with what happens to God when he works among us, aligned with the ultimate triumph of the Lamb." John Howard Yoder, *The Politics of Jesus* (Grand Rapids: Eerdmans, 1994), 238.

Chapter 19: Visiting Prisoners

1. Eric Schlosser, "The Prison-Industrial Complex," *Atlantic Monthly* 282 (December 1998): 52. Even the early twentieth-century figures represented a dramatic increase from earlier times. "Nobody in the colonial period had yet advanced the idea that it was good for the soul, and conducive to reform, to segregate people who committed crimes, and keep them behind bars." Indeed, one scholar has found only nineteen cases of people sent to jail in New York between 1691 and 1776, and there were no federal prisons at all (except for soldiers and sailors) until 1891. Lawrence M. Friedman, *Crime and Punishment in American History* (New York: Basic Books, 1993), 48, 269.

2. Elliott Currie, *Crime and Punishment in America* (New York: Henry Holt and Company, 1998), 15.

3. Schlosser, "The Prison-Industrial Complex," 52.

4. Currie, *Crime and Punishment in America*, 13.

5. Norval Morris, "The Contemporary Prison," *The Oxford History of the Prison*, ed. Norval Morris and David J. Rothman (Oxford: Oxford University Press, 1995), 215.

Other examples: We celebrate our currently low rates of unemployment, but, in 1996, while the "official" rate of unemployment among men was 5.4 percent, if the 1.1 million men in state or federal prison had been counted in, it would have risen to 6.9 percent. In other words, about a fourth of American males not holding down jobs were in prison. A parallel analysis increases the unemployment rate among black males from 11 percent to nearly 18 percent. The largest number of mentally ill Americans in any sort of institution are in jails and prisons. (Unemployment data from *Economic Report of the President*, 1997; prison statistics from Bureau of Justice Statistics, *Prisoners in 1996*. Cited in Currie, *Crime and Punishment in America*, 33.)

6. Currie, *Crime and Punishment in America*, 29, 57.

7. In 1991 one-third of federal inmates were getting substance-abuse treatment. By 1997, though the percentage of inmates with substance-abuse problems was clearly higher, only 15 percent were receiving such treatment—this largely because of cutbacks in programs, made in spite of the fact that those who participate in them are much less likely to commit crimes after their release—73 percent less likely to be rearrested in the first six months, for instance. Jonathan Alter, "The Buzz on Drugs," *Newsweek*, September 6, 1999, 26–27.

8. For a rich discussion of biblical views of imprisonment, see Lee Griffith, *The Fall of the Prison* (Grand Rapids: Eerdmans, 1993).

9. Timothy Gorringe, *God's Just Vengeance* (Cambridge: Cambridge University Press, 1996), 3–4.

10. Martin Luther, *Sermons on the Gospel of St. John*, ch. 1, 12th sermon, trans. Jaroslav Pelikan, *Luther's Works* vol. 22 (St. Louis: Concordia Publishing House, 1957), 167.

11. Martin Luther, *Lectures on Galatians* (on Gal. 3:13), trans. Jaroslav Pelikan, *Luther's Works*, vol. 26 (St. Louis: Concordia Publishing House, 1963), 280.

12. Karl Barth, *Church Dogmatics* 2/2, trans. G. W. Bromiley et al. (Edinburgh: T. & T. Clark, 1957), 492; 4/1, trans. G. W. Bromiley and T. F. Torrance (Edinburgh: T. & T. Clark, 1956), 258.

13. John Milbank, *Theology and Social Theory* (Oxford: Basil Blackwell, 1993), 421–22.

14. See, for instance, Stanley Hauerwas, *Against the Nations* (Minneapolis: Winston Press, 1985), 11–12.

15. Charles W. Colson, *Against the Night* (Ann Arbor: Servant Publications, 1989), 188–90.

16. Charles W. Colson, *Kingdoms in Conflict* (Grand Rapids: Zondervan, 1989), 465.

17. Will D. Campbell and James Y. Holloway, "*. . . and the criminals with him . . .* " (New York: Paulist Press, 1973), 148.

18. I am grateful to Scott M. Brannon for conversations which have shaped this chapter in a number of ways.

Part 4: Resurrection

1. Kurt Marti, *Leichenrede*, quoted in Jan Milič Lochman, *The Faith We Confess*, trans. David Lewis (Philadelphia: Fortress Press, 1984), 247.

Chapter 20: Hopes of Resurrection

1. Wolfhart Pannenberg, *Systematic Theology*, vol. 2, trans. Geoffrey W. Bromiley (Grand Rapids: Eerdmans, 1994), 346–47.

2. The writer of 1 Enoch, who thinks of Sadducees as sinners, has them declare:

> As we die, so die the righteous,
> And what benefit do they reap for their deeds?
> Before, even as we, so do they die in grief and darkness.
> (1 Enoch 102:6–7)

The Essenes apparently expected some kind of resurrection, but the references in the Dead Sea Scrolls to resurrection are skimpy and cryptic. See for instance 4Q521, "A Messianic Apocalypse," and 1QH 3.19–23, "Thanksgiving Hymn 2," in Geza Vermes, *The Complete Dead Sea Scrolls in English* (New York: Allen Lane, Penguin Press, 1997), 391–92, 245.

3. See D. S. Russell, *The Method and Message of Jewish Apocalyptic* (Philadelphia: Westminster Press, 1964), 369–70.

4. See for instance 4 Maccabees 14:5, where the seven brave brothers who died under torture are described, not as awaiting resurrection, but "as though running on the highway to immortality."

5. See Pheme Perkins, *Resurrection: New Testament Witness and Contemporary Reflection* (Garden City, N.Y.: Doubleday, 1984), 37.

6. See, for instance, 1 Enoch 104:2; 4 Ezra 7:78; 2 Baruch 51:10; 4 Maccabees 17:4–6.

7. 2 Baruch 51:10; see Russell, *Method and Message*, 378.

8. 2 Baruch 56:2, 37:2, 64:2–3; Russell, *Method and Message*, 379.

Chapter 21: What Happened When Jesus Was Raised?

1. Hermann Samuel Reimarus, *Fragments*, trans. Ralph S. Fraser (Philadelphia: Fortress Press, 1970), 245.

2. For a recent variant, see John Dominic Crossan, *Who Killed Jesus?* (San Francisco: Harper San Francisco, 1994), chapter 6.

3. "For if Jesus Christ is not risen . . . the whole Christian church is based on an illusion and the whole of what is called Christianity is one huge piece of moral sentimentalism, to which we cannot say farewell soon enough." Karl Barth, *The Knowledge of God and the Service of God according to the Teaching of the Reformation*, trans. J. L. M. Haire and Ian Henderson (London: Hodder and Stoughton, 1938), 87.

4. "Christ . . . meets us in the word of preaching and nowhere else. The faith of Easter is just this—faith in the word of preaching." Rudolf Bultmann, "New Testament and Mythology," in Hans Werner Bartsch, ed., *Kerygma and Myth* (New York: Harper Torchbooks, 1961), 41.

5. See, for instance, John Dominic Crossan, *The Historical Jesus* (San Francisco: Harper San Francisco, 1991), 404; Sallie McFague, *Models of God* (Philadelphia: Fortress Press, 1987), 59.

6. Stephen T. Davis, "'Seeing' the Risen Jesus," in Stephen T. Davis, ed., *The Resurrection* (New York: Oxford University Press, 1997), 128.

7. John Calvin, *Institutes of the Christian Religion* 3.25.8, trans. Ford Lewis Battles (Philadelphia: Westminster Press, 1960), 1002.

8. In the Book of Tobit, which would have been familiar to the authors of the New Testament, an angel appears to eat and drink, but this turns out to have been a vision (Tobit 12:19).

9. See Karl Barth, *Church Dogmatics*, 3/2, trans. Harold Knight et al. (Edinburgh: T. & T. Clark, 1960), 452; 4/1, trans. G. W. Bromiley (Edinburgh: T. & T. Clark, 1956), 334–35.

10. Rowan Williams, "Between the Cherubim: The Empty Tomb and the Empty Throne," in Gavin d'Costa, ed., *Resurrection Reconsidered* (Oxford: Oneworld, 1996), 91. See also Rowan Williams, *Resurrection* (Harrisburg, Pa.: Morehouse Publishing, 1994), 5, 79–80, 117, and Joachim Jeremias, *New Testament Theology*, vol. 1 trans. John Bowden (New York: Charles Scribner's Sons, 1971), 303.

11. Ignatius of Antioch, Letter to the Ephesians 19.1, *Ante Nicene Fathers*, vol. 1, 57.

12. Resurrection "on the third day" might be an exception. More of that later.

13. One of the oddities of scholarly discussion of these matters is that many authors treat the resurrection narratives in Luke's Gospel as obviously legends but Luke's descriptions in the book of Acts of Paul's experience of the risen Jesus as obviously historical.

Paul speaks in this way of his own experience in Galatians 1:15 and 1 Corinthians 9:1. In 1 Corinthians 15 he seems to be quoting a traditional formula of how Christ "was seen," first by Peter, then by various groups of others, and last of all by Paul himself. 1 Corinthians 15:3–5 uses a number of phrases ("sins" in the plural, "in accordance with the Scriptures," "the twelve") that appear nowhere else in Paul, so he seems here to be quoting an earlier formula, which would go back to the earliest Christians. The Greek verb form can mean "was seen," "allowed himself to be seen," or "was made visible by God" (it was a way of avoiding the direct use of the divine name).

14. Other passages that might hint of a heavenly luminousness: Acts 7:55; Mark 9:3; Rev. 1:13–16.

15. See Matthew's reference to a rumor alive "to this very day" that the disciples had stolen Jesus' body (28:15).

16. See Shebuoth 4.1, *The Mishnah*, trans. Herbert Danby (Oxford: Oxford University Press, 1933), 413. An early critic of Christianity dismissed the resurrection as based on the testimony of "hysterical females." Origen, *Contra Celsum*, 2.55, trans. Henry Chadwick (Cambridge: Cambridge University Press, 1953), 109–10.

17. There would certainly have been symbolic reasons for imagining a resurrection "on the third day." Hosea 6:2 speaks of God "raising up" the nation on the third day. Jonah was delivered from the whale on the third day (Jonah 1:17), and Matthew 12:39 and Luke 11:29 both refer to Jesus fulfilling the sign of Jonah. See Thorwald Lorenzen, *Resurrection and Discipleship* (Maryknoll, N.Y.: Orbis Books, 1995), 267. But I'm not sure all this quite explains the very early custom of worship on the first day of the week. See Williams, *Resurrection*, 105. Much has been made in the scholarly literature of Hosea 6:2, but it is never clearly cited in the New Testament.

18. See David Hume, "Of Miracles," *An Inquiry concerning Human Understanding* (Indianapolis: Library of Liberal Arts, 1955), 123.

Chapter 22: Bodily Resurrection and Eternal Life

1. Plato, *Phaedo* 64a, trans. David Gallop (Oxford: Oxford University Press, 1993), 9.

2. Seneca, *Ad Lucilium Epistulae Morales* 24.18, trans. Richard M. Gummere (New York: G. P. Putnam's Sons, 1917), 177. Aristotle's conviction that the body was important to full humanity represented a minority view among classical philosophers.

3. Tertullian, *On the Resurrection of the Flesh* 9, *Ante Nicene Fathers*, vol. 3, 551–52.

4. Athenagoras, *The Resurrection of the Dead* 15, *Ante Nicene Fathers*, vol. 2, 157, translation altered. See also Irenaeus, *Against Heresies* 5.6.1, *Ante Nicene Fathers*, vol. 1.

5. Augustine, *Letter* 148.5.16, *Nicene and Post-Nicene Fathers*, 1st ser., vol. 1, 503.

6. Gregory of Nyssa, "On the Soul and the Resurrection," *Ascetical Works*, trans. Virginia Woods (Washington: Catholic University of America Press, 1967), 261, translation modified.

7. There are suggestive passages—"I the Lord do not change" (Mal. 3:6); "The Lord is the everlasting God" (Isa. 40:28); "From everlasting to everlasting you are God . . . for a thousand years in your sight are like yesterday" (Ps. 90:4)—but there is a "very serious shortage within the Bible of the kind of actual statement about 'time' or 'eternity' which could form a sufficient basis for a Christian philosophical-theological view of time." James Barr, *Biblical Words for Time* (London: SCM Press, 1962), 138.

8. Plotinus, *Enneads* 3.7.3, trans. Stephen MacKenna (Boston: Charles T. Branford [no date]), 99.

9. Thomas Aquinas, *Summa contra gentiles* 1.66, *On the Truth of the Catholic Faith*, vol. 1, trans. Anton C. Pegis (Garden City, N.Y.: Image Books, 1955), 219.

10. In particular, Martin Heidegger, *Being and Time*, trans. John Macquarrie and Edward Robinson (New York: Harper and Row, 1962); and *The Concept of Time*, trans. William McNeill (Oxford: Basil Blackwell, 1992); and book 11 of Augustine's *Confessions*.

11. Karl Barth, *Church Dogmatics*, 2/1, trans. T. H. L. Parker et al. (Edinburgh: T. & T. Clark, 1957), 612.

12. T. S. Eliot, *Four Quartets*, *The Complete Poems and Plays* (New York: Harcourt, Brace, and World, 1971), 136.

13. Gregory of Nyssa, *On the Soul and the Resurrection*, *Ascetical Works*, 269–70.

14. Ibid., 263.

15. Augustine, *The City of God* 22.26, trans. Henry Bettenson (Harmondsworth: Penguin Books, 1972), 1079.

16. Karl Barth, *Church Dogmatics*, 3/3, trans. G. W. Bromiley and R. J. Ehrlich (Edinburgh: T. & T. Clark, 1960), 90.

17. Gerard Manley Hopkins, "That Nature Is a Heraclitean Fire, and of the Comfort of the Resurrection," *Poems and Prose* (London: Penguin Books, 1985), 66.

Chapter 23: The Resurrection Narratives in the Gospels

1. To be precise: "Feed my sheep" twice, and "Feed my lambs" once.
2. See Hans Urs von Balthasar, *Mysterium Paschale*, trans. Aidan Nichols (Edinburgh: T. & T. Clark, 1990), 260–61.
3. Raymond E. Brown, *The Gospel according to John XIII–XXI* (Garden City, N.Y.: Doubleday, 1970), 1049. I followed Brown's argument here in my earlier book, *Narratives of a Vulnerable God.*

Chapter 24: Baptism

1. Ignatius, *Letter to the Ephesians* 18.2, Cyril C. Richardson, *Early Christian Fathers* (New York: Macmillan, 1960), 93.
2. Athanasius, *Against the Arians* 1.12.47, *Nicene and Post Nicene Fathers*, 2d ser., vol. 4, 333.
3. See for instance Tertullian, *On Baptism* 4, *Ante Nicene Fathers*, vol. 3, 670; Ambrose, *On the Mysteries* 3.8, *Nicene and Post Nicene Fathers*, 2d ser., vol. 10, 318.
4. Ambrose, *Of the Holy Spirit* 1.6.76, *Nicene and Post Nicene Fathers*, 2d ser., vol. 10, 103.
5. See, for instance, Thomas Aquinas, *Summa Theologica* 3.66.7, trans. Fathers of the English Dominican Province (Westminster, Md.: Christian Classics, 1981), 2380; Martin Luther, *Large Catechism* 226, trans. John Nicholas Lenker (Minneapolis: Augsburg Publishing, 1935), 164.
6. My friend David Willis taught me, with characteristic passion, these points about baptism.
7. The issues are laid out with characteristic clarity by Robert W. Jenson, "Baptism," in Carl E. Braaten and Robert W. Jenson, *Christian Dogmatics*, vol. 2 (Philadelphia: Fortress Press, 1984), vol. 2, 318.
8. Karl Barth, *The Teaching of the Church Regarding Baptism*, trans. Ernest A. Payne (London: S.C.M., 1948), 40–41.
9. See Wolfhart Pannenberg, *Systematic Theology*, vol. 3, trans. Geoffrey W. Bromiley (Grand Rapids: Eerdmans, 1998), 265.
10. Roland H. Bainton, *Here I Stand* (Nashville: Abingdon-Cokesbury Press, 1950), 367.
11. Calvin, *Institutes of the Christian Religion* 4.15.4, 1306–07.
12. Aquinas, *Summa Theologica* 3.66.11, 2385.
13. Luther, *Large Catechism* 224, 162.

Chapter 25: The Christ Who Reigns

1. Karl Barth, *Church Dogmatics*, 3/2, trans. G. W. Bromiley and T. F. Torrance (Edinburgh: T. & T. Clark, 1960), 453.
2. John of Damascus, *The Orthodox Faith* 4.2, *Nicene and Post Nicene Fathers*, 2d ser., vol. 9, 74, translation altered.
3. John Calvin, *Commentaries on the Epistle to the Ephesians* (4:10), trans. William Pringle, *Calvin's Commentaries*, vol. 21 (Grand Rapids: Baker Book House, 1989), 275.
4. John Calvin, *Second Defence of the Faith concerning the Sacraments in Answer to Joachim Westphal*, *Tracts and Treatises*, trans. Henry Beveridge, vol. 2 (Grand Rapids: Eerdmans, 1958), 290.
5. Karl Barth, *Church Dogmatics*, 4/2, trans. G. W. Bromiley (Edinburgh: T. & T.

Clark, 1958), 153. Christ "ascended higher than all the heavens, in order to fill the whole universe" (Eph. 4:10).

6. Paul Tillich, *Systematic Theology*, vol. 1 (Chicago: University of Chicago Press, 1951), 240.

7. Ernst H. Kantorowicz, *The King's Two Bodies* (Princeton: Princeton University Press, 1957), 339.

8. Karl Rahner, "The Theology of Power," *Theological Investigations*, vol. 4, trans. Kevin Smyth (Baltimore: Helicon Press, 1966), 406.

9. See Norman K. Gottwald, *The Tribes of Yahweh* (Maryknoll, N.Y.: Orbis, 1979).

10. See Walter Brueggemann, *Theology of the Old Testament* (Minneapolis: Fortress Press, 1997), 609–10.

11. "Providence . . . has brought into the world Augustus and filled him with a hero's soul for the benefit of mankind. A Savior for us and our descendents, he will make wars to cease and order all things well. The epiphany of Caesar has brought to fulfillment past hopes and dreams." Inscription at Priene, celebrating birthday of Augustus in 9 B.C., quoted in Frederick W. Danker, *Jesus and the New Age* (Philadelphia: Fortress Press, 1988), 24.

12. Augustine, *The City of God* 4.3, trans. Gerald G. Walsh et al. (Garden City, N.J.: Doubleday, 1958), 87.

13. *The Epistle to Diognetus* 5, 7, *Ante Nicene Fathers*, vol. 1, 26–27.

14. Justin Martyr, *First Apology* 39, *Early Christian Fathers*, trans. Cyril C. Richardson (New York: Macmillan, 1970), 266.

15. C. John Cadoux, *The Early Christian Attitude to War* (New York: Seabury Press, 1982), 149–50.

16. Clement of Alexandria, *Exhortation* 10, *Ante Nicene Fathers*, vol. 2, 202.

17. Origen, *Against Celsus* 8.68, *Ante Nicene Fathers*, vol. 4, 665.

18. Miroslav Volf, *Exclusion and Embrace* (Nashville: Abingdon Press, 1996).

19. See Michael Battle, *Reconciliation: The Ubuntu Theology of Desmond Tutu* (Cleveland: Pilgrim Press, 1997).

20. Philip P. Hallie, *Lest Innocent Blood Be Shed* (New York: Harper and Row, 1979).

21. Calvin, *Institutes*, 2.15.4, 499.

22. Hans Urs von Balthasar, *Heart of the World*, trans. Erasmo S. Leiva (San Francisco: Ignatius Press, 1979), 117–18.

A Note on Language

1. It's a dramatic feature. God is called "Father" 115 times in the Gospel of John alone, as opposed to fewer than twenty times in the whole Old Testament.

2. See Mary Rose D'Angelo, "*Abba* and 'Father': Imperial Theology and the Jesus Traditions," *Journal of Biblical Literature* 111 (1992): 611–30; James Barr, "*Abba* Isn't 'Daddy,'" *Journal of Theological Studies* 39 (1988): 28–47.

3. See Marianne Meye Thompson, *The Promise of the Father* (Louisville: Westminster John Knox Press, 2000).

4. Karl Barth, *Church Dogmatics* 1/1, trans. G. T. Thomson (Edinburgh: T. & T. Clark, 1936), 447.

Index of Scriptural References

General Index